HOW TO MAKE IT BIG AS A CONSULTANT

Cohen's Maxims

compensation   Compensation, whether in the form of profit, salary, or job satisfaction, is the by-product of your contribution to society and is in direct proportion to this contribution. It is an error to make compensation the focus of your life's work. You will not reach your full potential, and you will have cheated society of the full benefits of your talent and ability.

duty   Whatever your occupation, you have a duty to the society of which you are a member. If you are a soldier, your duty is to protect that society. If you are in business or industry, your duty is to create and manage the jobs, wealth, and products of that society. Therefore, failure will be harmful not only to you but to society, just as success will be beneficial not only to you but also to society.

individual ability   Every individual has the potential to do great things. To reach this potential, you must discover your special abilities and qualifications. This means that you should always attempt new tasks and accept responsibility for untried assignments whenever they are offered.

leadership   A leader accepts responsibility. This means that the welfare of those you lead must always come before your own well-being. Therefore, while your primary duty is the accomplishment of your organization's mission, the welfare of your subordinates comes second, and your own welfare last.

planning   Successful actions are results not of accidents or luck but rather of an analysis of the situation and the preparation and proper execution of plans. Because of a changing environment and other variables, plans will not always succeed as originally conceived. But planning will maximize your successes and minimize your failures.

responsibility   If you are assigned a task, you are responsible for its successful completion. There are no acceptable excuses for failing to fulfill this responsibility, and this responsibility cannot be shifted to others.

risk   Never be afraid to take risks. If you work for someone, risks are part of what you are getting paid for. If you work for yourself, taking risks is the only way you can become successful.

self-confidence.   Self-confidence comes from successfully completing increasingly difficult tasks and assignments. Give your maximum to every project, no matter how insignificant or formidable.

success   Success does not come from working hard. Success comes from playing hard. Therefore, if you want success, you must position yourself so that the duties you perform, no matter how difficult or challenging, are considered play by you and not work. If you do this, not only will you gain success, you will have fun doing it.

HOW TO MAKE IT BIG AS A CONSULTANT

Second Edition

William A. Cohen

amacom
American Management Association

This publication is designed to provide accurate and authoritative
information in regard to the subject matter covered. It is sold with
the understanding that the publisher is not engaged in rendering
legal, accounting, or other professional service. If legal advice or
other expert assistance is required, the services of a competent
professional person should be sought.

Library of Congress Cataloging-in-Publication Data

Cohen, William A., 1937–
     How to make it big as a consultant / William A. Cohen.—2nd ed.
          p.   cm.
     Includes bibliographical references and index.
     ISBN 0-8144-5941-2 (hardcover)
     ISBN 0-8144-7860-3 (pbk.)
     1. Business consultants.   I. Title.
HD69.C6C57   1990   90-55203
658. 4'6—dc20   CIP

First AMACOM paperback edition 1993.

Printing number

10   9   8   7   6   5   4   3   2   1

This book is dedicated to the memory of my father
Sidney Oliver Cohen
who, even on his deathbed,
never failed to give excellent
counseling and advice whenever it was requested.

CONTENTS

Preface   xi

1   The Business of Consulting   1

What Is Consulting? • How Big Is the Consulting
Industry? • Why Does Anyone Need a Consultant
Anyway? • What Makes an Outstanding
Consultant? • How Much Money Can You Make as a
Consultant? • How Do People Become Consultants?

2   How to Get Clients   20

Direct Methods of Marketing • Indirect Methods of
Marketing • Marketing Consultant Services in the
Public Sector

3   Making the Initial Interview a Success   66

Looking and Acting Like a Professional • Seven
Essential Questions • What to Do When the
Interview Is Over • The Company Audit

4   How to Write a Proposal   76

Why a Written Proposal Is Necessary • How to
Write a Good Proposal • The Structure for a Letter
Proposal • Converting a Proposal Into a Contract

5   Pricing Your Services   85

Three Price Strategies • Other Considerations •
Methods of Billing • Disclosing the Fee

**6   What You Must Know About Consulting
Contracts**   96

Why a Contract is Necessary • Methods of Incurring
a Contractual Obligation • Elements of a Contract •
A Sample Contract

**7   Planning and Scheduling the Consulting
     Project**   **108**

   The Project Development Schedule • Developing a
   PERT Chart

8   Negotiating With Your Client   **119**

   Six Steps in Contract Negotiation as Seen by Uncle
   Sam • Goals and Objectives of the Party With Whom
   You Are Negotiating • Preparation: The Key to All
   Contract Negotiations • Being Wary of Telephone
   Negotiations • The Negotiation Plan • Negotiation
   Gamesmanship

9   How to Solve Your Client's Problems Easily   **132**

   The Harvard Case Study Method • The Charles
   Benson Problem: A Case Study • Psychological
   Techniques for Problem Solving

10 The Importance of Ethics in Consulting   **151**

   Business Ethics: Not Always Clear-Cut • Typical
   Problems Pertaining to Ethics in Consulting

11 Making Professional Presentations   **165**

   Objectives of Presentations • Five Keys to a
   Successful Presentation • Overcoming Stage Fright
   • Answering Questions

12 How to Run Your Consulting Business   **181**

   Selecting the Legal Structure for Your Consulting
   Firm • Other Legal Necessities • Clients' Use of
   Credit Cards • Stationery and Business Cards •
   Insurance and Personal Liability • Keeping
   Overhead Low • Necessary Records and Their
   Maintenance • Tax Obligations

**13 What a Computer Can Do for You in
     Consulting**   **225**

   How the Computer Revolutionized My Writing and
   Consulting Practice • How the Computer Can
   Double or Triple Your Productivity • What You
   Need to Know About Computers • What Kind of
   Computer Should You Buy? • What Kind of Printer
   Should You Buy?

Epilogue   **237**

Contents

Appendix A **References Useful to Consultants** **239**

Appendix B **Sample Consultant's Brochure** **243**

Appendix C **The Consultant's Questionnaire and Audit** **253**

Appendix D **An Extensive Consulting Proposal** **283**

Appendix E **Associations of Consultants** **307**

Index **309**

PREFACE

I didn't start out in life to become a business consultant. I know that I am not alone in this, for I have talked to hundreds of other consultants, both full- and part-time, and very few started out with that intention. Most of them must have had an early experience like mine. Because my entrance into the consulting field was unplanned, the first time I performed consulting services I had no one to ask for advice.

Experience in other fields had taught me that whenever I lacked knowledge about something, my first step should be to find a book on the subject. So I did just that. I visited several bookstores; I checked with the libraries. But I found few books with the information I needed. How much should I charge? Was a contract absolutely necessary? Did I need a business license or some other kind of license? What could I do as a part-time consultant without running into a conflict of interest with my full-time employer? How much could I make if I decided to devote full time to consulting? Also, if I consulted full-time, how much time would I need to spend marketing my services versus actually consulting, and how should I go about marketing my services, anyway? I was plagued by these and numerous other questions, but I had nowhere to turn for answers.

Eventually I learned, but mainly it was the hard way— through experience. I made numerous mistakes, which in some cases cost me money and in all cases wasted time and brought frustration. However, I did finally learn what to do and how to do it, and I began to make money. I consulted for Fortune 500 companies, for small businesses, for start-up companies, and for the government, and this endeavor continues to this day.

Then some years ago, within a few months of each other, I received my Ph.D. and became a full-time university professor. (I might interject here that becoming a successful business consultant in many specialties does not require a Ph.D., an MBA, or in fact any business degree at all. But more about that later.) In any case, becoming a business professor did not curtail my consulting activities. If anything, it intensified them.

At my university, I noticed that many students had a tremendous interest in business consulting—and not just business students. I was persuaded to develop an interdisciplinary course at California State University at Los Angeles on the subject of consulting for business. As this course developed, we did not stop at theory; every quarter I invited practicing consultants from many fields to share their experiences. The speakers ranged from those in small, one-person operations to staff consultants employed by multimillion-dollar corporations. My speakers included both full- and part-time consultants, and both men and women.

So popular did this course become that it attracted not only business students from all disciplines but also psychologists, chemists, anthropologists, attorneys, and English majors. Many of those who took the course were older students from outside the university, including engineers, pilots, and many company executives and professionals who wanted to leave their corporate jobs or to consult part-time. We even attracted a number of professors, who sat in on these lectures at various times to pick up what they could.

Partially due to the success of the business consulting course, another program for which I had responsibility also prospered. This was the Small Business Institute at the university, of which I was the director. The Small Business Institute program, conducted at universities around the country under the sponsorship of the U.S. Small Business Administration, furnishes consulting services to small businesses. The consulting is done by business students, supervised by professors. Over a period of years, we developed one of the largest Small Business Institutes in the country and several times won district, regional, and national awards for the top performance among participating universities. The Small Business Institute program allowed students in the consulting course to do hands-on projects as a part of their education.

Soon we had many requests for help from outside the university. In order to make this program mobile, we developed a consulting seminar that I gave several times a year. These seminars were attended not only by neophyte and would-be consultants but also by many consultants with considerable experience in their various professions. They generously shared their experiences and knowledge with other seminar students, and with me.

As a result, this book is based not only on my own experience but also on that of many others—including numerous guest lecturers, professors, and students who have accomplished more than three hundred different consulting engagements for as many different small businesses. It is also based on the face-to-face interchange of ideas from consultants in many different fields and geographic locations.

Had I had this book in my hands when I first started out, I would have saved myself thousands of wasted hours and much frustration. I would have avoided countless blunders, including journeys down blind alleys, while I struggled to learn how to promote my practice, develop long-term client relationships, and, in one case, get paid for services already performed.

This book contains the collective experiences of hundreds who have endeavored to earn their livelihood through the practice, either full- or part-time, of business consulting. Its aim is to help you to build a successful, rewarding business consultancy.

This revised edition not only updates every chapter but contains an expanded appendix section and two new chapters: one on negotiating (Chapter 8) and one on the use of computers in consulting (Chapter 13).

1

THE BUSINESS OF CONSULTING

Independent consulting has to be one of the most incredible businesses around, with advantages found in no other way of making a living. Consider working hours. You probably have some time of the day when you work best. Most people do. Some people work better in the morning, others in the evening, and a very few people work equally well all day. But in independent consulting, it doesn't make any difference, because you can pick your own hours. *You* can decide when you work and when you do not. You can always work at your best time.

Are you in a job where you don't like your boss? Must you work with people whom you just do not care to be around? Well, in independent consulting you decide whom you wish to work for and whom you do not wish to work for, as well as whom you do and do not work with. Whether you do or do not work for a particular client is entirely up to you.

Are you dissatisfied with your current salary? In consulting you set your own fees; *you* decide how much you're worth and how much you want to make. If you are worth more right now, today, you can give yourself a raise.

Do you prefer to work at home? In consulting you can make $100,000 or more working out of your own home without worrying about parking, driving, or the expense of an outside office. In fact the office in your own home is tax-deductible.

Finally, are you concerned about making the big plunge of going into your own full-time consulting practice? No need to risk this. You can start in consulting part-time and ease your way in. Many successful consultants have started through part-time work after their full-time jobs, at nights and on weekends. And if you follow the instructions in this book, you will soon be able to build a successful consulting practice; you will not have to quit your full-time job until you are fully ready and certain that you will be successful.

What Is Consulting?

Consultants operate in many, many different fields. Import-export, management, engineering, and marketing are some of the more common ones. There are consultants in archeology and clothes selection. There are even consultants to help authors overcome writer's block. In my classes and in seminars around the country, I have met experts from all those fields and more. All had become or had the potential for becoming successful consultants. They had widely varying backgrounds and consulted in many different business areas. As I was writing the first edition of this book, my wife called my attention to an article in the *Los Angeles Times* that told the story of an enormously successful consulting business run by a young mother. She worked about six days every month, advising businesses on which records to keep and which to throw away.

A consultant is simply anyone who gives advice or performs other services of a professional or semiprofessional nature in return for compensation. This means that regardless of your area of interest or expertise, you can become a consultant. Everyone has a unique background, with special experiences and interests that are duplicated by few others and are in demand by certain individuals or companies at certain times.

Many of my students ask whether it is necessary to have an advanced degree in order to be a consultant. The answer is definitely no. Although the orientation of a consultant is clearly professional, I have known many successful consultants with limited formal academic training. The important thing is that you have the necessary experience, qualifications, and skills to help with a task that an individual or company wants performed. Where you obtained these skills is of far less importance. I must add, however, that if it is your intent to work as a management consultant for a major consulting firm and not on your own, a Masters of Business Administration (MBA) degree will probably be required. But if you are on your own, whether or not you obtained your expertise from a university is not crucial. I know of a successful import-export consultant with no degree, and an expensive consultant to top managements of major corporations who has no MBA, only an undergraduate degree in sociology.

How Big Is the Consulting Industry?

Because consulting encompasses so many different aspects of life, it is very difficult to measure precisely the total dollar volume for consulting services currently performed in the United States. Most people are able only to estimate the value of consulting services being performed for business. A recent article in *Fortune* estimated that the size of the industry had reached $10 billion annually and is growing at 20 percent every year—even faster overseas.[1] Others have estimated an even higher figure—$15 billion a year.[2]

Consulting for Business

Even business consulting encompasses a very, very wide area of activities. Jerome Fuchs, author of *Making the Most of Management Consulting Services* (New York: AMACOM, 1975), categorizes consulting activities into eleven different areas.

1. General management, encompassing organizational planning, strategy, and other general management tasks

2. Manufacturing, including production control, facilities management, and so forth
3. Personnel, having to do with development and training, recruitment, selection, management of employee benefits programs, and similar activities
4. Marketing, covering such topics as new product introduction, pricing, promotion, and development of distribution channels
5. Finance and accounting, including cost accounting, valuation, tax advice, and investment programs
6. Procurement and purchasing
7. Research and development, and potential product selection and screening
8. Packaging, including aspects such as packaging machinery, design, and testing
9. Administration, including office management and administrative procedures
10. International operations, which has to do with import, export, licensing, tariffs, and joint ventures
11. Specialized services, which catches all the many other areas, such as executive recruiting or telecommunications

Consultants News, a newsletter of the consulting industry, surveyed 583 companies to find out what types of consulting expertise they offered. (Appendix A contains the address for *Consultants News* as well as a list of other references helpful to consultants.) Here are the results:

Consulting Expertise Offered	*Number of Firms Offering*
General management	219
Personnel	143
Marketing	126
Organizational planning	113
Manufacturing	112
Management development	100
Strategic business planning	97

Administration	96
Finance and accounting	89
Marketing strategy and organization	82

Types of Consulting Firms

Consulting firms may also be defined by other aspects of their business, including size, location, and the type of client they serve. This means you can speak about:

1. *National general management firms.* These are large firms such as McKinsey and Company, Booz-Allen, or Arthur D. Little, which do millions and millions of dollars in consulting business every single year. How much is millions and millions? In a recent year, McKinsey and Company did more than $500 million in consulting revenue.[3]
2. *Major accounting firms with consulting divisions.* Most national CPA firms today, including all of the Big Six, have divisions that do management consulting in addition to their regular accounting activities. Arthur Anderson did more than $800 million in consulting revenue, primarily as a result of its information systems work.[4]
3. *Functionally specialized firms.* These organizations specialize in certain particular areas of business. Such a firm might deal only in market research or in strategic planning.
4. *Industry-specific firms.* These are large national or international firms dealing only with certain industries or certain types of operations. An example would be Theodore Barry, International, which was once known primarily for its work in the utility industry.
5. *Public sector firms.* These firms specialize in consulting primarily with the government—either national, state, or local—or nonprofit organizations such as universities or hospitals.
6. *The so-called think tanks.* These very large firms,

such as Rand and SRI International, may have many or very few customers. The Aerospace Corporation, located in Los Angeles, deals mainly with the U.S. Air Force.

7. *Regional and local firms.* There are numerous consulting firms that operate in a single and limited geographic area, even though their annual sales may be quite large.

8. *Sole practitioners.* This is an area many new consultants seek, and well they might. There are more than fifty thousand such consulting businesses in America; more than half of these are one-person operations, and another 20–25 percent have between two and ten people.

9. *Specialty firms outside of business.* This may actually be one of the largest areas of consulting, although it is rarely counted because the focus is outside the area of business. Such firms may consult on health, etiquette, dress, or even personal behavioral management.

This wide variety indicates that the opportunities in the consulting business are tremendous. Many of the local or regional firms, and even the larger firms, started small with a sole practitioner and grew to be multimillion-dollar giants.

Why Does Anyone Need a Consultant Anyway?

You may ask yourself why it is that a large company hires a consultant, at sometimes very high compensation, when it already has staffs of experts who, one would think, should be even more qualified than the consultant. In a television broadcast several years ago, *60 Minutes* asked this very question about consultants to the government. After all, if the government employees themselves are qualified, why the need to hire consultants? And why pay them more than the employees themselves are being paid?

Actually there are very good reasons why both the

government and business organizations use consultants. In fact, not only are they hired, they are hired again and again and held in considerable esteem. Because it is good business to find a need and then fill it, it is very important for you to understand exactly what these reasons are. Let's look at each of them in turn.

1. *The need for personnel.* Sometimes even the largest companies lack personnel at specific periods of time or for specific tasks. They may need assistance during a temporary work overload, or they may require unique expertise that is not needed on an ongoing basis every day of the year. Temporary assistance might be needed, for example, when a company bids for a government contract. During this period, it is required to put out a great amount of work over a short period of time. The staff personnel may not be available to do this without stopping other important projects, so consultants are hired. Or a company may need unique expertise on a short-term, project basis. Take direct marketing, an area I frequently consult in: Many businesses use direct marketing only occasionally, so it does not make sense to hire a full-time expert whose salary could easily exceed $50,000 per year. Therefore, a company is perfectly happy to hire a consultant at fees of from $50 to $300 an hour to accomplish a specific task. The need for personnel also provides the motivation for the search consultant who is paid by client companies for finding specific executives or professionals. The large fees these consultants earn are an indication of the demand for their services.

According to *Business Week*, executive search is no minor business. In 1989, John H. Byrne, in "The New Headhunters," estimated top billers in executive search as follows:

Firm	Annual Revenue ($ millions)	Number of Consultants	Number of Searches
Korn/Ferry Int'l	$91.5	258	2,350
Russell Reynolds	91.0	181	2,000

Firm	Annual Revenue ($ millions)	Number of Consultants	Number of Searches
Spencer Stuart	81.7	137	1,800
Heidrick & Struggles	55.0	118	1,185
Boyden Int'l	34.6	100	1,150
Peat Marwick	27.5	91	1,010
Paul R. Ray	16.2	39	410
Ward Howell	13.9	45	610
Jackson & Coker	13.6	60	535
Nordeman Grimm	9.5	17	151

2. *The need for fresh ideas.* Not infrequently a company has a problem, and management feels the employees are too close to it to understand all the ramifications. It makes sense then to bring in someone from outside—someone with competent problem-solving skills but not necessarily knowledge of the business. In fact, sometimes the individual's very ignorance (assuming, of course, a talent for problem solving) helps to provide the answer. Peter F. Drucker, perhaps the world's greatest and certainly the most famous management consultant, has frequently said that he brings to the problem not so much his experience in a specific industry as his ignorance. He has a tremendous ability to penetrate through a confusion of factors and recognize the main issue, and thus to recommend ways to solve the problem. His services are well worth the fees he charges.

3. *Company politics.* At times the solution to a problem may actually be known, but for various political reasons it cannot be presented by those who understand the problem. For example, a division of a major company once proposed that the company enter a new market with one of its products, which would have required an investment of millions of dollars. The potential in this new market was highly controversial within this company. Because the new product would come from the division that suggested it, the division's recommendations would be considered prejudiced. However, by hiring an outside consultant to study the same issues, the

division succeeded in accomplishing the same thing. The consultant was assumed to be more impartial and less likely to be influenced by company politics.

4. *The need for improved sales.* No company can exist without sales. This is true no matter how knowledgeable its president or senior staff, how skilled its financial people and accountants, or how innovative its engineers in developing or manufacturing new products. A company that needs to increase sales in a short time frame will sometimes look outside its own marketing staff for help.

5. *The need for capital.* Every company needs money. The need for capital is extremely common in start-ups. But it is also very common in successful companies. In fact, the more successful a company, the more capital it needs. The need for capital is a continuing problem with many companies. An individual who has expertise in finding sources of capital will be in continual demand.

6. *Government regulations.* Government regulations, if not obeyed, can result in fines, imprisonment, or even the closing down of the business. No company is immune to government regulations, and all companies need to ensure that they fulfill these regulations in the most efficient and effective manner. At the same time, they wish to minimize any negative impact on their business and, if possible, use the regulations to help the operation of their business. These regulations concern many areas: equal employment opportunity, age discrimination, consumer credit protection, safety standards, veterans' rights, and numerous others. If you have knowledge in any of these regulatory areas or can become an expert in them, there is a real market for your consulting services.

7. *The need for maximum efficiency.* All organizations need to operate in as efficient a manner as possible. An organization that operates at lower efficiency than it is capable of will eventually have problems. More efficient competitors will take away its market and drive it out of business. Inefficiency leads to high costs, making prices uncompetitive. Slippages, delays, and low productivity all result from ineffi-

ciency. If you know how to increase the efficiency of an organization, you have something important to sell as a consultant.

8. *The need to diagnose problems and find solutions.* One reason that the MBA degree is so sought after by many businesses is that the graduates with these degrees are supposed to be very adept at diagnosing problems faced by business and developing solutions for them. Anyone who can do this is in demand. The more general problem solving you do and the better you become at it, the more your name will get around. Large consulting firms have capitalized on the need of businesses to have their problems diagnosed and recommendations for solutions made. For this reason, these firms have sought to hire MBAs from the top schools at extremely high starting salaries in order to build and maintain a reputation for problem solving. Even some individual practitioners such as Peter F. Drucker are nationally and sometimes internationally known for their problem-solving talents, which means that they are in great demand.

9. *The need to train employees.* The operation of any business is becoming more and more complex, and today many employees are continually trained throughout their careers. Managers need different types of training for leadership, organizational, and planning skills; computer operators need additional training with the latest equipment, techniques, software, and programming. In fact developments are occurring so rapidly that virtually every single functional area of business needs continual training. If you are an expert and can teach skills in any area that is in demand, you have a niche in a type of consulting that commands large fees from industry.

10. *The need for a complete turnaround.* A friend of mine, who made a worldwide consulting reputation as a "workout specialist," was often called in by a bank or a group of investors to take over a company in danger of bankruptcy. He would come in as president and do whatever was necessary to turn the company around. Sometimes he was president of several companies simultaneously, when

he'd spend a good deal of time in flight, continually going from one distressed company to another. Once the company was in shape, off he would go to the next project. Since many companies find themselves in extreme conditions, when the investors are willing to put up a fight, there is a need for a troubleshooting consultant who can pull off a complete turn-around.

Turnaround specialists command heavy-duty fees—as much as $30,000 per month.[5] William Brandt became a turn-around consultant while working on a doctorate in sociology. A friend asked him to help a failing coal mine. Once involved as a consultant, he never stopped. Brandt, only thirty-nine years old, has built his Development Specialists, Inc., into a $4 million practice.[6]

Signals Indicating the Need for a Consultant

According to James E. Svatko, senior editor of *Small Business Reports,* the following situations signal the need for outside expertise from a consultant:

- Lack of a written business plan
- Unexplained low morale
- Steady, constant increases in costs
- Regular cash shortages
- Chronic delays or late deliveries of products
- Loss of market position
- Overworked staff
- Excessive rework without achieving objectives
- Continual supply deficiencies
- Lack of information about the competition or market[7]

Remember, these are the reasons that businesses normally need consultants. There are also thousands of other areas in which both businesspeople and nonbusinesspeople may need assistance. For example, consultants are making millions of dollars today by teaching people how to manage their time, control stress, lose weight, and keep fit. If you have specific knowledge in almost any area—from handicrafts to hypnotism, mathematics to merchandising—you may have skills that are in demand by some segment of the population.

How Do Potential Clients Analyze Consultants for Hire?

James Svatko's analysis of the consultant-client relationship led him to recommend that companies answer the following questions before deciding whether to hire a consultant. You should answer these five questions yourself before submitting your formal proposal to a client.

1. Can you add something worthwhile to the company's total output?
2. Will your expertise bring the company any closer to its goals?
3. Can you make the company work more effectively?
4. Will you save the company time?
5. With the budget available, can you do a comprehensive and effective job?[8]

If your proposal doesn't prove that you can do these things for your client, either rework your proposal or don't submit one.

What Makes an Outstanding Consultant?

Being a consultant and being an outstanding consultant are two different things. After talking with many top-flight consultants around the country, I have identified seven areas that make the difference.

1. *Bedside manner.* This refers to your ability to get along with your client. Here it's not so much what you say, but how you say it. Doctors with much knowledge but poor bedside manners often find that their patients prefer to go to doctors with much less experience or ability. Developing a pleasant bedside manner so that your clients have confidence

in what you say can be as important as your technical knowledge.

2. *The ability to diagnose problems.* To stay with the doctor analogy, we know that the doctor has access to all sorts of medicines to help cure a patient. But if he or she makes an incorrect diagnosis, the medicine may hurt more than it helps. Similarly your ability to diagnose the problem correctly is extremely important. It is one of the most significant criteria of an outstanding consultant.

3. *The ability to find solutions.* Of course, having diagnosed a problem, you are expected to recommend the proper actions to correct the situation. Chapter 9 is devoted entirely to problem solving. With practice you will be able to solve complex problems consistently by suggesting the right course of action for your client to take.

4. *Technical expertise and knowledge.* Perhaps you expected this would be the most important skill for a good consultant, and it is true that technical expertise in a field is important. Expertise comes from your education, your experience, and the personal skills you have developed. But it may be in any one of a variety of areas, and it may develop in a variety of ways. G. Gordon Liddy, known primarily for his association with the Watergate break-in, today commands a six-figure income as a security consultant. Note that even a background that includes incarceration in a penitentiary does not affect your ability to be a good consultant and to make a major contribution to the benefit of your client.

5. *Communication skills.* Charles Garvin, from the well-known Boston Consulting Group, has done extensive consulting in the area of business strategy since the early 1960s. From more than twenty years' experience, Garvin has identified three major attributes that every good consultant needs. He believes the number one attribute is superior communication abilities. (Analytical skill is second, and the ability to work under pressure is third.)

Some years ago, a study of how companies viewed recent business school graduates was conducted by Dr. Allen Blitstein. Dr. Blitstein wanted to know two things: the most important factors in why new graduates were hired, and the major factors that indicated success on the job after hiring. You may have thought that such factors as grade point average or perhaps the school attended would be of primary importance. But not so. According to the employers who did the hiring, the ability to communicate was far more important. And that was true both for getting hired and for success on the job. You should study Chapter 11, on presentations, with particular interest.

6. *Marketing and selling ability.* Regardless of the technical area you are interested in, whether it is a functional area in business or something entirely different, you must learn to be a good marketer and a good salesperson. Not only do consultants sell an intangible product, they also must sell themselves. Chapter 12 discusses how to market your business and yourself; every secret I have learned from my own experiences or from other consultants I reveal to you in this chapter.

7. *Management skills.* Last, but not the least in importance, is the ability to manage a business or a practice and to run projects. In my mind, an outstanding consultant must also be a good manager. As with other skills, the ability to manage can be learned. To assist you in this process, Chapter 12 shows you how to manage your business efficiently. In addition, throughout the book I give step-by-step instructions for many processes that will help you perform as a skilled manager.

Dick Brodkorb is the chairman and chief executive officer of a consulting company in Costa Mesa, California, called Decision Planning Corporation. Dick frequently speaks to my classes in consulting. He has identified two groups of skills that he feels are most important in making a good consultant. He calls them The Big Three and The Big Four. The Big Three are (1) communication skills, both written and oral; (2) technical command of a subject; and (3) the ability to get along with others.

He suggests that neophyte consultants first master The

Big Three, and then move on to The Big Four. The first of The Big Four is analytical skills (not necessarily quantitative); second, sensitivity to others is extremely important; third, you should have a tolerance for the consulting life-style, which may require intensive hours of work on some projects; and finally, you need to have a strong personal drive to be successful.

In summary there are certain things you must know in order to be a consultant. These are:

- How to become expert in your field
- How to get clients
- How to diagnose and solve problems
- How to run your practice

All these topics, and a lot more, are covered in this book.

It's important to recognize that you may not need actual hands-on experience in your technical area of interest at first. One of my MBA students went to work for one of the largest consulting firms in the country with no hands-on experience at all, using solely what he had learned as a student. Peter F. Drucker once said that although he consults internationally for major corporations, he has never been a practicing manager, with the single exception of serving as dean at Bennington School for approximately two years in the 1940s.

How Much Money Can You Make as a Consultant?

No one should embark on a career as a consultant primarily to make money. Still, money is needed to live, and it can provide the freedom to choose what one wishes to do in life and for whom, so this is a valid question.

In the early 1980s, Professor Laurie Laurwood of Claremont Graduate School surveyed 150 California consulting firms, both sole practitioners and major firms. She found that the average firm did $250,000 a year in business. Other surveys of sole practitioners at about the same time indicated that a typical first year's gross for a consultant ranged from $20,000 to $40,000, and that the average consultant billed at between $300 and $600 a day.

Today those figures would be below the average. Large firms bill considerably more. William Bain, the founder of Bain and Company, said recently, "Consultants today routinely get billed to clients at $28,000 a month each."[9]

A very large consulting firm can charge millions of dollars or more for a single job.[10]

I discuss pricing your services in detail in Chapter 5, but for now, when you are considering the potential of the business, it is important to realize that you will not be able to bill for every minute of every day. Some time must be spent in marketing your services. Therefore, it's important to consider the ratio of billable time to time spent marketing, which is not billable. Howard L. Shenson, who has given seminars around the country on consulting, estimates that new consultants should plan to spend at least one third of their time the first year marketing their services, and only two thirds in actual billable time. After the first year, marketing time can be reduced to 15 or 20 percent. Other estimates for marketing time have ranged as high as 40–50 percent. Many independent consultants note that, once established, they spend almost no time marketing, since they either receive additional clients through referrals or spend all their available time on established clients.

When you are estimating how much you can actually make as a consultant, it is better to start with the assumption that in the first year you will spend about half of your time marketing your services. You may not actually need that much, but it's safer than expecting to spend most of your time on work billed to your clients and then finding that you have grossly overestimated your first year's sales.

How Do People Become Consultants?

Individuals get into consulting in many strange ways, and no two stories are exactly alike. You may be interested in hearing how some consultants got their start.

Howard L. Shenson was a Ph.D. student at the same time he was teaching and serving as department head at California State University at Northridge. He received numerous requests from companies in the local area, and he soon was engaged in a variety of consulting activities in addition to his teaching and research. As the months went by, he realized he was spending more and more time consulting, and he was finding it more fascinating than his academic work. Finally he decided to devote himself entirely to full-time consulting, and he found not only better job satisfaction but far greater compensation than he could ever earn as a professor.

Hurbert Bermont, author of the self-published *How to Become a Successful Consultant in Your Own Field* and a successful consultant in the publishing industry as well as a consultant's consultant today, got his start when his boss called him in one day and fired him. Bermont said he went through total shock at the time, but he later realized it was a favor in disguise. In desperation Bermont called around and found a friend who agreed to let him use his office, secretary, and telephone for a nominal sum in exchange for training his friend's new secretary. He was able to attain as a client the most prestigious and successful name in his business by working for the company at the right price—nothing. This door opener eventually led to a paying contract with the company and, more important, gave him a major client with which to impress other prospective clients. At the end of six months, he was earning almost as much as it had taken him twenty years to reach in his previous career.

Phil Ross started out as an actor who worked as a salesperson with a manufacturing company between jobs. Because of his unique abilities not only to sell but to educate and motivate, he soon became national sales director. When he became dissatisfied with company policies, he began looking for another job, using a national executive search firm. In the process, he was recruited by that firm to become an executive recruiter, or "headhunter." Search consulting probably calls for more sales skills than any other type of consulting, since the consultant must be able to convince a company to become a client *and* persuade a fully satisfied employee to consider leaving his or her current organization and become a candidate for a job with a different company. Phil mastered these skills and excelled as a search consultant, and soon he was appointed national training director. After several years, Phil left to start his own executive search firm and eventually founded THE PROS, a consulting firm that assists corporations worldwide with their personnel and recruitment problems.

Luis Espinosa was born in Mexico and was my student at California State University at Los Angeles. He wanted to become a consultant for a major consulting firm. Using special job-finding techniques that got him face-to-face interviews with principals of top consulting firms, he was soon hired by Theodore Barry, International. After only two years, he was recruited as a top-level strategic planner for a bank in Mexico City with $20 billion in assets. He then went on to a similar high position as an internal strategic planning consultant with an American bank.

This points out yet another advantage of consulting. Not infrequently, consultants who are highly visible to top management so impress their clients with their performance that they are catapulted immediately into senior executive ranks at extremely high salaries. Several years ago, *Business Week* carried the story of Ilene Gordon Bluestein, who became director of corporate planning at the Signode Corporation in Glenview, Illinois, at age 28, only four years after leaving school. The point here is that those four years were spent in consulting. Bluestein wasn't the only success mentioned. This article told of others who used consulting as a springboard to corporate success. All were young, held senior positions, and made large salaries. And every single one had been a consultant.

John Diebold opened a consulting operation in his parent's house in Weehawken, New Jersey. Had he prepared a résumé, the most recent item would have been the fact that he had been fired from another consulting group. The reason? He had tried too hard to convince a company to buy a computer. That was in 1954. Three years later, he bought the company that had fired him. Today his firm, The Diebold Group, has branches around the world. Some call him The Prince of Gurus.[11]

In this chapter, I've supplied an overview of the entire consulting business. I hope I've opened your eyes to some of the potentials—both in the life-style of a consultant and in the compensation you might receive—as well as to different consulting areas that you might enjoy. Finally, although I've mentioned stories of several individuals who have become consultants, it's important for you to realize that it is not so important *how* you become a consultant as that you actually *become* one. There are many routes to becoming a consultant, but the bottom line—success—is what counts. This process starts in Chapter 2 with your learning how to get clients.

Notes

1. Anne B. Fisher, "The Ever-Bigger Boom in Consulting," *Fortune* (April 24, 1989), p. 113.

2. Gregory J. Millman, "Taking the Con Out of Consultants," *Business Month* (February 1990), p. 44.

3. John Byrne, "What's a Guy Like This Doing at McKinsey's Helm?" *Business Week* (June 13, 1988), p. 82.

4. Ibid.

5. William Keenan, Jr., "Should You Turn to a Turnaround Specialist?" *Sales & Marketing Management* (October 1988), p. 66.

6. Lois Therrien, "William Brandt: Putting Small Businesses Back in the Black," *Business Week* (August 21, 1989), p. 99.

7. James E. Svatko, "Working With Consultants," *Small Business Reports* (February 1989), p. 61.

8. Ibid., p. 59.

9. Ann B. Fisher, op. cit., p. 120.

10. Howard P. Allen, "Are Management Consultants Worth Their Hire?" *Business Forum* (Fall 1988/Winter 1989), p. 31.

11. Frank Rose, "The Prince of Gurus," *Business Month* (April 1989), p. 67.

2

HOW TO GET CLIENTS

This chapter discusses one of the most important aspects of any consulting business—getting clients. No matter how expert the consultant and no matter what the field, without clients the business and the practice cannot exist. In this chapter, you will find not only conventional methods of marketing your practice and obtaining clients but also some ways that may not be so obvious. I call these "indirect methods" of marketing your services. Although they take longer, they can greatly expand your practice. To build a dynamic practice, you should integrate both direct and indirect methods into your marketing program.

Direct Methods of Marketing

With the six direct methods of marketing listed as follows, you approach potential clients directly and let them know that you are available:

1. Direct mail
2. Cold calls
3. Direct response space advertising
4. Directory listings
5. Yellow Pages listings
6. Former employers

Let's look at each in turn.

Direct Mail

With direct mail, you send potential clients a letter or a brochure or both advertising your services. An example of a page from a catalog used in direct mail is shown in Figure 2-1. It is very similar to a direct mail letter. Note that it talks directly to the client's needs and tries to avoid sounding pompous or distant. The writer is attempting to establish direct communication with the potential client. By suggesting the firm's past accomplishments, the writer implies the kinds of things that can be done for a new client in the future. Finally the piece doesn't leave things hanging; at the very end, the prospective client is asked to call at once for additional information or to set up a consulting appointment.

Direct Mail Letters. Writing direct mail letters for any purpose is an art. Not everyone can write compelling copy for direct mail letters. However, it is not necessary that you be able to do so. There are plenty of good copywriters around who make this their business, and plenty of super-successful consultants have their advertising copy written by someone else. The cost may be several hundred to several thousand dollars, but for a good direct mail letter, it is an investment well-made.

To find a good copywriter, look for one who already has a track record in direct response work. He or she knows how to write copy for direct results, and that's what you're looking for.

Where can you find someone like this? Try the English or advertising department of your local college or university. Sometimes you'll find outstanding free-lancers masquerading as professors or graduate students. Direct marketing clubs or associations of copywriters can sometimes recommend candidates for you to check out; check the associations in your telephone book. You can also consult the Yellow Pages; look under "Copywriters." Other good sources are

Figure 2-1. Example of an effective direct mail piece.

AN OVERVIEW OF
SALES AND MARKETING CONSULTING
WITH STEVEN WEST AND HIS GROUP

There are many occasions in which the complexity or importance of a problem or a situation mandates the use of an outside consultant.

Outside consultants maintain a detached objectivity. They don't get emotionally involved in the internal politics or fixed way of thinking of the past. Consultants bring with them fresh ideas. They are emissaries of new information. Often, they will cross-pollinate ideas between clients and act as a conduit for new technology. Consultants bring with them specialized talent. This highly specialized talent can be hired to solve a particular problem, define a particular opportunity and then that assignment can be completed. Consultants become part-time, pro tempore members of your staff. They give you depth and allow you to maintain a lean and mean payroll. And consultants will often work on a fixed fee basis, so that you know exactly what your costs will be. There are no guesses and no equivocation.

Steven West and the New York Marketing Group are considered to be the world's leading sales and marketing consultants. Their 7 operating divisions can bring sharpness of focus and expertise to bear upon unique and complex problems at your company. They combine a no-nonsense, real life experience with the most sophisticated cutting edge technology. Their unique blending of pragmatic, straight-line thinking, coupled with advanced strategies and tactics in sales and marketing, are fitted to your company's needs to find solutions to problems. But their solutions are focused on reality —not in graphs-charts-philosophies-models.

New York Marketing Group and its affiliates are the largest private sales and marketing consulting company in the world. More than 50 specialists each focus in on specific areas of sales and marketing consultation. Under the direction and leadership of Steven West, this group can marshal its resources to assist you in solving your unique corporate problems.

More than 1/8 of the Fortune 500 companies and half of America's largest banks utilize Steven West and his associates to help solve their unique consulting problems. Companies such as Revlon, Sears, Wang, Citicorp, Manufacturers Hanover, Data General, GTE, Nynex Telephone Company and Bell South are just a few of the clients who utilize Steven West's services.

Many smaller companies whose names, no doubt, would mean nothing to you, are active users of Steven West and his company's services. You need not be a multi-billion dollar, multi-national company to take advantage of the expertise of this group.

Fees, seniority and experience level can be adjusted to suit your respective budgets. This group can readily undertake projects in the millions of dollars. Conversely. projects of a few thousand dollars are welcome with the same level of enthusiasm.

Whether your requirements are for a few days of consultation, or an in-depth, on-going relationship, Steven West and his associates will be happy to explore working with your company.

A Word of Caution—The New York Marketing Group and Steven West will not accept any assignments that they feel would not be fruitful for their clients. If what you have in mind is not going to work, or if there is a probability that it is unlikely to work, your project will not be accepted.

Recently, a top executive at Baush & Lomb said, "In talking to my friends in the business community, what sets aside Steven West and his group from all other sales and marketing consultants, is their batting average. 96% of the time they will find the solution that you are looking for. If they don't think that you are barking up the right tree, they'll politely reject the assignment." This is professionalism in its ultimate development. For information call:

(718) 479-3700

There are 7 specialized areas of consultion in which you can utilize Steven West and his group.

THE NEW YORK MARKETING GROUP
61-47 188th Street
Fresh Meadows, NY 11365

Courtesy of The New York Marketing Group.

the direct marketing professional magazines: *Direct Marketing, DM News, Target Marketing,* and *Direct.* Their classified and space advertisements contain listings of many free-lance copywriters. Your local library either has or can get these publications for you. In all cases, ask for a sample of the copywriter's work before you contract with him or her.

If you don't mind dealing with someone who may not be local, let me recommend Dr. Luther Brock, "The Letter Doctor." Dr. Brock has been in the business of writing direct response copy for years, and his expertise has brought him deserved renown. He can be reached at 2911 Nottingham, Denton, Texas 76201. His telephone number is (817) 387-8058.

Writing Your Own Direct Mail Copy. You can write your own direct mail copy, but you must be a competent writer and be willing to work at doing this special type of selling in print.

There are numerous formulas around to help you write direct mail copy. My own formula consists of five steps:

1. Get attention.
2. Develop interest.
3. Demonstrate benefits.
4. Show credibility.
5. Deliver a call to action.

Write in the first person. Write simply, with your potential client in mind. And keep it personal. Define your target audience exactly. Focus on that individual reader as you write your copy.

Let's say you are consultant John Smith. We'll create a direct mail piece and go through it step by step.

Getting attention. First, you want to get attention. You do this with a headline. However, usually it isn't written as a headline. Instead make it the first paragraph in your letter. It is an extremely important paragraph because it must "hook" your prospective client instantly. If it fails to do this, your letter goes right into the trashcan unread.

To construct this paragraph, try to think of the most important thing you've done that would be important to your target audience. Let's say you're a marketing consultant specializing in increasing sales for small to medium-size companies. Think through the assignments you've had and what happened as a result of your work. Look for five to ten great accomplishments and then pick the most important. If you are a new consultant, you might consider what you did while working for someone else. It really doesn't matter whether these accomplishments were achieved for a client or a boss. What is critical is that good results came about due to your work.

Finally, craft your attention getter. Keep reworking the paragraph to minimize the number and complexity of words and maximize the dramatic effect.

Let's say you finally come up with the following:

> A few weeks ago, a client called to thank me. He's the president of a $5 million export company. The sales plan I put into effect for him caused his sales to increase by 541 percent in two months. And, as he told me, this increase came with no increase in costs. No wonder he was so excited!

Can you imagine the president of a small or medium-size company throwing that letter away without reading further? I can't. Not if it's written on high-quality bond paper, with an impressive letterhead, and the letter is addressed to him or her by name. Every company of that size wants to increase sales. If you've increased a similar company's sales by 541 percent at no cost increase in such a short time, maybe you can do the same for the prospect's company. He or she would have to be a fool not to at least read further.

Now that you have your prospective client's attention, develop his or her interest.

Developing interest and demonstrating benefits. You can develop interest and demonstrate benefits at the same time.

All you need to do is state the reason for your letter and list some more of your accomplishments from the five to ten that you selected earlier.

> I am writing to you because I am a marketing consultant specializing in increasing sales for companies like yours. If you are interested in increasing your company's sales dramatically at low cost, you may be interested in some other things I have done:
> - Trained seven salespeople of a $20 million clothing manufacturing company. Their sales increased by an average of 46.3 percent after six months.
> - Conducted a marketing audit for a $2 million company making small industrial parts. This company increased its sales by $441,000 the first year and cut selling costs by 4 percent at the same time.
> - Developed and helped implement a marketing plan for a new product for a $75 million pharmaceutical company. First-year sales were $11 million—twice that of new products introduced in the past.
> - Created a sales and promotional plan for a start-up newsletter for a small publishing company. The newsletter was profitable after only eight months. Second-year profit objectives set prior to my plan were exceeded by 111 percent.

Note that there are few adjectives but a great many numbers. Numbers add credibility even as you develop interest and show your prospective client some of the benefits he or she could receive. Again it is like your attention-getting paragraph. Your prospective client knows that if you can do these kinds of things for other organizations, you can do similar things for his.

Showing credibility. Up to now, everything you've stated consists only of *your* words. It's important to have a third party confirm your abilities. The best way I've found is to

quote from letters from clients and former clients—or from
former bosses if you are a new consultant. After you have
been a consultant for a while, you're going to get letters of
thanks. Then all you need to do is ask if you can quote the
writer in your sales literature. But how do you get endorsements when you are just starting out? The best way is simply
to ask for them.

If you've done a good job for someone, telephone and
ask him what he thought about your work. Was he happy
with the results? Did anything good happen? If your client
was pleased, ask if he'd be willing to write a letter from
which you can quote. You might even offer to supply ideas
and figures that would help him write it. Once you collect
four or five good quotes, you are ready to confirm your
credibility:

> Here is what some of my clients have said about my
> work:
>
> "John Smith is the World's Best Consultant for small
> and medium-size companies."—*George Able*, president,
> ABC Service Company.
>
> *****
>
> "You tripled my sales in three months and saved my
> company."—*Hugo Mondesto*, president, Q. T. Limousine
> Service.
>
> *****
>
> "Your sales training really did wonders. Now all of my
> salespeople are superstars."—*Joe Fine*, The Cutting
> Edge, Inc.

In some cases, you may not be able to get permission to
extract from a letter for your direct mail. In that case, use
initials only and disguise the company name like this:

> "The ROI for your services was 500 percent plus.
> Thanks." ———, president, a medium-size travel
> agency.

Another way of showing credibility is with a brief statement of your educational and technical or consultant experiences?

> I have a B.S. in engineering from California State University at Los Angeles, and an MBA from the University of Michigan. I have managed marketing activities and consulted in marketing for twelve years.

Delivering a call to action. Research has demonstrated conclusively that if your prospective client doesn't act immediately, he or she will probably never act. So the final part of your direct mail letter should be a call for immediate action. To do this, be very clear and explicit about what you want your prospective client to do. Usually you'd like him or her to call or write you to set up a face-to-face interview. You can call your prospective client to action like this:

> Please call or write me at no cost or obligation for a face-to-face interview so you can judge for yourself whether I can help you. *One cautionary note:* Please call or write immediately. The majority of the work I do is done by me personally; I believe that's one of the secrets of my success. But I get booked early. Even if your ideas are not firmed up yet, I recommend calling or writing now. That way it is more likely that I will have the time available to help you.

I recommend using a P.S. as well. The reason is that a P.S. is almost always read. Some people read the P.S. even before they read the rest of the letter. Use the P.S. to stimulate the action you want. If you can, it helps to offer something free in return for action:

> P.S.   I have prepared a special booklet, *How to Get the Most out of Marketing Consultants,* for my clients. If you call or write, I will send you a copy with my compliments, while they last.

The "while they last" and the free offer provide additional incentives for your prospective client to respond right away.

Of course there are many ways of writing a direct mail letter to get clients. To help you, I recommend the following books: *Words That Sell* by Richard Bayan (Westbury, N.Y.: Asher-Gallant Press, 1984); *The Copywriter's Handbook* by Robert W. Bly (New York: Dodd, Mead & Co., 1985); and *On the Art of Writing Copy* by Herschell Lewis (Englewood Cliffs, N.J.: Prentice-Hall, 1989).

Brochures

The basic purpose of any brochure is, first, to advertise your type of work and, second, to convince the reader that you are the most capable individual available to do this work. Therefore, if you are going to develop your own brochure, write it to answer the two questions "What is it that I do?" and "Why am I the best?" Answering these questions may require that your brochure have different sections. Such sections might include descriptions of the kind of work you do; specific examples of problems you have solved for clients in the past, along with benefits they have accrued from using your services; reasons why your services are better than those offered by competitors; your experience, background, and special qualifications that make you unique; a list of previous clients (if available); and perhaps even some testimonials from previous clients. If you haven't done any consulting previously, you can write down accomplishments that you attained when you were an employee working for someone else. As long as these accomplishments were in your area of consulting expertise and benefited whomever you were working for at the time, it is unimportant whether the beneficiary was an employer or a client. There are a number of good books available to help you in preparing your own brochure. Here are a couple: *How to Prepare Professional Design Brochures* by Gerre Jones (New York: McGraw-Hill, 1976) and *Better Brochures, Catalogs, and Mailing Pieces* by Jane Maas (New York: St. Martin's Press, 1981).

Designing Your Brochure. Before you even begin to design your brochure, decide what it is supposed to do and who your target market is. Consultant brochures can have very different objectives. One consultant whose area was strategic planning wanted her brochure to continually remind her clients and prospective clients of her expertise. Her brochure was a twenty-page manual on strategic planning, printed on glossy paper. It cost a fortune, but she maintained that it was well worth the investment.

Another consultant I knew produced a multicolor glossy brochure with numerous photos. It cost him $20,000 for only one thousand copies. He told me that most of his prospective clients barely looked at his brochure and few read any of it. Yet he was entirely satisfied. His consulting practice was in a highly technical area of composites and composite structures. The brochure demonstrated conclusively that he was a force in the industry, and he said that the brochure enabled him to capture significant business that he previously could not obtain.

However, most of us want something simple that we can use with our direct mail letter or get to prospective clients in other ways. We would like a brochure that will help us get in the door for a face-to-face interview or reinforce our capability and help close the sale of the engagement during or after the interview.

The target market is also important. An expensive brochure says that you are high-priced. That's fine if your market has the money. That's why the big consulting houses have fancy and expensive brochures. But if your clients are small businesses, and your pricing is anything but high, you may scare off prospective clients.

Deciding on the objective for your brochure as well as your target market will help you to decide on type of printing, paper, size, and other factors. It will also help you to decide what should go in your brochure.

The basic contents of a brochure include who you are, what you do, how you work, what you've done, and how to contact you. Who you are can be handled by your qualifications and a photo. I like to include a photo because it lets people know there is a real person behind the name. A list of the kinds of things you do gives your prospective clients some idea of how they can profit from using you. How you work can be in the form of a case history of an assignment or just a description of your method of operation from initial meeting to assignment completion. In the section on what you've done, you can list your accomplishments as described for your direct mail letter. Just remember to use few adjectives but lots of numbers, dollar figures, and percentages. You can also include a client list and a page with quotes regarding your performance, as in your direct mail letter. Finally, make certain you include your address and phone number.

Once you know what your brochure is going to contain and its approximate size, you can begin to work out a rough layout. It is important to do this before you begin to write copy. If you have only the equivalent of two sides of an 8½- × 11-inch sheet of paper, there may not be sufficient space for everything you want to include. Do a rough layout and you'll know.

Only after the layout is done should you begin to write copy. Again you can get a professional designer and copywriter to do all of this for you—or you can do it on your own. In the old days, I did everything myself except the final typesetting. But nowadays, with Harvard Graphics, Word Perfect 5.0 Fonts, and other computer programs available, you can probably do *everything* yourself if you want to.

Your brochure should be accompanied by your direct mail letter. The format of your brochure could be anything from a simple one-page flier to a slick, many-paged booklet, or something in between. Small consulting operations often get good results with a modest brochure, perhaps one 8½- × 11-inch sheet folded twice that describes the background of the company, the type of work it does, and the qualifications of the principal or principals. Many of the very large firms produce quite elaborate brochures covering all aspects of their practices, which are designed to impress clients with the stature, size, and accomplishments of the firms simply by the brochures themselves.

An excellent brochure, which falls somewhere in between, is shown in Appendix B. Mickey Rosenau, owner of the Rosenau Consulting Company of Santa Monica, California, has divided his brochure into different topic headings such as The Company, What We Do, Clients, Qualifications, Recent Assignments, Our Code of Professional Responsibility, Contractual Terms and Conditions, Case History, How We Work, Why Retain Rosenau Consulting Company, and Client Relationships. A brochure like this goes a long way toward making a sale even before the consultant meets the potential client face-to-face for the first time.

Locating the Right Mailing List. Producing your letter, your brochure, and their first-class envelope is not inexpensive. You can expect to spend as much as fifty cents or more including postage to get each direct mail package to a potential client. Therefore, you do not want to waste your mailing on individuals who have only a slight chance of being interested in your services. You want to reach those who are real potential customers—individuals who have the authority to hire you and would probably be interested in what you have to offer.

One source of help are those professionals who handle mailing lists: list brokers, managers, or compilers. These experts can be found in most Yellow Pages under the heading "Mailing Lists." They will discuss your needs with you and help you rent lists of potential clients interested in the particular services you offer. Usually you pay nothing for this advice on lists. The list broker gets paid a commission from the list owner when you rent the lists.

If you are located in a smaller town, the potential size of your market, depending upon your specialty, may be so small that a direct mail campaign is not advisable. On the other hand, you could do a direct mail campaign with the idea of promoting a national or international business. This, of course, may require travel on your part, unless you consult through the mail or by telephone, both of which are possible.

One consulting firm that successfully promotes its practice through the mail is the MTA Group Management and Technology Advisers, Inc., a small consulting firm involved in production for the publishing industry. It has spent as much as $45,000 a year on its direct mail campaign alone. The company also stays in touch with its client list of about six thousand companies by mailing out up to six different first-class packages (each containing a letter, a card, and a small brochure) and then sending the same mailings out a second time, all within the span of a year. In 1983 *DM News* reported an overall response rate of 1.8 percent for this firm's mailing.

If you would like to receive additional information or catalogs of lists, here are some representative companies to contact:

Addresses Unlimited—14621 Titus Street, Van Nuys, Calif. 91402 (213/873-4114)

AH Direct Marketing—2554 Lincoln Boulevard, Suite 1040, Marina del Rey, Calif. 90291 (213/827-5515; toll-free: 1-800/843-4662)

Ed Burnett Consultants—99 West Sheffield Avenue, Englewood, N.J. 07631 (201/871-1100; toll-free: 1-800/223-7777)

Compilers Plus, Inc.—466 Main Street, New Rochelle, N.Y. 10801 (914/633-5240)

Direct Media, Inc.—70 Riverdale Avenue, Greenwich, Conn. 06830 (203/531-1091)

Dunhill International List, Inc.—1100 Park Central Boulevard, South Pompano Beach, Fla. 33064 (toll-free: 1-800/223-1882)

Hugo Dunhill Mailing Lists, Inc.—630 Third Avenue, New York, N.Y. 10017 (212/682-8030; toll-free: 1-800/223-6454)

Dun's Marketing Services, a company of the Dun & Bradstreet Corporation—49 Old Bloomfield Avenue, Mountain Lakes, N.J. 07046 (toll-free: 1-800/624-5669)

R. L. Polk and Co.—6400 Monroe Boulevard, Taylor, Mich. 48230 (313/292-3200)

Fred Woolf List Co. Inc.—280 North Central Avenue, Hartsdale, N.Y. 10530 (914/946-4466; toll-free: 1-800/431-1557)

Alvin B. Zeller, Inc.—37 East 28 Street, New York, N.Y. 10016 (212/689-4900; toll-free: 1-800/223-0814)

Cold Calls

Cold calls are those made to prospects with whom you have had no prior contact. This method can be extremely effective in obtaining clients. However, it is time-consuming, and it involves significant rejection, which you must learn to cope with if you are to use this method.

Let's say you've decided to devote a single day to obtaining clients through cold calls. That means you should make from twenty-five to thirty actual contacts with individuals who have the authority to hire you. If even half this number retained your services, you would soon be extremely wealthy from consulting. As a matter of fact, you would have more consulting work than you could possibly handle. But the reality is that if one of these calls leads to a one-time engagement worth $3,000 to $5,000, the day has been well worth your time. If you consider that this is a satisfied client who will hire you again and again, this single success out of many calls was really worthwhile. However, twenty-five to thirty calls with one success usually means twenty-four to twenty-nine rejections, some of which will be rude and abrupt. Therefore, if you wish to use cold calling, you must train yourself to be prepared for the rejection that accompanies its use.

You can maximize your success in using the cold-call method by doing the following:

1. *Write out exactly what you want to say ahead of time.* Usually you should follow the outline of a good direct mail letter. That is, you should speak about benefits to your potential client and sell yourself by describing past accom-

plishments. (These could be things you did while employed full-time for someone else. The important thing is that you were the one responsible and actually did whatever it is you claim.) While planning what you are going to say, never forget that the object is *not* to make a sale over the phone, which is almost impossible to accomplish, but to get a face-to-face interview where you can close the sale. (I show you how to do that in Chapter 3.) So now you know how to tell a successful cold call: It always ends with an appointment for a face-to-face interview.

2. *Use creative ways to get around the secretary.* One of the most bothersome aspects about the cold-call method is that frequently executives who may wish to hire you have secretaries in place between you and them. Part of a secretary's job is to screen out job seekers and those wanting to sell something to the boss. Therefore, it is essential that you get through the secretary. One method is simply to avoid the secretary altogether. Call before 8:00 A.M. or after 5:00 P.M., and chances are the manager will answer the call directly. Another technique is to identify yourself by name and ask for the individual you wish to speak with, using his or her full name. If you do not have this name, call the company and ask the receptionist for the individual's full name, not just Mr. Smith but Don Smith. When the receptionist connects you with his secretary, say firmly, "This is Jim Black for Don Smith. Would you connect me please?" Or you can say, "This is Jim Black, president of the XYZ Consulting Group, for Don Smith. Would you connect me please?" If the secretary asks the nature of your call, say that it is a private business matter. If she refuses to connect you without having this information, ask her to forward the information to her boss and leave your number for him to call you back. The chances of getting through are better this way than if you say that you are calling to see if Mr. Smith is interested in hiring you as a consultant.

3. *Combine your calls with a direct mail campaign.* This one-two combination punch can work very well. Do the direct mail campaign first, then wait several weeks. This

gives the executive time to call you directly if she wishes, and you will have a greater chance of setting up an interview. After several weeks have gone by, you cold-call those who have not responded to your mailing. Now if the secretary asks the reason for the call, you can say that it has to do with a letter you wrote previously to Don Smith. If you're wondering whether to include in the letter a statement that you will call soon, my recommendation is no. For one thing, if you indicate that you will call, the executive who may otherwise have called may not do so, and it's always much better if she responds immediately rather than passively wait for you to call. Second, if you get very busy, either with other aspects of your marketing campaign or with consulting work, your call will be delayed, and you could lose a sale. The direct mail campaign, combined with a cold-call follow-up, works well because some executives who desperately need your services may not realize it from your letter. In a personal conversation, they may recognize that you can fulfill their need and will make an appointment for an interview.

Direct Response Space Advertising

Until fairly recently, the advertising of consulting services was not particularly common. Today a number of different types of consultants are using it successfully. Executive search consultants, for instance, advertise in magazines or trade journals in their areas of specialty. Since potential clients in certain industries prefer to deal with specialists, these ads are often successful. However, advertisements for other consulting services are less successful; some are even prohibited by professional consulting associations. Consultants tend to be equated with attorneys and doctors in terms of confidentiality and standards of professionalism. Since the ethics codes of these two professions have only recently permitted advertising, it is no wonder that the same has been generally true for consulting.

However, depending upon the type of services you offer, some sort of advertising may be effective and acceptable. If you decide to advertise, it is important that the ad be well-written, which means written with your potential clients in mind. Also be certain to place your ad in a medium likely to be read by your target audience. Don't be fooled by the total number of people reached by your ad. It is only likely clients who count. For this reason, don't advertise in your local newspaper unless everyone in the general population is a potential client for the services you offer.

Advertising is expensive. Further, learning how to write the copy that makes such advertising work is not easy. The type of advertising that you are interested in is *direct response space advertising*. Like a direct mail letter or cold calling by telephone, this type of advertising is intended to bring a direct response. At the very least, such an ad should result in inquiries that will lead to consulting engagements.

Even some professional writers cannot write this kind of copy. The copy must be so compelling that prospective clients needing your services would be foolish not to contact you. Most such advertisements use the AIDA formula—for *attention*, *interest*, *desire*, and *action*. A dramatic headline is used to attract people's attention. Their interest is immediately aroused in the lead-in paragraphs through the statement of specific benefit. Additional benefits are stated and talked about until their desire to respond to the ad is at a peak. At this point, the ad calls upon them to respond at once by taking specific action.

If you want to advertise your services, I recommend that you read the following books: *Building a Mail Order Business*, 2nd ed., by William A. Cohen (New York: Wiley, 1985); *Tested Advertising Methods*, 4th ed., by John Caples (Englewood Cliffs, N.J.: Prentice-Hall, 1974); and *How to Write a Good Advertisement* by Victor O. Schwab (North Hollywood, Calif.: Wilshire Book Co., 1980).

Directory Listings

There are many directories that list consultants and the particular services they provide. Some are free; some charge for listings. Usually this method of advertising is not very effective for a simple reason: Few potential clients use directories when seeking consultants. As a test, I once paid $300 to be listed in one of these directories. Over the period of a year, I received numerous letters about my listing, but every single one was from someone seeking to sell *me* something! Directory listings are not recommended unless the listing is free.

Yellow Pages Listings

Listings in the Yellow Pages of your telephone book may be effective for certain types of consulting practices. Clients who have never used a consultant before may turn to the Yellow Pages in search of services. If you decide to advertise this way, it is important that you buy a large ad. The psychology of this is simple: A larger ad will attract readership over a competitor's smaller ad. Second, many people assume that a large ad is placed by a large company and a small ad by a small company. A large advertisement for a small business may actually outpull a small ad placed by a multibillion-dollar organization. Try such an ad for one year. If it brings in clients, continue to use it. If not, simply maintain a listing in the Yellow Pages with no ad.

Former Employers

Many consultants get their initial cash flow going by selling their services to former employers. They are able to do this because, no matter what the circumstances of your departure (unless you were fired for incompetence), you have something to offer that company in expertise and experience. Retaining you as a consultant allows your former employer to use that expertise without the large overhead of an annual salary and benefits, even though as a consultant, you may get a much higher hourly rate than when you were an employee. A former employer may also wish to hire you simply to ensure that you will not go to work for a competitor, either as a consultant or as a full-time employee. In any case, it is certainly worth exploring. Approach your former employer, explain that you are now going into full-time consulting and that you would be happy to do for the company what you did in the past, as well as other related work.

Indirect Methods of Marketing

Indirect selling methods should be part of your overall marketing program. Their disadvantage is that they are long-term efforts. They usually do not immediately result in engagements. Thus, as attractive as they are for building a consulting practice, they cannot be relied on by themselves, especially in the early stages of your business.

Indirect methods of getting clients include:

1. Speaking before groups
2. Sending out newsletters
3. Joining and being active in professional associations
4. Joining and being active in social organizations
5. Writing articles
6. Writing a book
7. Writing letters to the editor
8. Teaching a course
9. Giving seminars
10. Distributing publicity releases
11. Exchanging information leads and referrals with noncompeting consultants

Let's look at each of these in more detail.

Speaking Before Groups

Speaking in public is an excellent way of building your consulting practice. In your community, there are undoubtedly numerous groups that use guest speakers, sometimes on a monthly or even a weekly basis. If the type of consulting you do—or something associated with it—is of interest to members of one of these groups, you can benefit from speaking to it.

Dr. Pedro Chan, an immigrant from Macao, China, used

this method to build his acupuncture consultancy for physicians. You can do the same thing. Simply pick a topic having to do with the services you offer, whether it's tax consulting, starting a new business, direct response marketing, or some other subject of potential interest. Then prepare a forty-five-minute talk that would be of interest and value to your audience. If you consult in direct marketing, you could speak on the topic, "Five Ways to Increase Direct Mail Response." If you consult in personnel matters, you might choose "How to Decrease Personnel Turnover" as your topic.

Now go to your telephone book and look for local organizations that appear to have meetings and therefore may use guest speakers. Call and ask to speak to the program chair. Explain what you have to offer and how the membership can benefit from your presentation.

After your speech, let your listeners know how to contact you for additional information. A business card is good, but a prepared handout,* with information about your presentation together with your telephone number and address, is even better. In the bio that you supply to the organization (which will be used to promote your appearance and to introduce you when you speak), make certain to include the fact that you are a consultant. In some cases, you will actually get paid for your presentation, but this is only a bonus. Your major objective is to gain exposure and eventually get additional clients.

Three books that will help you are: *Speak and Get Results* by Sandy Linver (New York: Summit Books, 1983); *Power Talk* by Niki Flacks and Robert W. Rasberry (New York: The Free Press, 1982); and *How to Write and Give a Speech* by Jean Detz (New York: St. Martin's Press, 1984).

You may also want to join the National Speakers Association and participate in their many programs for helping speakers. The Association even has a professional emphasis group for consultants. For membership information, contact the Association at 3877 N. 7 Street, #350, Phoenix, Arizona 85014.

---

*In the front of this book, you will see "Cohen's Maxims." This is a handout that I give all attendees at my courses and seminars.

Newsletters

The way to use a newsletter to get clients is not simply to dispense news but to dispense news of interest and value to potential clients and to remind the older ones that you are still around. Every time a client or potential client receives one of these newsletters with your name on it, he or she thinks of you. One method is to use newsletters written by someone else. These syndicated newsletters are mailed out with your firm's name imprinted on each copy. One organization that does this is Dartnell's Cambridge Associates, 164 Canal Street, Boston, Massachusetts 02114-1805. A sample of its newsletter *Executives' Digest* is shown in Figure 2-2.

Of course you can write your own newsletter with specialized information pertaining directly to services you offer. It doesn't have to be elaborate; you can type a master directly onto your business letterhead and have it reproduced by a quick printer. If the material is of value to your readers, you can be sure it will increase your credibility and help to build your practice.

A sample of one of these newsletters promoting consulting and seminars, by Phyllis Hillings & Company, is shown in Figure 2-3. Note how useful information and promotional materials are combined.

If you'd like to attend a seminar on the editing, design, and production of newsletters, contact Promotional Perspectives, 1955 Pauline Boulevard, Suite 100-A, Ann Arbor, Michigan 48103 (313/994-0007). This organization conducts seminars on the subject all over the country.

See also *Publishing Newsletters* by Howard P. Hudson (New York: Scribner's, 1982) and *The Newsletter Editor's Desk Book* by Marvin Arth and Helen Ashmore (Shawnee Mission, Kan.: Parkway Press, 1984).

Let me tell you a story about effective use of a newsletter. I was the head of a rapidly growing organization and had been hiring new people every few months, mostly through advertisements in *The Wall Street Journal*. Every time one of my ads appeared, headhunters would call offering to find the needed candidate for me; since I had never dealt with

(text continues on page 49)

Figure 2-2.   Sample newsletter.

February 1990

Executives' Digest

SUMMARIES OF TIMELY ARTICLES OF SPECIAL INTEREST TO BUSINESS MEN AND WOMEN

YOUR FIRM'S NAME HERE

(Or, at no extra cost, use your own title and masthead design)

Executives Wary of Budget Deficit
Sales and Executive Marketing Report, September 27, 1989, p. 48.

Eighty-seven percent of the CEOs surveyed by the Conference Board consider the federal budget deficit a "serious" problem, and almost 50 percent consider the problem "very serious."

To reduce the deficit, they suggest cutting back on farm supports, foreign aid, and defense expenditures. Only 33 percent of the CEOs would approve cuts in spending for Social Security, Medicare benefits, and unemployment payments.

Ninety percent urge higher excise taxes on tobacco and liquor. Slightly more than 50 percent think a value-added tax would be fair while almost 50 percent oppose it.

The Conference Board also noted: 1) 30 percent support spending levels for the Food Stamp program, but 48 percent suggest small cuts; 2) 35 percent back present spending levels for public housing, but 45 percent want reductions; 3) 30 percent favor current expenditures for the space program, but 54 percent want modest cuts; 4) nearly 32 percent support taxing social security benefits, whereas 45 percent are opposed; 5) more than 70 percent oppose increases in the personal income tax rate; and, 6) more than 74 percent oppose higher income taxes.

Don't Credit the Fraudulent
Consumer Finance Bulletin, July 1989, Vol. 4, No. 7.

Credit cards are convenient, but thieves can fraudulently use them. It is important to protect your cards and the information they contain.

Consumer Finance Bulletin suggests you: 1) Sign your card as soon as you receive it; 2) Make sure your card is returned after purchases—especially in busy stores and restaurants; 3) Don't carelessly discard receipts and carbons; 4) Don't write your credit card number on mailers or return cards that can be opened; 5) Avoid giving card numbers to telephone solicitors unless you initiate the call; and 6) Keep your cards in a safe place. Also, make a list of numbers so that you can notify the issuer in case of theft or loss.

Courtesy Dartnell's Cambridge Associates.

Chart the Organization
The Conference Board, Press Release, New York, NY 10022.

There is growing demand for corporate organization charts because of the continuing trends toward company mergers and restructurings. Companies are also beginning to see organizational design as a factor in competitive intelligence and business strategies.

The Conference Board is a prime source for organizational charts. It has a collection of up-to-date charts from 500 leading corporations in 17 different industries. They are used by CEOs and marketing executives to 1) examine competitive structures, 2) analyze structures of reorganized firms, 3) design new charts, 4) learn how leading companies organize management teams and workforces, and 5) learn about new job titles, staff directions, and operating relationships.

Information and samples can be obtained by contacting Linette Waters at (212) 759-0900.

Aim at Military Targets
Reprinted with permission of Sales and Marketing Management, September 1989, p. 29.

Many companies overlook the military market—an enormous, $169-billion, youth-oriented market apparently immune to recession and unemployment.

Look at it as "a military city," suggests Nat Kornfeld of Army Times Publishing. The "city" has a population ranking between New York and Los Angeles, with a high concentration of 18-to 34-year-olds. Sales at military exchanges and commissaries rival those of the largest supermarket and department store chains.

Some characteristics of the military market: Average family income is $47,400, a large portion of it disposable. Almost 67 percent own a bank credit card vs. 40 percent of all U.S. households. There are more two-car household families than the average. Military families also invest more in stocks and corporate and government bonds than the average U.S. household. Military personnel must take 30 vacation days annually and are major users of airlines, rental cars, and vacation resorts.

(continued)

Figure 2-2 *(continued).*

Page 2

Concern About Competitiveness
Management Accounting, September 1989, p. 24.

 Concerns about competitiveness seem to have peaked in the United States, say some experts. But some leaders think we can't afford to let competitiveness become just another fad. As Roger B. Smith, chairman and CEO of General Motors points out, corporate competitiveness requires sustained effort, constant innovation of products and services, and continuous improvement.

According to Smith, "There are no 'Number Ones,' only a transnational world moving toward economic independence with the United States still filling a central role. The real meaning of competitiveness is our ability to provide a high and rising standard of living for our people through the performance of our products in world markets."

As Smith notes, a number of factors determine how well the United States sells its products. Among them are the U.S.' economic values, the quality of its educational system, international currency exchange rates, international trade policies, tax laws, and governmental regulations.

Smith believes the United States needs to keep its productivity high, invest in technology and people, understand what quality means, introduce constant innovation, and develop products with new features and capabilities.

He believes the United States needs to create a lean production system in every facility. Also needed are training and retraining, and good management and leadership. There should also be a commitment to teamwork and a sense of urgency and acceptance of change as a way of life in order to create "America the Competitive" in the best sense of the concept.

"Greatness cannot be achieved without discipline."
                                          —Al Fracassa

Communications and Business Strategy
TBS Briefs, Temple, Barker & Sloane, 1989.

Poor communications can doom any business strategy, says David Gaylin of Temple, Barker & Sloane, Inc.

"When drafting a business strategy, managers should keep in mind its organizational implications," says Gaylin. "The greater the degree of change required, the greater the organization's need for information."

Gaylin thinks business strategies should be motivational. Without understanding the commitment, a business strategy cannot succeed. A good business strategy must: 1) Describe the realities that gave birth to its need; 2)Explore the strategy in a manner appropriate to the audience; 3) Describe the network for the strategy; and 4) Define the role and contributions of the individuals involved in the strategy's implementation.

By building commitment to the strategy throughout the organization, the strategy can help provide a truly competitive edge.

Persevere for Peak Performance
The Office Professional, Professional Training Associates, 212 Commerce Blvd., Round Rock, TX 78664, 1989.

Worldwide competition provides the United States with a major reason to improve performance. We attribute others' success to low wages, but there are other factors.

About 72 percent of all U.S. students graduate from high school vs. 92 percent in West Germany. And 13 percent of all Americans are illiterate compared to 5 percent in Japan. Japanese students attend school 240 days a year. Korean children 250 days, and U.S. students 180 days. Also, U.S. firms invest much less time in training.

In his book *Peak Performers,* business writer Charles Garfield says U.S. firms must: 1) Decide to excel; 2)Learn from setbacks; 3) Sustain commitment; 4) Define individual and team missions; 5) Build group pride; 6) Seek individual excellence; 7) Persist even when goals seem unreachable; 8) Put restlessness to work; 9) Integrate natural talents and acquired skills; and 10) Pay attention to preferences.

Credit Card Service Boosts Sales
Entrepreneur, October 1989, p. 130.

Banks and other financial institutions can help you boost sales with credit card programs, no matter how small your business. And that means more sales, because the cards increase the probability, speed, and magnitude of customer spending.

American Express says 40 percent of its members spend more at businesses where their cards are accepted. A MasterCard International study shows that families make 32 percent of their transactions and spend 36 percent of their dollars using cards. The percentage of dollars spent at retail establishments totals 43 percent compared to 28 percent for personal checks and 20 percent for cash.

For businesspeople, the cards present opportunities to improve cash flow without extending credit. If you can prove your creditworthiness, you should be able to establish a credit card program. You'll need to provide a financial statement, a list of suppliers, credit references, and perhaps a list of customers. Getting approval for a credit card program is usually easier if you have a "storefront," but home businesses can also qualify.

Once approved, you will receive a start-up kit and instructions on how to run the operation. You will learn specifics such as checking the signature of the charge slip against the one on the card, verifying the card's expiration date, checking bulletins listing cancelled cards, etc. Most credit card processors are now computerized, with on-line verification obtainable within 4 to 15 seconds.

With a credit card program, you can expect processing charges, interchange fees, authorization service charges based on the dollar value of the transactions, and other operating costs.

Note: The material summarized on these pages represents a cross section of current comment and opinion. We do not necessarily concur in the opinions herein presented.

Make Voice Mail "Listenable"

Nation's Business, August 1989, p. 56.

The use of voice mail is growing, but some people feel that talking to a machine is "like talking to a wall." There are seven ways you can humanize a voice mail system for the benefit of employees and clients. Here they are:

1) Give the caller the choice of talking to a person or a voice machine. This makes the caller feel as though he or she is in control.

2) Make sure messages are returned promptly, increasing the client's confidence in your company.

3) Don't surprise people who don't expect voice message systems. Let clients know you have voice messaging. List your voice message mailbox on your business card.

4) Make sure your employees don't use the voice mail system when they can use a telephone.

5) Persuade management to support the system. If they don't support it, subordinates won't use it, either.

6) Frequently change your messages to make them sound more personal.

7) Monitor the use of voice mail. Provide training for employees reluctant to use the system.

"We fear to know the fearsome and unsavory aspects of ourselves, but we fear even more to know the godlike in ourselves." —Abraham Maslow

Making EC Good for the USA

Europe, September 1989, p. 16.

This year will be important for everyone exporting to Europe, says Eugene McAllister, Assistant Secretary of State.

The European Community (EC) could become an open market for U.S. products. Founded in 1957, the Community now has 12 members — most of whom have experienced substantial growth.

During the 1970s and 1980s, European business was in a quagmire. This poor business climate was referred to as "Euroscelerosis" because of trade delays, technical costs, and duplication of effort. Custom procedures accounted for about two percent of all intra-EC trade.

For the EC to become truly successful, a new and outward orientation is needed. Restrictive rules of origin, quotas and local content requirements, and special standards, certifications, and testing processes may make trading with the EC difficult — something the United States hopes to avoid.

Considerable progress has been made in approving more than 100 of nearly 300 directives, but major issues still need to be resolved. Among them are harmonization of value-added taxes, a single currency and a common central bank, and free movement of labor.

Looking at VDTs

American Optometric Association, Press Release, September 11, 1989.

About 50 to 75 percent of the workers using video display terminals (VDTs) experience vision problems. But there are many ways to help alleviate these vision hazards.

The American Optometric Association suggests 1) annual eyesight examinations; 2) advising the optometrist about the kind of work you do; 3) taking breaks from watching the video screen — usually 15 minutes every hour or two; 4) minimizing glare from windows by using shades, drapes, and blinds; 5) reducing task lighting to about one-half that of the overhead office lighting; 6) placing a glare filter over the VDT screen; 7) adjusting furniture and the VDT, including screen brightness and contrast; and 8) placing reference materials at the same distance as the VDT to minimize head and eye movements.

For more information, write for a free copy of "VDT User's Guide to Better Vision." Send a stamped, self-addressed business envelope to American Optometric Association, 243 N. Lindbergh Blvd., St. Louis, MO 63141.

Great spirits have always encountered violent opposition from mediocre minds. —Albert Einstein

Coping with AIDS in the Workplace

American Financial Services Association, Press Release, July 24, 1989.

More than 40 percent of all AIDS-infected people are now actively employed in the workplace. With no cure for AIDS in sight, as many as 750,000 to 1.5 million people may be infected with the disease but not yet ill, constituting a time bomb that is ticking away.

AIDS victims are frequently discriminated against in housing, public accommodations, business establishments, city services, and educational institutions. Many of the victims are black (29 percent) or Latins (14 percent). But whites still make up the majority of the infected (55 percent).

Laws to protect AIDS-infected individuals include the Federal Vocational Rehabilitation Act and the Fair Employment Housing Act. In 43 states, laws prohibit discrimination on the basis of physical handicaps or disabilities.

To cope with these problems, employers should consider: 1) establishing corporate guidelines for lawfully handling such cases; 2) developing health education programs; 3) arranging for employee counseling of newly diagnosed cases; 4) evaluating current employee benefits programs to determine appropriateness to employees suffering from AIDS; and 5) establishing an atmosphere of trust so that employees affected will come forward without fear of retribution.

The complete text of articles summarized on these pages are often available from the original publishers. We'd be glad to give you the addresses of these publishers.

(continued)

Figure 2-2 *(continued)*.

Page 4

Knowing Spanish is the most important foreign language requirement for executives moving up the ladder, according to a survey reported in *The Boston Globe*. Of the respondents, 44 percent indicated Spanish was the most important language to learn; Japanese at 33 percent was followed by French 8 percent, Chinese 6 percent, German 5 percent, and Russian 1 percent. Still essential, of course, is the ability to communicate well in English.

The chief information officers (CIOs) of Fortune 500 companies now receive an average $162,000 in annual compensation, according to Heidrick & Struggles. Responding CIOs of non-industrial companies earn $17,000 more than their industrial counterparts. The typical CIO is 48 years old, white, male and married to his first spouse. He works 57 hours a week, and spends less than 25 percent of his time in business travel.

Consider how prospects read your sales letters. They usually read the salutation first, then the signature of the person who sent it, and then the P.S. Then they return to the salutation and scan the first paragraph to see if the content interests them, says the *Business-to-Business Direct Marketing Handbook*.

CONVERSATION PIECES

Finding ways to keep workers happy is becoming more difficult. After a few years of work, workers sometimes exhibit a vague uneasiness or a decline in satisfaction with their positions. To ensure employee satisfaction, companies are offering many different benefits. For example, one company emphasizes good wages, benefits, and working conditions. Another company gives employees greater control over their work lives. Managers at another firm are judged by the number of problems raised by subordinates. And another major corporation emphasizes improving performance.

Flexible hours may not be as important to accountants as they are to some workers. An Accountants on Call survey indicates that only 20 percent of the respondents consider flexible work schedules "essential." Of the respondents, 53 percent said they already have flexible hours, but 49 percent said that they are not essential, and 28 percent said they aren't at all important.

DEs (Displaced Executives) are likely to find job hunting even more difficult, according to outplacement specialists. The average job search now takes 5.9 months (vs. 5.1 months in 1988). However, DEs will receive more severance pay, and many DEs will get a salary that is 9 percent higher than they did when changing jobs in 1988.

"Visual impact is 85 percent of the message when you first meet somebody, what you say is only 15 percent," says *Executive Strategies*. The publication also suggests that the cut and fit of your clothing are more important than how much they cost. You should think of image as a marketing issue. Paying attention to packaging the product can help you get the best price.

Check your earnings history every three years for social security purposes, suggests the Social Security Administration. If you've worked long enough to qualify for retirement benefits and can estimate future earnings, you can figure out future benefits and target your retirement date. This step is important because correcting mistakes becomes difficult after the statute of limitations runs out in three years, three months, and fifteen days. Check with your local Social Security office or call 1-800-2345.

THIS SPACE IS FOR
YOUR MESSAGE OR ADVERTISEMENT
(OR USE THIS ENTIRE PAGE)

With your name on the front of this publication and your ad in this space, you can send this helpful and interesting little newsletter to your list of clients and prospects *every month*.

It's *inexpensive*. It's *exclusive*, since we won't sell it to a competitor in your area while you are distributing it. And, there's *no* long term *contract*.

Write or phone for complete details on putting this publication to work for you.

DARTNELL'S
CAMBRIDGE ASSOCIATES

A DIVISION OF THE DARTNELL CORPORATION
164 Canal Street • Boston, Massachusetts 02114-1805
(800) 468-3038 • (617) 723-5969 • FAX (617) 227-6982

Figure 2-3. Sample brochure.

ETIQUETTE UPDATE

Premier Edition   *Summer 1989*

OUTCLASS YOUR COMPETITION!
Good Manners Make Good Business Sense

In any business of social setting, knowing what to do and when to do it will put you at ease and make the person you are dealing with more comfortable. Individuals and companies both benefit by using tact and style with others.

> *"A company becomes a company you want to do business with because of the people who work in it, so business etiquette has a very definite relationship to the bottom line."*
> — Letitia Baldrige
> (the doyenne of etiquette)

As the executive of a successful corporation, you are aware of the importance of customer satisfaction. A recent study for the White House Office of Consumer Affairs concluded that "96% of unhappy consumers never complain about discourtesy but up to 91% will not buy again from the business that offended them. In addition, the average unhappy customer will tell his or her story to at least nine other people and 13% of unhappy customers will tell more than 20 people."

As an individual, you will be in a better position for advancement if you appear confident, poised and successful when attending meetings or other business events. Your ability to handle colleagues, clients and superiors with confidence will be noted by those who have the power to promote you.

Phyllis Hillings & Company is offering a summer of seminars to corporations and individuals who wish to reinforce their positive image or to create a more effective professional presence. Business Etiquette, Table Manners and Public Speaking are three areas to be studied. Calendar and course descriptions appear on page 2.

INNOVATIONS
PH&C Expands Services

Phyllis Hillings & Company has recently moved to The Commons, Suite 265, an office compound located at 140 South Lake Avenue in Pasadena. Situated in the heart of the financial district, it is minutes from the 210, 134, and Pasadena freeways. The telephone number is (818) 304-0088.

PH&C is also pleased to announce the formation of its public speaking division, *Standing Ovation*, headed by Pamela Hillings Tegtmeyer. Ms. Tegtmeyer holds a degree in speech and theater and is the recipient of numerous awards in the field. *Standing Ovation* will present monthly workshops on public speaking to help people gain presence, confidence and the skills needed to deliver a more effective talk, business presentation, or announcement. Private consultations are also available on an hourly basis.

Bonnie Sill has joined the company as Director of Business Development. Ms. Sill has an extensive background in domestic and international sales.

Good Advice – Never bring a date, friend, or relative to a business or social engagement unless their name or "and guest" is written on your invitation.

INSIDE —

New Seminars		
	Description	2
	Schedule	2
	Registration	4
Tips on Tipping		3
New Children's Classes		3
Manners Survey Results		3
Conference on Women		4

Courtesy Phyllis Hillings & Company.

(continued)

Figure 2-3   (*continued*).

NEW SEMINARS ANNOUNCED FOR SUMMER:

PUBLIC SPEAKING
Conquer the #1 Fear

Whether representing your company or yourself, you will be able to hold the attention of your audience and gain its approval if you appear confident when speaking. Topics will include how to organize, start, and end a speech; seven tips to control stage fright; how to introduce a speaker, deal with distractions, or present or receive an award; the necessity of maintaining eye contact, and more. You will be videotaped twice during the session, giving you an idea of how others perceive you.

Offered four times:
**MONDAY, JUNE 26
THURSDAY, JULY 20
TUESDAY, AUGUST 15
MONDAY, SEPTEMBER 18**
6:30 - 9:30 p.m.
The Commons
140 South Lake Avenue, Pasadena

The seminar price of $75 includes refreshments, portfolio, videotaping, and validated parking.
LIMITED TO 20

STRICTLY BUSINESS
Represent Your Company with a Maximum of Confidence and a Minimum of Stress

If you are confident in knowing what to do and how to do it, you will maintain a competitive edge that will be advantageous in today's fast-paced business world. When you practice accepted etiquette skills, you enhance your success rate in getting an order, gaining a client, and keeping a customer. This seminar is ideal for the person seeking advancement. It will cover the essentials of meeting and introducing people graciously, greeting guests in the office, telephone etiquette, proper dress, male/female office protocol, entertaining clients, and other appropriate subjects.

WEDNESDAY, JULY 12
7:30 - 9:00 a.m.
The University Club
129 South Oakland, Pasadena

The seminar price of $50 includes breakfast, "Etiquette at a Glance/At Table" booklet, portfolio, slide presentation, and complimentary parking.
LIMITED TO 20 - Reservation Deadline July 5

ETIQUETTE FOR THE 90'S
A "Crash" Course in General Etiquette

Find out all the things your mother didn't have time to teach you and be reminded of the things she did! You will learn how to introduce people correctly, how to respond to various invitations, the art of making conversation, the value of thank-you notes, the essentials of good table manners, showing respect for older people, the benefits of *please* and *thank you*, and much more. Also included are tips on proper dress and the importance of a well-groomed appearance.

Offered three times:
**MONDAY, JULY 10
THURSDAY, AUGUST 10
THURSDAY, SEPTEMBER 21**
6:30 - 9:30 p.m.
The Commons
140 South Lake Avenue, Pasadena

The seminar price of $65 includes refreshments, portfolio, slide presentatio, and validated parking.
LIMITED TO 40

AT TABLE
Enjoy the Polish and Power of Social Poise

This seminar is designed especially for the adult who wishes to be more sophisticated in table manners and restaurant etiquette. You will be served a four-course dinner in the oak-paneled Grecian Room of The Biltmore Hotel where your current knowledge of table manners will be refreshed during discussions and demonstrations of making/receiving toasts, proper guest/host duties, power seating at a business meal, ordering from a French menu, using a sommelier, the only proper way to hold a knife and fork, eating difficult foods, tipping, paying the bill, and other areas of concern.

MONDAY, JULY 24
6:30 - 9:30 p.m.
The Biltmore Hotel
506 South Grand Avenue, Los Angeles

The seminar price of $125 includes dinner, wine, portfolio, "Etiquette at a Glance/At Table" booklet, slide presentation, and valet parking.
LIMITED TO 20 - Reservation Deadline July 17

Register now for the seminars you prefer to create a more positive professional presence. All seminars are limited in size to allow for more personalized attention. Use the registration form on the back page to reserve your place and get ready to *outclass your competition!*

- 2 -

TIPS ON TIPPING
How Much, To Whom: A Guide to Giving

Tipping is an accepted tradition in our society. If you are aware of the proper amounts for various services, you will be able to enjoy your meal without worrying about what to do when it ends.

Waiter • The waiter or waitress customarily receives 15%. If the restaurant is particularly elegant or special services have been performed, increase it to 20%. Figure it on the pre-tax amount and round it off to the nearest dollar or half-dollar.

Captain • The captain is the one who seats you and distributes the menus. If he prepares dishes especially for you or performs duties other than just seating you, he should receive a gratuity of 5% of the bill or $5.00, whichever is greater. It is passed to him with a word of thanks as you exit.

Bartender • If you have a drink at the bar before being seated, the bartender should receive 15% of the bar bill at the time you leave the bar, even though you may not pay the bar bill separately. Unfinished drinks should be carried to the table for you.

Wine Steward • The wine steward (sommelier) should receive 15% of the wine bill if he makes suggestions and serves the wine. The tip is handed to him with a word of thanks as you are leaving.

Musicians • Strolling musicians, *IF* they play requests for you or your guests, should receive two to five dollars, depending on how many of your requests they perform. A pianist should receive a minimum of $2.00 for playing a request. Do not assume he would prefer a drink.

Parking • Parking attendants should be handed one or two dollars (depending on the type of establishment) when they bring up your car. If there is a charge for valet parking, fifty cents to a dollar is sufficient. If a doorman calls a taxi for you, hand him one dollar upon entering the cab. Do not tip the parking attendant or the doorman on your arrival.

Coat Check • If you check one or two coats, tip one dollar. Add a dollar if you check three or four items.

Washroom • Washroom attendants should receive a minimum of fifty cents for just sitting. If they hand you a towel or offer colognes or special soaps, make it a dollar.

In general • Tipping should be carried out as subtly as possible. It is perfectly proper to add up the bill, but don't make comments on how expensive or how reasonable it is.
• If the bill is delivered on a tray, replace it face down. If it comes in a wallet, insert the money or a credit card into the wallet and leave it on the table in front of you. If you pay by credit card, it is proper to add the gratuity to the bill or to leave it in cash. Do not forget to sign the receipt if you are charging.

PASADENA'S TEN MOST WELL-MANNERED
Second Annual List Published

Results of the second annual "Ten Most Well-Mannered Persons of Pasadena" were announced recently. The polite people are:

Dick Davis .... Partner and Vice President of Podley, Caughey & Doan Realtors
Judy Gain .... Manager, Treasury Operations at Avery International
David Hotchkin ..... Senior Vice President, Anchor West Financial
Leonard Marangi ... Managing partner, Hahn & Hahn law firm
Richard Mastain .... Regional Vice President, Prudential Asset Management
Donna Mathewson Executive Director, American Institute of Architects–Pasadena and Foothill Chapter
Linda Mitchell .... Philanthropist
Nancy Payne .... Realtor, William Wilson Company; Philanthropist
Anne Pursel........... Member of the Pasadena School Board
Tricia Trent............ Founder and Executive Director of Top Performance

CONGRATULATIONS TO ALL!

Nominations are already being received for the '89-'90 contest. Whether you telephone or mail in your suggestion, please include the name and address of your nominee and your own name and telephone number so you can be contacted for additional information.

This year's survey will feature the addition of the five companies in the Pasadena area with whom you most enjoy doing business. Already suggested are Bristol Farms and Federal Express. Customers are much more likely to write letters of complaint—seldom of praise—so, if there is a business you enjoy dealing with, please send in the name so it might be on the honored list.

Good Advice — If you will be doing considerable business with a person from a foreign country, read up on the customs and courtesies of the country so that you will not commit any social blunders.

YOUNG MANNERS
New Series Announced for Children

Due to numerous requests, a series of classes on manners for children will be offered for the first time this fall. Pamela Hillings Tegtmeyer will be the instructor and Sue Bicknell, mother of four, will coordinate the series. The scheduled dates for the series are September 16, 23, 30, and October 7. If you wish to be included on a special mailing list for these seminars, please call the office or send in the reservation form on page 4. Also, please include the names of any friends who may be interested.

Good Advice-
Do not call a client by his or her first name until asked to do so, particularly if you are dealing with an older person.

- 3 -

(continued)

Figure 2-3 *(continued)*.

SOUTHERN CALIFORNIA
CONFERENCE
ON
WOMEN

Phyllis Hillings & Co on Program

    Ann Sullivan Tully, a fashion consultant from New York and Dallas with many years of experience in the fields of dress and design, will be joining Ms. Hillings to present a seminar on the importance of the combination of appropriate dress and proper actions. This seminar will be featured at the first annual Southern California Conference on Women to be held September 5, 6, and 7 at the Anaheim Marriott.
    Ms. Hillings and Ms. Tegtmeyer also have been asked to present one of their popular seminars on Business Etiquette at the event. The conference is expected to attract over 10,000 women to the three-day series of seminars, workshops, and prominent luncheon and banquet speakers.

A Practical Guide to Being the Best
Etiquette at a Glance:
At Table
**Table Manners for
Sophisticated Dining**

Now available through mail order or at one of our seminars, this is the first in a series of **Etiquette at a Glance** booklets. *At Table* is filled with helpful information and contemporary etiquette reminders. Whether you are to be host or guest, whether you will be at table in a restaurant or a home— your own or someone else's—this booklet will help you feel secure that your manners are impeccable. Included are sections on seating arrangements, toasting properly, styles of eating, tipping and paying the bill, as well as proper use of utensils--and which are which. It reminds you when to pick up your napkin, the only proper way to hold your knife and fork, and gives other concise information you can read enroute to the restaurant.

BOOKLET	$4.95
Tax	.32
Postage & Handling	1.00
TOTAL	$6.27

Use the registration form below to order gift copies now!

Good Advice-
    It is always polite to offer your hand when meeting someone; never refuse to shake a proferred hand.

- -
CLIP & MAIL

SEMINAR REGISTRATION

PUBLIC SPEAKING 6:30- 9:30pm $75	**STRICTLY BUSINESS** 7:30- 9:30am $50	**AT TABLE** 6:30- 9:30pm $125	**ETIQUETTE FOR THE 90'S** 6:30- 9:30pm $65
☐ Mon., June 26	☐ Wed., July 12	☐ Mon., July 21	☐ Mon., July 10
☐ Thurs., July 20			☐ Thurs., Aug. 10
☐ Tues., Aug. 15	☐ Please put me on the mailing list for the Children's Seminars.		☐ Thurs., Sept. 21
☐ Mon., Sept. 18	☐ Please send me _____ copies of *Etiquette at a Glance: At Table*. I have included $6.27per book in my check.		

NAME: _____

COMPANY: _____

ADDRESS: _____

_____

TELEPHONE: [Home] _____ [Office] _____

AMOUNT ENCLOSED: _____ Please duplicate Registration form for each additional person.

PLEASE MAKE CHECK PAYABLE AND MAIL TO: *Phyllis Hillings & Company
140 South Lake Avenue, Suite 265
Pasadena, CA 91101*
       CANCELLATION POLICY: Full refund if requested before reservation deadline.

headhunters and knew that they were expensive (fees up to 30 percent of an executive's annual salary), I turned them all down. However, one day I received a friendly letter from a recruiter, along with a free subscription to his newsletter. Over the next two to three months, I continued to receive this newsletter, which I found useful. When I next needed to recruit, I hired this headhunter to help me. That newsletter helped earn the headhunter a $7,500 fee on that one placement, not to mention the potential for future business.

Professional Associations

Membership in professional associations can be an excellent way to obtain clients over the long term, for two reasons: First, your participation lends you the credibility of the association even if you yourself are unknown; second, professional associations are excellent for making contacts, especially if you take an active role. Plan to participate actively in programs, e.g., hold office. Over the years, many clients have come to me because of my active role in associations.

Social Organizations

Social organizations are more for contacts than credibility. They include alumni associations, tennis or bowling clubs, or health studios; I have even obtained clients from fellow members of a martial arts club! When a social relationship is established, a client relationship often follows. Individuals see you, get to know you, and begin to trust you. If they happen to have a need in an area you are consulting in, they may well think of you. With very little direct effort, you may acquire a contact.

Organizations, both social and professional, are a basis on which you can build long-term relationships. It's no wonder that "relationship marketing" is now considered an important idea for all businesses.

Writing Articles

Naturally, if you are going to write an article, it must pertain to the type of consulting you do, and it must be interesting and valuable to the reader. Perhaps most important of all, the biographical information that you include with the article should note that you are a consultant.

The first consulting assignment I ever received was the result of an article I had written for a magazine called *Ordnance*. The executive vice-president of one of the largest aerospace companies in the country saw my article and found it particularly interesting, as he had headed a project having to do with the very product that I wrote about. He contacted me immediately for a possible consulting engagement.

Famed management consultant-trainer Howard L. Shenson tells the story of a consultant who wrote a single article and syndicated it to ninety different in-house publications. It resulted in so many requests for his services that he had to go into business as a consultant broker, brokering the offers that came his way, because he simply could not handle so much business on his own.

I've used this marketing method to promote not only my consulting services but other activities as well. One example concerns a book that I wrote, *Building a Mail Order Business,* published in its first edition by Wiley in 1982. To assist the promotion of this book, I wrote an article entitled, "Can Anyone Make a Million Dollars in Mail Order?" and self-syndicated it around the country to magazines and newspapers, offering each an exclusive in its geographic area or industry. (As long as the publications know what kind of rights you are offering, this is entirely legal and ethical.) In this manner, I multiplied my readership for this one article many times over. You can see a sample of my cover letter as well as a sample article printed under the title, "Imagination Is the Key to Making a Million," in Figures 2-4 and 2-5.

One day my publisher called and asked if I would be willing to go on radio station KLBJ in Austin, Texas, and naturally I agreed. This radio appearance, which was actu-

(*text continues on page 54*)

Figure 2-4. Cover letter to editor promoting article about mail order books.

Dear _____ :

Recent research that I completed has uncovered a business that can be run out of the home on a part-time basis, yet which can and has produced a number of millionaires. In fact, its current sales volume exceeds $100 billion every year, and it is so lucrative that more than half of the "Fortune 500" companies are engaged in it.

The business that I am referring to is the mail order business . . . and readership demand for information about the subject is so great that many major book publishers, including McGraw-Hill, Prentice-Hall, and Harper & Row, have published books on the subject. Interestingly, almost every one of these books stays in print over the years and continues to sell. For example, one of Prentice-Hall's books on mail order is in its twenty-fourth printing. John Wiley has just published my book entitled BUILDING A MAIL ORDER BUSINESS: A COMPLETE MANUAL FOR SUCCESS.

The reason that I am writing to you is that I have just completed a short article that explores the question, "Can Anyone Make a Million Dollars in the Mail Order Business?" I know that the answer, which is based on the research that I did for my book, will surprise you. It certainly surprised me . . . and I know that it will surprise and interest your readers as well.

I am enclosing this article for your review. I can offer it to you on an exclusive basis to your newspaper in your city. However, like many hot items that may be due in part to present economic conditions, the demand for this information is time-sensitive. Therefore, I can only reserve my offer to you for 30 days. Please let me hear from you as soon as possible.

Sincerely,

William A. Cohen, Ph.D.
Professor of Marketing
California State University,
   Los Angeles

Figure 2-5.   Article about mail order books in *Salem Evening News.*

living   THE SALEM, MASS., EVENING NEWS—FRIDAY, JUNE 25, 1982   **19**

Imagination is the key to making a million

By DR. WILLIAM A. COHEN

More than eighty years ago, Richard Sears and Julius Rosenwald got together to build Sears, Roebuck & Co. into what would eventually become a $10 billion corporation. In the process, these two entrepreneurs built themselves into the world's first mail order millionaires.

Since the time of Sears' beginning, countless part time and full time entrepreneurs have been attracted by the apparent ease with which inexperienced business people could enter this profession of selling products through the mail and emerge with a fortune. What is surprising is not that many have failed. Many have. But the unexpected fact is that in both good times and bad, many have succeeded.

Just before the depression of 1929, a young man by the name of Robert Collier wrote a book in less than two months called, "The Secret of the Ages." In the first six months after writing the book, Collier made more than a million dollars selling the book solely through the mail. He went right on selling the book through the 1929 depression. In fact, although the book has never appeared on any best seller list, it wouldn't surprise me if "The Secret of the Ages," was one of the biggest sellers of all time since it has never been withdrawn and is still being sold through the mail today.

Now it could be that Collier's achievement was a fluke . . . if so many others hadn't done the same thing with similar products.

Brainerd Mellinger, famous for his self-published course on import-export, built a huge multi-million dollar business around his product. Joe Karbo wrote his book, "The Lazy Man's Way to Riches" in 1973. Before he died in 1980, he sold more than a million copies at ten dollars each. His family continues to sell the book today.

Melvin Powers, a famous mail order publisher in North Hollywood, started with a single small book on hypnotism. Today he has more than 400 books in print and has sold millions of books in the interim.

Of course, there are a great many products besides books which are sold through the mail. In a recent year, more than $2.7 billion in general merchandise including home furnishings, housewares and gifts were sold as well as another billion dollars each in ready to wear clothing and collectibles. This is the stamping ground of mail order wizards like Joe Sugarman in Chicago who built a $50 million a year business selling electronic products in only seven years right out of his garage.

Sixty-nine year old A. J. Masuen of LeMars, Iowa, went from door-to-door salesman to more than $1 million a year selling first aid kits and supplies through a mail order catalog. Two high school boys, Len and Rick Hornick started their multi-million dollar mail order business selling hand-carved wooden ducks to hunters and collectors. Today they employ more than 100 expert craftsmen to make their ducks, and they mail out a 32-page catalog to almost a million customers four times a year.

What qualities does the would-be mail order entrepreneur need? Three qualities are absolutely essential: imagination, persistence, and a high degree of honesty. Imagination is needed in order to be able to visualize the special appeal which will compel a potential customer to buy your product. If you have imagination, you can sell almost anything by mail.

Mail order pro Ed McLean proved this by selling thousands of an unpopular model of a Mercedes-Benz automobile which conventional automobile dealers hadn't been able to sell. Mail order experts Hank Burnett, Christopher Stagg, and Dick Benson proved it by selling sixty airplane tickets at $10,000 each for an around-the-world flight. But perhaps the king is Joe Cossman. With no more business experience than being an ex-serviceman, Cossman sold 2,118,000 ant farms, 1,583,000 potato spud guns, 1,600,000 imitation shrunken heads, and 1,508,000 home garden sprinklers and many other products . . . all by mail.

Persistence is required because success is rarely instantaneous and there are always obstacles and set-backs. Cossman spent over a year working on his kitchen table encountering false leads, problems, and failures at the same time holding down a full time job during normal working hours before he finally hit his first success. And even that first successful project required hard work and numerous obstacles that had to be overcome. Less persistent entrepreneurs would have quit long before.

Absolute honesty is required because a successful mail order business is built on trust, repeat sales, and satisfied customers. After all, you are asking your customers to send money, sometimes a great deal of money, to someone he does not know and cannot see. Cheat your customer even a little, and you've lost that customer forever. Without repeat customers, you might just as well invest your time and energy in a dried up oil well. The potential for a successful enterprise might have existed once, but now its gone for good.

The basic principles which you must understand to be successful in mail order have to do with product selection, structuring your offer, testing, where and when to advertise, and what to put into your advertisements. It takes a book to do justice to all of these subjects in detail, so we'll look only at the rudiments.

While it is true that a mail order expert can sell just about anything through the mail, some products just naturally make better mail order products than others. To increase your chances of picking a winner, look for a product that is light weight, nearly unbreakable, has a broad appeal to a large segment of the population, and has a large margin for profit. This last requirement means you have to be able to buy low, and sell high. Believe me, you are going to need this high profit margin in order to pay for your advertising costs, and at first to pay for your mistakes during the learning process.

You should try to get a product which allows you to sell it at three or four times the cost of the product to you. Now clearly you can't do this with a high priced product. But for most products under $25 this should be your goal.

This brings us to the important subject of testing. Successful mail order dealers test almost everything. They test which offer is best. They test different types of appeals. They test different prices. And they test different media in which to advertise. Testing is mail order's secret weapon. It is also the secret which allows a mail order operator to fail with four products out of five and still walk away with a million dollars or more.

How is it done? You spend a little money for a test. A complete failure tells you to drop the whole project. A marginal failure or a marginal success says to experiment and rework some aspect of the project. A major success gives you the green light for a larger investment. In this way you can afford to lose a little money on several dismal failures. But when your testing indicates a clear success, you can move immediately to capitalize on what you know to be a winner. The idea is not to risk a lot of money until you are certain of success.

While there are no guarantees, the potential does exist for just about anyone to make a million dollars or more in this business if they have imagination, persistence, and honesty and if they follow the basic principles that have proven to be successful.

(Dr. Cohen is professor of marketing at California State University, Los Angeles. He has just published a book entitled, "Building A Mail Order Business: A Complete Manual For Success," which is in its second printing.)

ally done from my office in California through a telephone
hookup, led to additional radio and television appearances
around the country and in Canada. But the interesting thing
is, this first appearance resulted from the article I had written. Someone in Austin had read the article, requested a
copy of the book, and felt that it might be an interesting
subject for a half-hour talk show.

Three books that may be helpful in the area of marketing
and publishing articles are *A Complete Guide to Marketing
Magazine Articles* by Duane Newcomb (Cincinnati: Writer's
Digest Books, 1975); *How to Get Published in Business/Profes-
sional Journals* by Joel T. Shulman (New York: AMACOM,
1980); and *How to Write "How To" Books and Articles* by
Raymond Hill (Cincinnati: Writers Digest Books, 1981).

Writing a Book

Writing a book is much like writing an article—except
that there is more to it. Having your book published demonstrates expertise in a certain area because the reader knows
that your writing has passed a rigorous screening by the
publisher. Publication gives you a credibility edge over your
competitors who do not write. I continue to receive a considerable number of requests for consulting that result from my
books. Recently I had a most unusual request. The president
of a small company, who had read both *The Executive's
Guide to Finding a Superior Job* (published by AMACOM in
1978 and released in its second edition in 1983) and the mail
order book mentioned previously, asked if I would locate a
senior director of marketing for his company. Although I
indicated that I hadn't done headhunting in some years, this
potential client said that he had read both my books and felt
that the combination of a former headhunter and an expert
in direct response marketing was just what he needed. The
result was my first search assignment in years.

For more information on writing books, see *The Book
Market: How to Write, Publish and Market Your Book* by Aron
Mathieu (New York: Andover Press, 1981); *The Non-Fiction
Book: How to Write and Sell It* by Paul R. Reynolds (New

York: William Morrow, 1970); *How to Get Your Book Published* by Herbert W. Bell (Cincinnati: Writer's Digest Books, 1981); and *How to Write a Book Proposal* by Michael Larsen (Cincinnati: Writer's Digest Books, 1985).

Writing Letters to the Editor

Letters to the editor can have the same result as other types of writting: building credibility. To be effective as a marketing tool, the letter should contain comments resulting from your expertise in a certain field, and you should identify yourself as a consultant in the area on which you are commenting. However, you should understand beforehand that the editor makes the decision on whether to publish your letter. Far more letters are received than could ever be published. To maximize your chances, make sure your letter is timely and well-written.

Teaching a Course

Teaching a course at a community college or a university can also lead to consulting assignments. Naturally the course must be in your area of expertise. Also make sure you teach this course at night, since this is when business executives are more likely to be continuing their education. My own teaching has led to major consulting assignments with large companies, locally as well as internationally. My only cautionary note here is that you must not consult with individuals while they are your students. This would be a conflict of interest. When I am asked about consulting while I am also serving as an instructor, I indicate that I would be happy to talk about the student's becoming a client after the course is over.

Giving Seminars

Giving seminars is much the same as teaching a course. Attendees at seminars tend to be responsible individuals with companies interested in the topic. If your seminar has to do with the area of your consulting services, this can easily lead to additional assignments. I know of several consultants who depend solely on this method to promote their practice; the fees they receive for giving the seminar are only a secondary consideration. You don't even need to do the administrative work of setting up your own seminars. Contact any local community college or university. Many offer seminars and are always on the lookout for new talent. They will require an outline of the seminar that you wish to give, its target market, the hours of attendance, the price, and a strong description of your background and expertise for giving the seminar.

Here are some books that can help you: *How to Organize and Manage a Seminar* by Sheila L. Murray (Englewood Cliffs, N.J.: Prentice-Hall, 1983); *Selling by Seminar* by Michael J. Enzer (Homewood, Ill.: Dow Jones-Irwin, 1986); *Running Conventions, Conferences and Meetings* by Robert W. Lord (New York: AMACOM, 1981); *Expanding Your Consulting Practice With Seminars* by Herman Holtz (New York: Wiley, 1987).

Publicity Releases

Every newspaper, trade journal, magazine, or other publication depends on a constant flow of news. They are interested in what you have to say, as long as what you have to say is of potential interest to their readership. Any time something of importance happens in your field, there is probably a story in it for some publication. Many times you will be surprised that what you consider common knowledge is new and quite interesting to many people, including potential clients. It is easy to write a publicity release. Just tell your story in a terse, straightforward style like that used in a newspaper article. A potential mailing list for your publicity release should include newspapers and other media such as trade journals whose target readership contains potential candidates for your services. Directories that list such media are available in your local library. Your librarian will be happy to help you find what you need.

Exchanging Information
With Noncompeting Consultants

Once you have established your area of expertise in consulting, you will find that there is a noncompeting-consultant network made up of other consultants who provide different services, much like doctors who deal in only one specialty and refer their patients to other specialists when required. Let's say that you specialize in organizational development, and a potential client or one of your established clients is seeking marketing consulting. You can recommend another consultant who will be able to help your client. In turn this marketing consultant can recommend your organizational development services to his or her clients when needed. To participate in this kind of network, use the cold-calling or direct mail techniques described earlier in this chapter, only this time target noncompeting consultants. Offer these other consultants an exchange in which you will recommend their services to your clients or potential clients if they will do the same for you. Make certain that they have a good supply of your business cards and brochures, and ask for the same from them.

Of course, before you make such an arrangement, you must be sure that this consultant will do a good job in the area in which you refer clients to him or her. You won't build much of a practice by referring people to consultants who fail to do a good job.

It is always important when clients contact you to find out how they happened to get your name. In many cases, this will be a referral, and once referrals begin coming in, it is a sure sign that you are well on your way to a successful practice. But in order to know which of the direct methods or indirect methods to continue and which to eliminate, you should always ask the question, "Can you tell me how you got my name?"

Marketing Consultant Services in the Public Sector

There is a tremendous opportunity for consultant services in the public sector. For the same reasons that large businesses use consultants, federal, state, and local governments have a real need for external services and will probably continue to spend millions or even billions of dollars to obtain them. Consulting services used by the government include advice on or evaluation of agency administration and management in such areas as organizational structures and reorganization plans; management methods; zero-base budgeting procedures; mail-handling procedures; record and file organizations; personnel procedures; discriminatory labor practices; agency publications; internal policies, directives, orders, manuals, and procedures; management information systems; program management such as program plans; acquisition strategies; regulations; assistance with procurement of solicited or unsolicited technical and cost proposals; legal questions; economic impacts; program impact; mission and program analysis; and much, much more. There are also various research and development and technology assessments done by external consultants, even though the government officially does not classify these areas as consulting services.

Consulting for the Government

Bernard Ungar, deputy director of the General Accounting Office, the congressional "watchdog" of the U.S. government, wrote that consulting services were being accomplished in eleven categories of federal product/service codes. These were:

1. Management and professional services
2. Special studies and analyses
3. Technical assistance

4. Management reviews of program-funded organizations
5. Management and support services for research and development
6. Technical representatives
7. Quality controls
8. Special medical services
9. Public relations
10. Training
11. Engineering development and operational systems development stages of research and development[1]

How Do You Get on the Government Bandwagon?

The basic method of locating opportunities to sell to the government is to use the *Commerce Business Daily (CBD)*, a newspaper published by the U.S. government five days a week. It's expensive—a yearly subscription by mail will cost you several hundred dollars—so I don't recommend that you order a subscription until your business in the government sector is high enough to warrant it. Fortunately the *CBD* is also available in many public libraries. Many states also publish business opportunities periodically (for example, California provides the *California State Contracts Register*). Contact the contracting office of your state to see if such a publication is available.

With regard to using the *CBD* or state publications, I recommend that you not bid directly on consulting opportunities unless you have had prior contact with the government agency. Simply responding to an advertisement in the *CBD* or a similar publication usually produces nothing but the wasted time and money in putting the proposal together. You need face-to-face contact with your prospective customers to convince them that you are better than the competition, and rarely can you do this with a proposal alone. The way to use these publications effectively is to consider the advertisements as a source of future clients and to make appointments for face-to-face meetings so that a later Request For Proposal will find you well-prepared.

Another method of locating opportunities in the government is to contact the Small Business Administration (SBA) in your area. Almost every government agency needs some type of consulting service. Whether it needs *your* services is another story. That you must investigate. Your local SBA office can help. Let it know that you are a business consultant and explain your area of expertise. Frequently it can refer you to someone within the agency who can help you find government contracts. The SBA also hires small-business consultants to help counsel its own small-business clients.

The Buying Process

The government buying process usually begins with an Invitation For Bid (IFB) or Request For Proposal (RFP). With an IFB, usually you just state a price for whatever is wanted; with an RFP, in addition to a price, you must submit a technical proposal documenting your method for accomplishing whatever services are requested. It is important to recognize that submitting an IFB or an RFP does not guarantee you a contract. Usually other firms are competing for the same work. Low price is always of importance; in fact, with the IFB, low price determines who wins the contract, assuming that the firm is otherwise qualified. With the RFP, however, other factors may be of equal or even more importance—one reason preproposal marketing is so important.

The Importance of Preproposal Marketing

Some years ago, I did considerable research on the factors that influence the winning of small ($2 million or less) government research and development contracts. Two popular theories seemed to indicate that marketing was more important than technical approach or even the price attached to a particular proposal. One of these was *consumer acceptance theory.*

According to consumer acceptance theory, the consumer may achieve three levels of intensity in his or her relationship with any product or service: acceptance, preference, and insistence. Consumer acceptance, the lowest level of intensity, means that the customer may have had some contact with the product or with some promotional effort. This contact leads to a decision on acceptability. Customer preference suggests a more satisfactory experience over a competing product and implies that the product will be favored over the competition's. Insistence, the highest level of intensity, is the stage in which the customer will take the product almost regardless of price or hardship and will brook no substitution. This stage, according to the theory, can be reached by a full knowledge of the product based upon considerable experience.

The other idea that was important to this application of marketing was the *merchandising theory. Merchandising* here means fitting the product to the potential customer's wants and needs. According to the main aspect of this theory, merchandising must be the central part of any marketing program. The market must be segmented in order to zero in on a specific customer, and the approach must accommodate the fact that this customer has a number of sometimes conflicting wants and needs that must be satisfied. These wants and needs are influenced by the customer's physical or mental state, his background or conditioning, the immediate situation that confronts him, and, most importantly, what he knows about the product either directly through its use or vicariously through communication with others. These wants and needs are of different relative values and may change. The desire for a particular product is influenced by its accessibility, including such factors as price, the customer funds available, and the effort required to secure it. Suppliers are likely to see a product from an entirely different perspective than the customer's. Yet the potential exists for presenting the product in such a fashion that it does satisfy the most important of the customer's wants, needs, and desires, or for altering the product within certain limits in order to accomplish the same purpose. To do this requires presentation to the customer; feedback from the customer; analysis of the customer's wants, needs, and desires; and calculation of the best way to satisfy them.

Thus, both theories, based on practice in the consumer-industrial world, argued for heavy investment in preproposal marketing for small government research contracts. And in fact, actual research with several different companies indicated the tremendous importance of the marketing done before the proposal was ever submitted. During this preproposal marketing, not only would the product or service be sold, but also critical information on how much the customer had to spend, the scope of the activities, and the kind of product or service he expected and thought he would receive would be established and made known to the seller. In some cases, win ratios increased from 0 to 100 percent by the simple influence of preproposal marketing. Preproposal marketing activities are absolutely critical for selling consulting services to any organization. Unfortunately, many consultants forget this when attempting to deal with the government.

The Marketing Sequence

The sequence of marketing to the government involves six steps. All of these are built around the notion of preproposal marketing.

1. Locate potential clients.
2. Screen.
3. Visit and make presentations.
4. Maintain contact and gather intelligence.
5. Prepare the proposal.
6. Negotiate the contract.

Locating Potential Clients. Potential clients can be located, as mentioned earlier in this chapter, through the *CBD*, the state register of opportunities, the SBA, or other government directories. Make a list that includes every potential client in the government.

Screening. The initial screening should be accomplished by telephone. Go right down your list and call each potential client one after the other. Indicate what types of consulting services you provide and try to pinpoint the interests of the potential client. If there is no interest, it is better to establish this now, when the only cost is a telephone call. Finally, try to establish an appointment for a face-to-face presentation. If this must be done at some other location, such as out of state, these visits should be coordinated so that you can make several on one trip.

Visiting and Making the Initial Presentation. For the initial presentation, organize yourself ahead of time and know exactly how much time you have. If it's thirty minutes or forty-five minutes or an hour or two hours, you should know this ahead of time and limit your presentation to these requirements. Also ask your contact how many people will be present. This will help you to plan your presentation and to know how many handouts or brochures to bring. I cover presentations in more detail in Chapter 11; for now you should understand that you must organize ahead of time and take enough brochures and other handouts so that all your potential clients can have a copy.

Maintaining Contact and Gathering Intelligence. Probably the most important part of preproposal marketing is not only to continue to sell at every meeting, but also to learn about forthcoming contracts before they are published in the CBD and similar publications. Also try to learn the scope of activity and how much money is available for these forthcoming contracts. Tell your potential client the approach you would recommend, and why. In some cases, these approaches will be incorporated into the RFP. This may seem like giving away ideas to competitors, but actually it's not necessarily bad, since you should be better-prepared than they to do whatever it was you proposed. At the same time, you should be honest and forthright in selling your ideas and disagreeing (tactfully) with your potential client when information stated is at odds with facts as you know them or if the cost will be more or less than the agency anticipates. In this way, by the time you respond to the proposal, both you and your potential client should understand exactly what is going to be requested, what you are going to propose, and approximately what these services should cost.

Preparing the Proposal. The proposal should contain no surprises. It is a sales document, one that confirms your outstanding ability, not a vehicle for presenting something new that you have not discussed with your potential client, even though you may think of something at the last minute. The reason for this is that no matter how lengthy your sales document (and some proposals are no more than a single-page letter), you do not have sufficient space to explain everything in detail. You will probably not be permitted additional verbal discussions once a proposal has been requested, so you may not be able to explain a new idea sufficiently. Any question that goes unanswered could work to your disadvantage in a competitive review process. Also, no matter how unique and advantageous your new idea might be, time is needed to sell the idea to your potential client's boss. Remember that any bureaucratic organization, including the U.S. government, tends to avoid and minimize risk. New ideas that have not been previously sold during the preproposal marketing phase have high risk from the perception of your potential client. Restate what you have already sold, and bid in accordance with the funds and scope of the effort as you uncovered them during your prior contacts.

Negotiating the Contract

Negotiating is a basic skill that is part of your stock in trade as a consultant. You will negotiate with clients, subcontractors, members of your client's organization, other consultants, vendors, and many others. So don't assume that negotiating a public service contract is simply a matter of signing a contract for a proposal. It is rare that any proposal is accepted exactly as made. There may be considerable discussion and give-and-take regarding terms, price, delivery, and performance. See Chapter 8 for more help.

Some recommended books are *How to Sell to the Government* by William A. Cohen (New York: Wiley, 1981); *The $100 Billion Market: How to Do Business With the U.S. Government* by Herman Holtz (New York: AMACOM, 1980); and *The Entrepreneur's Guide to Doing Business With the Federal Government* by Charles Bevers, Linda Christie, and Lynn Price (Englewood Cliffs, N.J.: Prentice-Hall, 1989).

To summarize, clients will not automatically come to you. You must market your consulting service. But if you do this well, in accordance with the guidelines in this chapter, you will soon build a successful consulting practice.

Note

1. Bernard L. Ungar, *Government Consultants GAO/GGD-88-99FS* (Washington, D.C.: General Accounting Office, 1988), p. 1.

3

MAKING THE INITIAL INTERVIEW A SUCCESS

In this chapter you are going to learn how to prepare for and conduct the initial interview with your prospective client. Along with general instructions about how to dress and how to act, I will give you essential questions that you must ask in order to learn all you can about the potential assignment, which will eventually enable you to confirm your understanding of the engagement. In addition I will point out nonverbal signs to look for and explain what each means, and I'll give you listening techniques that will help you to understand your client's feelings and intentions.

Looking and Acting Like a Professional

The first impression you make with your client should be the very best. In some cases, you can never overcome the effects of a questionable image in your client's mind. In large part, this initial image is made up of your appearance and your behavior. You want to look like, and act like, the professional that you are.

Dress is extremely important because it helps you make a good first impression. There are only two rules: Dress as neatly as possible, and try to look as much as possible like your client. For most business consulting, a conservative suit and tie for men and a suit for women are appropriate. However, if after several engagements you observe that in your client's industry a different type of dress is common, follow the second rule and dress like your client. Two good books on the subject are *Dress for Success* by John T. Molloy (New York: Warner Books, 1980) and *You Are What You Wear* by William Thourlby (New York: New American Library, 1980).

In this first interview, be professional but not pompous. You should always strive to be friendly, understand your potential client, and build empathy. Think back to the different medical doctors you have met over your lifetime. Some are professional and friendly, and you feel a real trust with them. Other doctors, who may be of equal if not greater competence, somehow build a wall between you and them, and you trust them less. The same is true with the business doctor, the consultant. You must maintain a professional attitude, and at the same time you must be tactful, friendly, and empathetic.

Seven Essential Questions

During the first interview, there are seven questions that you absolutely must ask in order to better understand the client's problems and to help you to decide whether to accept the assignment.

1. *What problem needs solving?* Whether the client contacted you or vice versa, it is important to find out exactly why the client is seeing you. Something is bothering the client. Some clients will spurt it out immediately; others will say very little, not wanting to reveal the full story until they know more about you. Nevertheless it is important that you draw them out and understand exactly why they are seeing you.

2. *Exactly what does the client want you to do?* What are the specific objectives of the assignment? Even though in this first interview your primary purpose is to gain information, and even though you are still feeling out the situation, it is important to have objectives explained explicitly once the reason for the assignment has been determined and you have talked to your potential client at some length about the task. For example, maybe this is a personnel problem; does she wish to decrease employee turnover? Does she wish to increase sales? Is there a problem in new product development, with too many unsuccessful products? Whatever your client's objectives might be, it is important for you to know exactly what they are.

3. *How will you know if the objectives have been met?* At first glance, this might seem obvious. If turnover is bad, the objective will be met when turnover is reduced. If sales are not what they should be, the objective will be met when sales increase, and so forth. However, you can easily see that there is much room for a difference of opinion. Will your client be satisfied if turnover decreases 10, 5, 1, or 25 percent? Or if sales increase 5, 10, or 15 percent? What you're looking for here is an exact figure so that both you and your client will know when the specified objectives have been met.

4. *Are there any particularly sensitive issues that you should watch out for?* Any organization made up of human beings contains political problems of one sort or another. As an outsider attempting to insert yourself into and analyze a particular problem, you may stumble into difficult political situations in the organization. For some types of consulting and for some clients, this will not be very important. For others, however, there will be some very sensitive issues that your client will not want you to disturb. Certain individuals or subjects may be off limits for interviews. If you are not sensitive to these political issues, you could end up leaving the company in a much worse situation than when you came, even though ostensibly you solved the client's problem. Take pains to ask about and to understand the politically sensitive

issues. Pay attention to detail so that you don't stumble around like a bull in a china shop but rather demonstrate the finesse of a real pro.

5. *Who will be your main point of contact?* Usually it's the individual who contacted you first, but this is not always the case. The only way to find out is to ask. Be certain that you have the name, title, and telephone number of this key individual.

6. *Will there be a backup contact?* Even if your main contact plans to be available throughout the assignment, request a backup contact. Your primary contact may have to leave on an unforeseen trip or be absent from the company just when you need him or her to make an important decision. So you lose time, and you may be forced into making a poor decision that could easily have been avoided. So always ask for the name of someone else in the company with the necessary authority on your project, and get his or her title and telephone number as well.

7. *What authority does each player have?* This is a key question. A player is anyone who has an impact on your engagement. If you do not take the time and trouble to identify the players, their responsibilities, and their authority, you could find yourself misdirected, either innocently by well-meaning individuals or deliberately by people in the company who do not wish you—or the individual who hired you—well. Some individuals may give you instructions or even verbal modifications of your contract even though they have no authority. Then you may find yourself in the difficult situation of being unable to bill for work requested by someone who had no authority to do so. Of course, beyond the loss of time and money, misdirection of this type could cause you to lose an important client.

Taking Notes

The only way to remember all you learn during the initial interview is to take notes. For this purpose, I recommend a notebook. I carry mine in my briefcase, and as soon as we start our conversation, I take it out and begin to take notes. If I don't understand a point, I ask the client to repeat what was said. Some consultant students have asked if a tape recorder wouldn't be a better way to record this information accurately, but I don't recommend it. A tape recorder is an intimidating device. Information that you are given as a consultant is frequently confidential; somehow pencil and notebook seem less threatening to a client's confidentiality. I have found that clients open up more if you use a notebook and a pencil.

I want to emphasize that in the very first interview you must find out everything that you possibly can. Never hesitate to ask for such information as the company's annual report or product brochures if you feel it will be useful to you. In fact, even after you have returned to your office, do not be afraid to call and ask for additional information if it will help you consider different ways to attack the client's problem.

Holding Off on Giving Advice

During the first interview, many new consultants are so eager to help the potential client and show that they recognize both the problem and the solution that they immediately begin giving advice. There are reasons you must not do this. One is that you don't really know enough about the situation yet to give advice. This is probably true in 95 percent of the cases. However, even in the 5 percent when the answer is obvious to you, do not volunteer anything unless you are already being paid for your time. After you have solved the problem, what reason does the client have to hire you?

I have made this mistake myself, but not anymore. Once a client called me about an exploratory interview and then suggested that I join him and his wife for supper at a nearby restaurant. The net result was that in addition to an hour during which I answered his questions, for the next two hours he and his wife pumped me for information over a delicious steak and drinks. For about a $30 meal, they received several hundred dollars' worth of consulting. On top of that, because I had apparently solved all their problems during our meeting and meal, they did not hire me. Why should they? Their problems appeared to be gone. Maybe the recommendations I made would have been different had I had time to think about them. Maybe I could have served my clients better. So both sides may have lost.

Interpreting Body Language

Psychologists have confirmed by research what sales-people have learned intuitively: What a buyer says may be less important than the message transmitted by the way he holds his body when he communicates with you. A potential client who speaks with arms folded across his chest, eyes avoiding yours, brow wrinkled, and fists clenched is probably feeling threatened by the situation and is not communicating openly with you. You are not getting all the information you could, and the client may not be convinced by what you are saying.

When you observe these physical signs, you should back off and try a different approach—anything to break this attitude and get the client to relax. A sign that you have been successful at this is that the client begins making direct eye contact and leans toward you. If he looks relaxed, with hands not clenched but open or extended, you have gotten through, and he is probably comfortable with the overall situation and is now ready for more open communication. But if he begins to turn his body away from you, avoiding direct eye contact again, you know he either does not want to discuss the issue you brought up or is suspicious of the particular approach you have taken. Again you are not getting through. To be successful, you must try a different approach.

Also watch to see if the client strokes his chin or neck, chews the end of a pencil, or leans back with his hands clasped behind his head. This indicates that what you say is being evaluated; the client is listening, and you are getting through. Continue to observe, and you will know whether you should continue that approach or attempt a new one.

Finally, you may observe a ready, almost eager attitude on the part of the client; he sits on the edge of the chair, leans forward, and catches your every word. Clearly you are making a favorable impression, and the client is demonstrating a readiness to act on your suggestions.

There are many complex issues involved in observing body language, and you need to know much more if you want to become an expert. But if you simply observe your client and think about what his body is telling you, you will learn quite a lot.

Two excellent books that will help you understand body language are *How to Read a Person Like a Book* by Gerard I. Nierenberg and Henry H. Calero (New York: Cornerstone Library, 1972) and *Body Language* by Julius Fast (New York: Pocket Books, 1970).

Making Use of Listening Techniques

Certain techniques of listening encourage various responses. You should use them to your advantage to draw the client out and obtain all the information you possibly can. Many of these listening techniques you already know, but you should review them to ensure you have them at your disposal and can use them consciously in your client meeting.

If you want to keep the other person talking, neither agree nor disagree with what is being said, but use neutral words in a positive way. "I see" or "how interesting!" or even "no kidding!" indicates your interest and encourages your client to continue talking.

On the other hand, if you wish to let your potential client know that you understand the information she has been giving you and want her to move to the next point, restate what has been said to you. Say something like "as I understand it . . ." or "in other words . . ." and then summarize.

If you wish to probe for additional information at the same time, you must lead the individual toward that information tactfully. Ask questions such as "Why do you think this is so?" or "Why do you think this happened?"

Finally, at some point you will want to summarize the

conversation and the ideas you've had. This is extremely important, because you will play back these ideas when you develop your proposal. You should do this recap when you control the interview. Take your time and use your notes to make certain you have it right. You can say, "Now, if I understand you correctly, these are the main objectives that you wish to cover, for the following reasons."

Identifying Emotions From Facial Expressions

You don't need to be a social scientist to identify happiness or sadness from the expression on a person's face. But other emotions may be more difficult to spot. The fact is, scientists have done considerable research in this area. According to Dr. Ronald E. Riggio, a psychology professor at California State University at Fullerton, your ability to do this even affects your charisma.

See if you can identify the human emotions on the ten faces shown in Figure 3-1. You may find the exercise more difficult than you thought. The answers appear at the end of this chapter.

Figure 3-1.   Ten common human emotions.

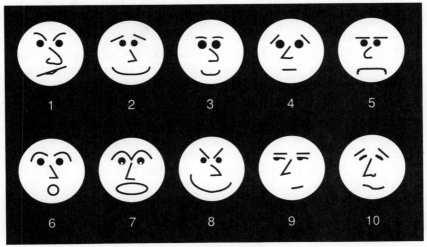

Adapted from Robert Riggio, *The Charisma Quotient* (New York: Dodd, Mead, 1987).

Like body language and listening techniques, your ability to instantly identify facial expressions can help considerably in working with your client and successfully completing the initial interview with a sale. If you want to know more, see Dr. Riggio's book mentioned in the figure.

What to Do When the Interview Is Over

For some short assignments and some special situations the client may wish to hire you on the spot. When you sense this—you will learn to recognize it with more experience— simply ask for the assignment. Tell your potential client how you bill and ask if she would like you to help her with the problem. As I explain in Chapter 6, even though this constitutes a verbal contract, it is very important that you follow up with a letter confirming exactly what you will do and the compensation you will receive.

However, many engagements, especially the larger ones, require a formal proposal and additional analysis on your part to determine the appropriate methodology, the time frame, and the price for your services. Therefore, at the end of the initial interview, you will not be in a position to offer a proposal, only to indicate when you will submit a proposal. If a letter of proposal is satisfactory, always ask if you can call should you have additional questions; if not, ask what form the proposal should take. You should also ascertain whether you are the only consultant being contacted or whether your proposal must compete with others. Most government proposals are competitive. Deciding whether you wish to bid on a competitivé contract is up to you. Many consultants refuse to bid on any type of contract and will politely withdraw if there is competition. My own recommendation is to consider all aspects of the situation, including your probability of winning.

Once you have established that a proposal is requested and when it is due, thank your client, make certain you leave your business card, and depart. If there is no specific deadline for your proposal, make sure you submit it as soon as possible. You never know what changes can take place in just a few days that would alter the demand for your services.

The Company Audit

To show you the scope of questions that might be useful in an initial interview, I have included as Appendix C a comprehensive checklist of questions, "The Consultant's Company Questionnaire and Audit." Do not think that you must ask each and every question at each initial interview. Also don't feel that because a question is not included, you may not ask it. In every situation, you should modify this list for the particular client before the interview. During the interview, if additional questions seem appropriate, make sure that you ask them as well.

Identification of Facial Expressions in Figure 3-1

1. Angry
2. Sheepish, embarrassed
3. Happy, contented
4. Puzzled, uncertain
5. Upset, disgusted
6. Surprised
7. Fearful
8. Sly, devious
9. Bored, disinterested
10. Tired, relaxed, relieved

If you got eight out of the ten right, you're doing pretty well. Five to seven is fair. Fewer than five says this is something you might want to work on.

4

HOW TO WRITE A PROPOSAL

If an agreement is not reached during the initial interview (and often it is not), the prospective client will expect a written proposal. In this chapter, we find out what a proposal must do and why it is necessary. All the essential elements of a proposal are listed and explained, and a proposal structure is provided.

Why a Written Proposal Is Necessary

A written proposal accomplishes five tasks that are important for you in getting on contract and beginning work as a consultant.

1. *The proposal finalizes the agreement.* Sometimes, even after an excellent exploratory interview, you have not yet made the sale. It is not unusual for a potential client to ask for a written proposal even though he is 90 percent certain about hiring your services. The proposal, then, is a sales document that ties together all the loose ends and closes the deal.

2. *The proposal documents what you are going to do.* The services you are going to perform in this consulting engagement should be clearly understood by both you and your

client. A proposal does exactly that; it spells out in black and white exactly what you are going to do so there is a documented basis for understanding.

3. *The proposal documents the time frame of your performance.* Just as what you are going to do is important, so is how long you will take in doing it and the time sequencing of each event. Sometimes the client will want to know partial information before the full project is complete. When the client wants information by a certain period, he may not hire you if he is not certain he will get it by that period. Documenting this time frame helps assure your potential client that he will get what he wants when he wants it.

4. *The proposal documents what you are going to receive for your services.* Unless you are independently wealthy, you aren't in business as a consultant just for fun, even though you may enjoy it immensely. The proposal specifies the compensation that you are going to receive for the services you propose to provide. Documenting this compensation can save you much trouble in getting paid later on.

5. *The proposal forms the basis for a contract.* As I demonstrate later in the chapter, the proposal can be the basis for a contract. In fact you can actually turn a proposal into a contract by adding a few sentences.

How to Write a Good Proposal

There are four points to remember in writing a good proposal.

1. *Keep the structure clear and logical.* I discuss structure later in this chapter.

2. *Use a professional but friendly style.* When you submit a proposal, just as in a face-to-face meeting, be professional but be friendly. In fact, if you are writing a letter proposal, you can be downright folksy; as long as you avoid stepping over professional bounds, it will only enhance your chances of being hired.

3. *Don't spring surprises in your proposal.* I mentioned this in Chapter 2, and although it sounds very simple, this is one of the hardest things to do. After you return from your initial meeting, you will frequently get new ideas that are different from what you and your client originally visualized. These ideas may be so good that you find it very tempting to include them in the proposal. Resist this temptation, unless you can check with your client first. There may be other reasons you don't know about why the client cannot accept these new ideas. He or she may need time to sell this idea to other employees, even top management in his or her company. If you surprise your client in the proposal, there may not be sufficient time to do this. Therefore, no matter how good the idea, unless you can clear it with your client before submitting it in the proposal, don't do it yet. You can propose it after you get the contract.

4. *Check before you send.* If at all possible, double-check the main points of the proposal with your client. If it's a short letter proposal, call the client and read it to him or her over the phone. For government contracts and some industrial contracts on a competitive bid, this may not be allowed. However, you should always ask. The worst someone can say is no. It is in everyone's best interest that the proposal be on the right track even before you send it. Don't assume that changes can be made after your client receives it.

The Structure for a Letter Proposal

Sometimes, especially with large or competitive contracts, the client will specify the structure of the proposal. (This is especially true of the government and large industrial companies). In this case, follow whatever structure is specified. However, a letter proposal is quite sufficient for most of your consulting engagements. Let's see what one looks like.

Opening

Simply state that you are writing to submit your ideas for the project discussed earlier.

Background

Begin by restating the background of the consulting situation. That is, restate your client's assumptions and other general facts in the case. This reassures the client that she has made an astute analysis of the situation. (If the client's assumptions are not correct, then you must convince her of this *before* submitting your proposal. If the customer is determined to use her assumptions, even if you have told her that they are incorrect and why, then you have a choice. You can use the client's assumptions or refuse the assignment. If you refuse, be as tactful as possible. The client will respect your stand and may contact you in the future.)

Objectives

State the objectives of the engagement precisely. Describe exactly what your client will learn or receive as a result of your work. I like to present these objectives in a way that makes them stand out visually—by using bullets, for example:

- Identify the least three secondary retail markets for new product line.
- Develop sales projections for six months and for twelve months.
- Recommend staffing increases to achieve sales projections.

Study Methods

Describe alternative methodologies for accomplishing the objectives. Discuss the advantages of each alternative and then indicate which method you propose to use, and why. When you describe the methodology, consider your audience. If your client is technical, use technical language; if not, don't confuse things with technical equations or terms. Stating all the alternatives, even those you do not intend to use, is extremely important, especially if you have competition. Competitors may propose alternative methods, and it is important that you show your client why these methods will not work and why the method you have chosen is the best. If you are convincing on this point, your potential client will use your proposal to help swing others to your way of thinking and to adopt your proposed methodology.

Potential Problems

Any project inherently has potential problems that could limit or detract from achievement. Don't omit or gloss over these potential problems; document them clearly, but also state how you will handle them if they occur. Clients smart enough to hire a consultant are smart enough to realize that potential problems exist. You cannot fool them into thinking that your approach is problem-free. In fact they will respect you more for anticipating the problems, as long as you have thought through what corrective actions you will take.

Data Flow Charts and Product Development Schedules

One type of a data flow chart is called a PERT chart. PERT (Program Evaluation and Review Technique) was developed for the management of complex multimillion-dollar projects for the government. It shows what tasks you will accomplish and in what order for most efficient management. It is more appropriate for very complex programs, but it can always be included in the proposal. If nothing else, it adds a bit of showmanship to your proposal and demonstrates the control you have over the project. A product development schedule will probably be sufficient for most projects. I discuss how to build both in Chapter 7.

The Finished Product

Your client will want to know what to expect by way of a finished product. Will you be furnishing a report? A staff study? Photographs? And how many copies will you provide? This last point can be important, because frequently the client will need to distribute the information to others, perhaps the board of directors or other managers in the company. Specify exactly what you will furnish and what it will contain, the number of copies, drawings, photographs, and other details. Include the date on which you will complete your study and submit your final report.

Cost and Payment Information

For most small contracts, it is not important to break down cost information unless the client requests it. However, the timing of payment is important. The client will want to know not only how much you want but when you want it. For example, do you want 50 percent of your fee up front and 50 percent at completion? One third at signing of contract, one third at some intermediate point, and one third at completion? Work-in-progress billing with monthly invoices, or everything in one lump sum when you submit your report? (The last, by the way, is not recommended.)

Converting a Proposal Into a Contract

The last paragraph is a close. It can—and should—be friendly, but it can also serve as a contract if you combine it with an authority to proceed. Here's how to do this in a friendly but professional way:

> Please simply sign at the bottom where indicated, for authority to proceed under these conditions, and return the original to me. However, if you have any questions or suggestions pertaining to this proposal or the work you would like accomplished, please do not hesitate to call me at 555-1234.

If you decide to use the suggested last paragraph and allow it to be converted into a contract, you may wish your attorney to review this information.

An example of a letter proposal is shown in Figure 4-1, and a more extensive proposal is in Appendix D. You can see that both structures are very similar.

Figure 4-1.   A typical letter proposal.

April 24, 19XX

Mr. Joseph Black
Unique Sales Co., Inc.
4571 Plainview Avenue
Pasadena, CA 91107

Dear Mr. Black:

We enjoyed the pleasure of meeting with you on Wednesday, April 18. We were amazed to learn that you had been in the mail-order business for over 33 years selling government surplus.

The purpose of this letter is to present our proposal for a research study based upon the objectives discussed in our meeting with you.

Please keep in mind that this is a proposal and subject to your ideas and suggestions.

A RESEARCH PROPOSAL FOR:

An Investigation of the Seasonal
Sales Trend of Unique Sales Co., Inc.

Background

Unique Sales Company is a mail-order company that sells to individual consumers as well as to governments of foreign countries. The company originally sold marine equipment but has now expanded its sales to other items, such as aircraft parts, auto parts, and hydraulics.

Unique Sales Company's main objective was to sell government surplus items; however, recently there has been a drastic cut in the availablity of government surplus items.

The sales trend of this company has its peak months around the first five to six months of the year; the other months are slow. In the eastern part of the U.S., the sales are very much affected by the weather. The more severe the winters are, the higher the sales are, because people stay at home and read the sales catalog.

Objectives

The primary objective of this study would be to gain an insight into the factors causing cyclical variations in sales for the mail-order industry and for Unique Sales specifically. Recommendations for Unique Sales' actions will be made upon evaluation of data collected.

More specifically, the following areas would be investigated:

I. Sales trends (cross section)
   A. Industrial-oriented mail-order house
   B. Consumer goods-oriented mail-order house
   C. Industrial/consumer-oriented mail-order house
II. Factors affecting sales
   A. Weather
   B. Product line
   C. Target market
   D. Advertising effectiveness

Study Methods

Several market research methods would be incorporated into this study.

The first would be an exhaustive search for all readily available secondary market statistics and data. This would be statistical information already published or obtainable at a nominal cost. Possible valuable sources for this information would be U.S. government agencies, trade associations, the National Weather Bureau, and trade periodical publishers, as well as the standard business bibliographies.

In addition, personal telephone calls would be made to selected individuals in this industry. These would be those recognized as the most knowledgeable in the industry. From these telephone calls an attempt would be made to obtain data not uncovered during the search for secondary information.

Potential Problems

In most secondary research studies, the existence of relevant market statistics and data cannot be determined until the actual study is begun.

Market statistics do not exist for all industries and, in some cases, exist only in the files of private firms. In these cases, the information is considered proprietary and is not generally released to the business community.

In many instances, the use of personal interviews can compensate for lack of published data and bring to the forefront valuable data otherwise not available.

Overall, even with possible information gaps, the research team is confident we can supply Unique Sales Company with a viable, well-documented report.

(*continued*)

Figure 4-1   (*continued*).

The Report

Our report would consist of a description of the study objective, design, and the findings reported at three levels of detail.

First would be what we see as the major findings or highlights of the study, including our conclusion and recommendations. This section would be followed by a more detailed and documented discussion and analysis of the findings. An appendix would contain brochures and other supplementary materials.

Cost and Timing

The cost of this completed study would be $1500, one-half payable on authorization to proceed and one-half payable on delivery of final report, two copies of which will be delivered in its final form.

The study will be compiled, and the reports delivered, four weeks after authorization to proceed.

We know that you are busy. Therefore simply sign below for authorization for us to proceed with this work. If you have any questions or suggestions to make regarding this proposal and the proposed study, please feel free to call us at once.

Sincerely yours,

_____

W. W. Smith
Director of Research

_____

Mark Tizon
Principal Consultant

Authorization to Proceed

I agree to the terms in the above proposal and grant authorization to proceed in accordance with these terms.

_____

Joseph Black
President
Unique Sales Company

5

PRICING YOUR SERVICES

Pricing is crucial. As well as determining the size of your billings and profits, it has an important effect on your image as a consultant. In this chapter, I discuss the three basic price strategies available to you as a new consultant and the different methods of billing for your services.

Three Price Strategies

The three basic price strategies available to you are a low-price strategy, a high-price strategy, and a meet-the-competition strategy. Let's look at each one in turn.

A Low-Price Strategy

A low-price strategy is basically penetration pricing. The idea is that you will enter the marketplace with a price lower than your already established competitors; you will attract clients because of your bargain prices. This strategy can work for new consultants, and with it you will be able to attract more business than you could otherwise.

However, there are some serious shortcomings. First, with consulting you are basically selling your time, so you will have to work harder than those established in your profession to make the same amount of money. This also means that your competitors will have additional financial resources to use in countermarketing campaigns if they choose. Second, price has an image connotation. In the minds of many, low price means cheap, and a low-priced consultant may be viewed as a low-quality consultant. You may be given only the less rewarding, grubbier types of assignments and not those that provide high exposure to top-level management. Finally, after choosing a low price, you may find it extremely difficult to raise your price later on as your practice grows.

For example, I have a friend, George W., who is a CPA specializing in tax consulting. When George first started out as an independent consultant, it was part-time and after-hours. To build his practice, he chose a low-price strategy; his billing rate was only 50 percent of the average rate for these services. Some years later, after his part-time practice had grown, George quit his full-time job and bought an established tax consulting practice whose clients were billed at more than twice the rate George had been charging. George now had two different rates for his clients. Since he was now full-time, it seemed to make sense to raise his fees to the higher rate. However, as soon as he did this, every one of his former clients quit or threatened to. George needed these clients, so he reversed himself and maintained two different prices. However, he was hardly comfortable with this solution. First, he felt he was cheating his new clients by charging them so much more. But George also felt he was cheating himself, since he clearly was now worth the higher figure even if his older clients wouldn't pay it. When George brought this problem to me for advice, my suggestion was to raise the lower rate slowly. George did this, raising his prices from 10 to 15 percent every year. In a couple of years, the amount charged his lower-priced class of customers was close enough to that of the higher-priced class that he could finally accept the loss of the clients who refused to go along with the single, higher billing rate.

A High-Price Strategy

Another option that any consultant has, whether new or old, is to adopt a high-price strategy. This one is somewhat more risky. You are telling the world that you are worth that money; your image is one of a high-quality consultant. However, your potential clients may not believe you. It goes without saying that you had better be what you advertise. The high-price strategy is, however, a viable one that many new consultants overlook, either because they are afraid they are not worth the money, because they somehow have a nagging feeling they are ripping off their potential client, or because they fear they will get no business if they choose to charge high prices. The truth is that in many cases, you not only are worth much more than you think but may be worth more than established consultants who are already earning big fees. Before you reject a high-price strategy, consider the following stories; they are all true.

• My student, Harry S., graduated with an MBA from California State University at Los Angeles and went to work for a major consulting firm. The day after he left the university, the firm that hired him billed Harry's time at $1,000 a day plus $300 overhead, a total of $1,300 a day.

• Some years ago, I got together with two friends. One had been the city manager of a major U.S. city and had retired into consulting; the other was general manager of a division of a major aerospace company. The former city manager said, "Boy, this consulting is great. Do you know that I'm getting $50 an hour?" This friend had more than thirty years' experience as manager of various cities and also had a Ph.D. At the time, I was billing $100 an hour, and I said, "Bob, you are not charging nearly enough. I'm billing at twice what you're billing at. I'm billing at $100 an hour." The general manager of the aerospace company looked at both of us and smiled. "You're both undercharging," he said. "We pay our consultants $250 an hour, and to my knowledge none of them are as qualified or as good as either one of you two."

• Several years ago, I received a telephone call from an individual who identified himself as Jerry S., a former student at my university. Jerry said that he had been referred to me, even though he had not been my student, and that he had graduated eight years previously with a bachelor's degree. He explained that he and his partner gave seminars for companies on management styles and had put together a workbook for the seminars. Since I was known as an expert in direct response marketing, he wanted some advice on how they might self-publish this workbook and sell it through the mail. During our talk, I became intrigued with Jerry's frequent mention that his clients were top management, and I finally asked him who his clients were. "Oh," he said, "we give special seminars for small groups of top management in each company. Usually there are no more than five to seven in each group." I asked about his pricing. "Oh, we go high, for image purposes," Jerry replied. "We charge $7,000 a day." I laughed and told him that he understood the marketing of his services very well. Seven thousand dollars a day was far above the average fees charged by many providing similar services who held Ph.D. degrees.

• A friend of mine, Mary T., was going to start a part-time consulting business doing copyediting for writers. I told her of my concern that people generally charge too little for their services, and I gave her a short talk on not being afraid to use a high-price strategy. At the time of this incident, copyediting services were going for approximately $10 to $15 per hour. But I thought she knew that. A week later, she told me she had her first client—at $40 an hour! I almost fell over when I found out how much she was receiving, and so did she when I told her that she was receiving three to four times the amount usually charged by experienced copyeditors. And by the way, her client was well-satisfied with her services and employed her again at this rate.

Note that in all cases, these consultants had little difficulty getting the higher fees they charged. In fact their clients were quite ready to pay them. Again the reason is the image value of the consulting services offered. Therefore, if you are good at what you intend to do as a consultant, do not be afraid to use this pricing strategy. More consultants err by not choosing to use it than by choosing it. It is not a rip-off if you are good at what you do. In some cases, you may find that clients will not even want to engage your services if you charge too low a price. They will feel that either your work is weak or you are inexperienced. Therefore, even from the standpoint of idealism and wanting to do the greatest amount of good, consider the high-price strategy.

A Meet-the-Competition Price Strategy

This means simply that you choose a price that is approximately the same as your competitors or potential competitors are charging. If you choose this particular strategy, you must offer something else in addition to your regular services. Otherwise, why should anyone deal with you? But if you do offer some differential advantage, and if you promote it to your potential clients, the meet-the-competition price can also be a successful strategy. Differential advantages may include quicker service, specialized additional service not offered by anyone else, around-the-clock availability to answer consulting needs, quicker results, or better results.

If you are going to choose this strategy, spend some time thinking through your differential advantage: What additional service can you offer above and beyond your competition?

Other Considerations

Two other considerations should be taken into account when you are considering your pricing strategy: industry pricing and client price adjustment.

Industry Pricing

Certain industries have accepted prices for certain services. It is very difficult to violate this norm and build a viable practice. For example, employment agencies, on receipt of a job order, send the client several candidates to interview. If one of their candidates is hired, the agency may be paid from 10 to 15 percent of the individual's annual salary. Executive search firms supply three or more candidates for a particular job; if one of their candidates is hired, they get up to 30 percent of the executive's annual salary. Sometimes they get paid on an hourly or per diem basis whether one of their candidates gets hired or not. They perform essentially the same service, but note the significant difference in pricing. Therefore, when you are developing your fee schedule, it is important to consider the industry you are in. Employment agencies are simply not going to be paid the same as search firms, no matter how good a job they do. Of course you can deviate from the normal range of pricing in your industry, but if you do, you may find it much more difficult to get and keep clients.

Client Price Adjustment

Some consultants charge different amounts to different clients, depending on who they are or how big they are. For example, sometimes the government (federal, state, or local) has certain restrictions on the amount it can pay consultants, by policy or by law. If you expect to do a lot of government work, this will affect your pricing strategy.

Similarly, small companies generally cannot afford to pay as much as large companies. The examples I gave of the aerospace company that paid consultants $250 per hour and the consulting firm that billed the recent graduate's time at $1,000 a day were large companies. Clearly, smaller companies cannot pay these kinds of fees. You are therefore faced with a decision about billing if you deal with both large and small firms. You must either base your billing on the size of the company, have one low price for all, or have one higher price for all. The higher price eliminates a certain segment of your potential market. So may the lower price, because of image. A two-price system may also lead to problems. You must make this decision yourself after considering all the factors in your situation.

Methods of Billing

Basically there are four different methods of billing: (1) Daily or hourly; (2) retainer; (3) performance; (4) and fixed-price. Let's look at each.

Computing Billings Daily or Hourly

Billing on a time basis is fairly common with consultants, but deciding whether to bill on an hourly or a daily rate takes some consideration; as with so many other things, it's a trade-off. Some consultants feel that just getting started on any project will take the better part of a day, so they won't bill at less than a full day's rate. Even if a client wanted just two hours of their time, they would bill their daily rate as a minimum. Other consultants, especially those who work part-time and those who want maximum flexibility in their scheduling, use the hourly rate. Billing hourly lets them work at home or at some other location; they can also work for a couple of hours on one project and a couple of hours on another, and in that way they work with several clients in a single day. Of course one can also bill for fractional hours.

If you are considering a daily or hourly rate, be very certain you don't price yourself so low you can't make a decent living. Even if you elect to go with a penetration-price strategy, be very careful when you set your fee. Sometimes new consultants get into the field simply because they do not want to work for someone else. They are perfectly willing to work for the same amount that they made at their previous job. At first glance, that seems perfectly logical. However, using your previous salary to set your hourly rate is a trap you should avoid. Let's try out some numbers (pay attention; this is important).

Let's say you are currently making $42,000 a year and your fringe benefits are worth another $5,000; that's a total of $47,000 a year. If you work forty hours a week times fifty weeks (considering that you will have two weeks vacation), that's two thousand hours a year; $47,000 divided by 2,000 is $23.50 per hour. So should your billing rate be $23.50 an hour? Absolutely not! This figure does not take into consideration the fact that when you are working on your own, you will have overhead to contend with. Even though you'll try to keep this overhead as low as possible, I think you'll be surprised how fast it adds up. For example, let's make the following assumptions about your yearly expenses.

Clerical support	$ 5,000
Office rent	8,000
Telephone	3,400
Automobile	8,000
Insurance, benefits, etc.	6,000
Marketing expenses	20,000
Entertainment	2,000
Professional dues and subscriptions	1,000
Accounting and legal fees	3,000
Miscellaneous	2,600
Total	$59,000

Therefore, to receive $47,000 income a year, the same that you got working for someone else, you must charge $47,000 *plus* the $59,000 overhead, for a total of $106,000 a year. That works out to $53.00 per hour. If you want to tack on a profit for your firm (if it is incorporated) over and above your salary, you must add something to this figure. If you want a profit of 10 percent, you now have a billing rate of $58.30 per hour. That's what you must charge to earn the same salary you were making when you worked for someone else.

Working on Retainer

With a retainer, you receive a constant monthly fee in return for a guarantee that a certain number of your hours will be available to your client. This has advantages for both sides. For you it gives a guaranteed income and cash flow, which can be very advantageous. In fact most consultants would be willing to take a retainer at a reduced fee in order to ensure that money was coming in every month. For your client, a retainer guarantees that you won't work for a competitor and that the client will get first priority on your time. An additional advantage to you is that if the hours are not used, you get paid anyhow.

Performance Billing

I discuss performance contracts in Chapter 6. Basically this means no money without results. For example, for every dollar saved through your recommendations you might get 25 percent. Keep in mind that:

1. Performance billing is a good marketing tool.
2. It's critical to put all terms in writing.
3. It's a mistake to tie performance to profits, since profits can be manipulated for accounting or taxation purposes.

Fixed-Price Billing

A fixed-price contract, which we talked about in Chapter 6, is one in which you agree to do a certain job and get paid a fixed amount for it. The number of hours you work on the project is entirely up to you; you must put in whatever it takes. With a fixed-price contract, you can make more money, but at a greater risk, since you must guarantee accomplishment.

For a fixed-price contract to be profitable, you must be sure to follow these five guidelines:

1. Give yourself a "pad" in your estimations; overestimate a little to allow for miscalculations.
2. Use good estimating techniques, as discussed in Chapter 7.

3. Control your costs closely.
4. Carefully document exactly what you are required to do.
5. Be sure all changes to the contract are put in writing.

There are some basic formulas for setting the fee in a fixed-price contract; a typical one is shown in Figure 5-1. In

Figure 5-1.　Basic formula for a fixed-price contract.

Four elements of the formula are:

1. Direct labor
2. Overhead
3. Direct expense
4. Profit

Sample Computations

1. Direct labor:

Consultant	12 days @ $400/day =	$4,800.00
Assistant	4 days @ $90/day =	$360.00
Secretary	5 days @ $56/day =	$280.00
		$ 5,440.00

2. Overhead (65% of direct labor):　　　　　　　　　3,536.00

3. Direct expense:

Air travel	$500.00
Rental car	$100.00
Special printing	$100.00
Travel expenses (hotel, etc.)	$250.00
	950.00
Subtotal	$ 9,926.00

4. Profit (10% of subtotal):　　　　$992.60

TOTAL PRICE　　　　　　　　　　$10,918.60

this formula, overhead has been included as 65 percent of direct labor. Obviously you must cover your overhead some way; this percentage method is an attempt to spread your annual overhead among your various clients. You do this by estimating what you think your yearly overhead expenses will be, converting that into a percentage of your estimated annual income, and then adding that percentage amount onto the labor costs of each contract. In this case, a billing rate of $50 an hour would yield $100,000 annual income; estimated expenses of $65,000 a year works out to 65 percent for overhead. This particular formula incorporates a profit of 10 percent. The profit percentage is somewhat arbitrary, although it may be regulated in government contracts or contracts with companies that limit consultants' profits by policy.

Disclosing the Fee

Sometimes only one of the different ways of presenting the fee to the client is acceptable. Some clients will not accept a daily or hourly rate; they prefer a fixed-price contract. Therefore, it is a good idea to calculate your fee using *all* the various methods. If one way is unacceptable to your client, try another. However, in disclosing the fee, it is generally best to provide the minimum amount of financial data required. Therefore, for a fixed-price contract, if possible indicate only the bottom-line price. In the example in Figure 5-1, indicate the price as $10,918.60. If you are billing on a daily rate, give just that rate—$400 a day plus expenses, for example.

Some clients, especially the government, require full disclosure. In such cases, you have to make a full presentation, such as that in Figure 5-1, showing exactly how your figures are arrived at. The average client probably doesn't care about your overhead. Certainly there is no value to you in divulging your overhead so that potential competitors could discover it as well. Simply include it within your daily or hourly rate or within the fixed price if your fee is stated in this fashion.

6

WHAT YOU MUST KNOW ABOUT CONSULTING CONTRACTS

In this chapter, I show why consulting contracts are necessary and how you can develop your own. I also discuss the different methods of incurring a contractual obligation, the different types of contracts, and the major elements of any contract. I include a sample contract to help you develop your own.

Why a Contract Is Necessary

Essentially a contract covers two very important bases for you.

1. *It ensures that you and your client both understand fully the services you are to perform.* For your part, this will prevent wasted time, wasted resources, and wasted effort. It will also help ensure that you have a happy client at the end of the engagement. And a happy client will give you more work in the future and good referrals to others.

2. *It will help you get paid.* Always keep in mind that

even though you really enjoy your work, you must get paid in order to survive. Consulting may be a lot of fun, but without getting paid you won't be around to enjoy it. Having a written contract that documents your compensation will help you to gently remind your client of the financial obligations. If all goes sour and you must sue to get paid (this rarely happens, but it could), a signed contract is almost a necessity.

Developing Your Own Contract

It is most definitely possible to develop your own standard consulting contract and to use it in every situation with only minor changes regarding the particular client, services, and compensation. I talk more about this later on in this chapter under "A Sample Contract," but note now that you should have your attorney assist you with this. Do not, however, dump the whole project on your attorney; it will cost you excessively. A better procedure is to develop each element yourself, using the information in this chapter, and rough out the contract the way you would like it. Use the sample contract shown in Figure 6-1 as a guide. Once your rough contract has been formulated, have your attorney review it and put it in final form.

If Your Client Has a Standard Contract

Sometimes your client will be a large corporation with a standard contract. You may be asked to use this contract rather than yours. Naturally the final decision is always up to you. You should have your attorney review it, but usually these contracts are not unfair, and you may find them entirely acceptable.

Methods of Incurring a Contractual Obligation

There are five basic ways that a consultant can enter into a contractual obligation: (1) The formal contract; (2) the letter contract; (3) order agreements; (4) purchase orders; and (5) verbal contracts.

Let's look at each of these in turn.

Formal Contracts

The formal contract is a written document describing the obligations of both parties. For most assignments, I would recommend that you formalize your engagement in this way. It will save you many problems, heartaches, lost fees, and misunderstandings later on. Figure 6-1 shows a sample contract, the basics of which I used in contracting with a major multibillion-dollar corporation.

Letter Contracts

A letter contract can be evolved from a proposal. It is in written form, but it is much simpler than a formal contract. However, it contains the basic elements of the contract, and though it may look like a letter, it qualifies as a contract.

Order Agreements

Order agreements have the force of contracts. They are typically used for the purchase of consulting services to be accomplished over a period of time. They commit both you and your client to contractual terms before work is authorized. For example, an order agreement may commit you to so many hours of consulting over, say, a year's period; it also specifies how much you will be paid. However, your client decides when to initiate the agreement. In other words, an order agreement ties both you and your client to terms, but not necessarily to a start date. In some cases, the order agreement will be combined with an option that gives the client flexibility on whether or not to actually use these services. But if the services are used, the terms are as set forth in the order agreement.

(*text continues on page 102*)

Figure 6-1.   Sample consulting contract form.

_____ , 19__

CONSULTANT AGREEMENT

AGREEMENT made _____ , between _____ ,
               date   name of client
with principal offices at _____
                                client's address
hereinafter called "Client" and _____
                                 name of consultant
of _____ hereinafter called "Consultant."
    consultant's address

1. <u>Services</u>. Consultant, as an independent contractor, agrees to perform, during the term of this Agreement, the following services: _____
_____
_____

under the terms and conditions hereinafter set forth.

2. <u>Products</u>. The term "Products" shall mean the client's line of _____

3. <u>Compensation</u>.
(a) Client shall pay Consultant at the rate of __ per hour for each hour that Consultant shall perform services during the term of this Agreement; provided that the number of hours does not exceed _____ without the written consent of Client.
(b) In addition to the hourly compensation provided herein, Client agrees to pay Consultant $_____ under the following conditions: _____
_____

4. <u>Term</u>. The initial term of this Agreement shall commence on the _____ day of _____ , 19 __ , and end on the last day of _____ , 19 __ , provided however that either party may terminate this Agreement at any time during the initial term of any extension term by giving the other party _____ days' notice in writing.

(continued)

Figure 6-1 *(continued)*.

This Agreement may be extended beyond the initial term or any extension term only by the written agreement of both parties prior to the expiration of the initial term or any extension.

5. <u>Designation of Duties</u>. Consultant shall receive his requests for services to be performed from

———————————————— , ———————————————— , ———————————————— .
      client's name   title   company and address

6. <u>Restrictive Covenant</u>. During the term of this Agreement, Consultant shall not make his services available to any competitor of Client in the specific field in which he is performing services for Client.

7. <u>Indemnity and Insurance</u>. Consultant shall indemnify and hold harmless Client, its officers and employees against all losses, claims, liabilities, damages and expenses of any nature, directly or indirectly arising out of or as a result of any act of omission by Consultant, its employees, agents or subcontractors in the performance of this Agreement.

If Consultant uses, or intends to use, a personal automobile in the performance of this Agreement, Consultant shall maintain throughout the term of this Agreement automobile liability insurance in accordance with the law of the State of ———————————————————————— and not less than

——— .

8. <u>Patent Rights</u>. Consultant agrees during the term of this Agreement and for a period of 12 months after the termination of this Agreement, to assign to Client, its successors, assignees, or nominees all right, title and interest in and to all inventions, improvements, copyrightable material, techniques and designs made or conceived by him solely or jointly with others, relating to Products, in the performance of this Agreement, together with all United States and foreign patents and copyrights which may have been obtained thereon, and at Client's request and expense, will execute and deliver all proper assignments thereof.

9. <u>Confidentiality</u>. Consultant shall not disclose, publish or authorize others to publish design data, drawings, specifications, reports or other information pertaining to the work assigned to him by Client without the prior written approval of Client. Upon

the expiration or sooner termination of this Agreement, Consultant agrees to return to Client all drawings, specifications, data and other material obtained by Consultant from Client, or developed by Consultant, in connection with the performance of this Agreement.

10. Reimbursable Expenses. The following expenses will be billed in addition to compensation:

(a) Travel expenses necessary in order to perform services required by the Agreement. Use of personal autombile will be billed at __ ¢ per mile.

(b) Telephone, telegraph, and telex charges

(c) Computer charges

(d) Printing and reproduction.

(e) Other expenses resulting directly from performance of services in the Agreement

11. Warranty. Consultant services will be performed in accordance with generally and currently accepted consulting principles and practices. This warranty is in lieu of all other warranties either expressed or implied.

12. Limitation of Consultant Liability. Client agrees to limit any and all liability or claim for damages, cost of defense, or expenses against Consultant to a sum not to exceed $ _____ , or the total amount of compensation, whichever is less, on account of any error, omission, or negligence.

13. Payment Terms. Terms of payment are as follows: $ _____ due on the signing of Agreement and $ _____ due _____ , 19 __ . $ _____ due on delivery of _____ . A ____ % per month charge will be added to all delinquent accounts. In the event Consultant shall be successful in any suit for non-payment, Consultant shall be entitled to recover reasonable legal costs and expenses for bringing and maintaining this suit as a part of damanges.

IN WITNESS WHEREOF, the parties have signed this Agreement.

_____

Consultant

_____

Client

Purchase Orders

A purchase order is an internal form authorizing you to do work and to bill for it. It is generally used by larger companies to acquire relatively low-cost products or services. Consulting services may be "ordered" on a purchase order rather than a formal contract because your client can do this quickly and simply, as compared with going through the formal contractual process, which could involve your client's legal staff and some time delay. Usually purchase orders have a limit specified by company management, say, $25,000 or under.

Verbal Contracts

Always remember that a verbal contract is still a contract. Verbal contracts are very common in consulting, but they are not always desirable. They are definitely not recommended in two situations: with new clients, and for large projects. If the nature of the consulting situation with a new client is such that a more formal written contract is not possible, try to get a significant part of the payment up front before you start work. Also be very clear with your client; spell out your objectives, what you are going to do, and how and when you are going to do it.

Types of Contracts

The four basic types of contracts in consulting, each with variations, are: (1) fixed-price contracts; (2) cost contracts; (3) performance contracts; and (4) incentive contracts.

There is no one best contract for all situations, but rather a one best contract for a particular situation. Therefore, it is important to know the advantages and disadvantages of each one of these contracts.

The Fixed-Price Contracts

A fixed-price contract is one in which you agree to do a certain job for a predetermined amount. With few exceptions, no price adjustment is made after the award of the contract, regardless of your actual cost in performing it. As the consultant, you assume all the cost risk. If your estimate is poor, you could actually lose money on a fixed-price contract. On the other hand, if you can reduce the cost below the original estimate, you have the potential for making increased profit. Therefore, the more certain you are of your cost and your potential for reducing it, the more willing you should be to take a fixed-price contract. Conversely, the more difficult it is to estimate a particular job, the more risk you assume and the less willing you should be to accept such a contract. With all types of contracts, it is important to have an accurate estimate, but with the fixed-price contract, it is crucial.

Cost Contracts

In a cost contract, you are paid on your actual cost of performing the services: that is, your time plus related expenses such as the cost of reproducing your reports. As long as you put the time in, you are paid.

Obviously this type of contract involves a very low risk to you as a consultant. However, some clients will not accept cost contracts; they want to ensure that the project is actually completed within a certain budget. Thus, even when costs are difficult to estimate, you may have to choose between a fixed-price contract and no contract at all. One solution may be to break the overall task into subtasks. Those subtasks that you can cost out with minimum risk can be taken under a fixed-price contract; others, under a cost or a preformance-type contract (performance contracts are described in the next section). Another solution may be to insert a "not-to-exceed" clause in the contract, so that you are paid for the work you actually do, but the client is guaranteed that your fee will not be higher than an agreed-upon amount.

The cost contract has several variations, two of which—cost plus fixed fee and cost plus incentive—are frequently used by the government for research and development projects. With the fixed-fee type of cost contract, the consultant is paid a total of the cost plus a fixed amount agreed to by both parties prior to performance. With the incentive-fee type, the consultant is paid the cost plus a variable incentive fee tied to different levels of performance agreed to in the contract. The incentive type of performance contract is discussed in more detail in the next section.

Performance Contracts

Pure performance contracts are rare. More commonly they may be made a part of a modified-cost or fixed-price contract, wherein increased performance may earn a higher fee or reduced performance a lower one. However, by themselves, performance contracts are useful in closing a deal (more about that later in this section).

With a performance contract, your payment is based solely on actual performance. Executive recruiters who work on contingency—that is, they receive a fee only if one of the candidates they recruited is hired by their client—are actually working on a performance contract. Performance contracts can also be based on an increase in sales, a decrease in turnover, or other measurable factors. One cautionary note here: Do not accept a performance contract based on profits. Profits have too many definitions and are too easy to adjust upward or downward for accounting and taxation purposes. Although you may have done a great deal to increase performance, that work may not show up in accounting profits at the end of a year.

I mentioned that pure performance contracts are rarely used except to close a deal. Here's how to use a proposed performance contract to help you come to terms with your potential client. Let's say you have been negotiating with a prospective client, and while he seems satisfied about most aspects of the project, he is not quite ready to finalize and sign a contract with you. Perhaps you have been thinking along the lines of a fixed-price contract, which you have costed at $5,000. To close the deal, you could say something like this:

Look, Mr. Smith, I am absolutely convinced that I can do this job for you and do it within the time period and at the price I indicated. However, I can see that you are hesitating, so let me make an offer that I don't think you can refuse. Let me design this marketing campaign for you, and if it doesn't increase your sales by at least 25 percent, you pay me nothing. However, if your sales increase by 25 percent or more, and I have every confidence that it will be more, then you will pay me the $5,000.

You can see how the performance contract works. Either you perform or you receive nothing. That's why it's such a great close during negotiations. Your prospective client thinks, *Well, now, if this individual is ready to take a performance contract, what have I got to lose? He must be convinced.* Sometimes your client will agree to *your original terms* rather than the performance terms.

Incentive Contracts

Incentive contracts are also tied to performance. A type of incentive may also be combined with a fixed-price or cost contract based on achieving certain preset objectives or goals. When setting these goals, you must help your client; be certain that the incentive-fee structure is not unrealistic on either side. Remember that you are trying to build a long-term relationship, and terms that are unreasonable to you or your client, even if agreed to at the time, could lose you business in the future.

A client once asked me to help him increase attendance at his seminars. In return I would receive, in addition to a fee, an additional $20 for every seminar attendee above an agreed minimum (which was his maximum the previous year). I was to receive this $20 bonus not for just this one seminar, or even all similar seminars in a single year, but for life. That is, as long as those seminars were given by my client and the attendance was higher than the previous year's top, with no increase in costs, I was to receive $20 for each and every attendee above that number, whether or not I performed any additional services for his company. In my opinion, these terms were unreasonable and unfair to the client. We finally restructured the compensation, retaining an incentive contract in which I would be reimbursed with a fixed amount up front and then an amount for each seminar attendee over the minimum; however, I would get this for three years, not for the rest of my life.

Elements of a Contract

There are five basic elements that should go in any contract:

1. *Who?* Who is the consultant, who is the client, and who are any other parties that are in any way involved in the project?
2. *What?* What services are to be provided to the client?
3. *Where?* Where are these services to be provided? What is the address of the client, what is the address of the consultant, and are there special locations involved in the consulting?
4. *When?* When are the services to be performed, and when is compensation to be paid?
5. *How much?* How much does the consultant receive for his services?

In addition to these five basic elements, other important conditions of the engagement should also be covered. These include:

- Competitive restrictions
- Patent rights
- Insurance coverages
- Confidentiality

A Sample Contract

Look again at the sample contract in Figure 6-1. Note how the contractual elements fit in. You can use this sample as a basis for developing your own contract. But don't forget to have your attorney go through it to ensure that everything applying to your situation has been taken care of and that your rights are fully protected.

7

PLANNING AND SCHEDULING THE CONSULTING PROJECT

Planning and scheduling all but the simplest of consulting engagements are absolutely essential. Not only are these steps necessary for preparing the proposal, but once you are on contract, having a firm and good schedule in hand will save you time and money and will increase the quality of your performance as a consultant. All organizations I ever worked with that had problems with project management have had one outstanding thing in common—a failure to properly plan and schedule their projects before they began to work. Proper scheduling is not difficult. In this short chapter, I give you a special form that will help you do this.

The Project Development Schedule

Refer to the project development schedule in Figure 7-1. Start with the column headed "Task." Your first job is to list every task associated with the consulting project that you intend to undertake. Next, figure out how long each task will

Figure 7-1. Project development schedule form.

TASK	1	2	3	4	5	6	7	8	9	10	11	12
TOTALS												

take to complete in days, weeks, or months (in Figure 7-1 the numbers at the tops of the columns represent whichever time period you choose), as well as hours. Note that the measurements of task *length* and task *time* are not identical. A market research survey may require eighty hours of labor, which would be two weeks of eight-hour days. An organizational audit that requires interviews with twenty different company executives may take four calendar weeks to complete (because of the difficulty of scheduling executive time), but only forty hours of your time.

You also need to decide who will accomplish each task. If you are doing all the work yourself, this is easy. But in some cases, you will have other consultants or even other organizations working for you.

Figure 7-2 shows a project development schedule in which the tasks have been determined. After you write each task down on the schedule, draw a double horizontal line, starting at the place where the task will begin and continuing to the right until the task is complete. Consider each horizontal row as being either days, weeks, or months after the authority to proceed. (Note that in the example in Figure 7-2, the time period being used is months.) Later, when you get the contract, you can write in the actual days, weeks, or months and use this schedule to manage the project. Convert the hours into dollar expenses for each period and total both hours and costs. Use a diamond figure like this ◇ to indicate critical dates—times when something of great importance to the project must occur, such as the date a report is due. (Later, when the critical task is complete, you will color the diamond in like this: ◆.)

Once you are on contract and have the authority to proceed, you can use the schedule as indicated in Figure 7-3. On a new form, substitute the actual dates for the estimated time periods. (On Figure 7-3, note that, e.g., month 1 is replaced by June, month 2 by July.) Copy onto your new form the double horizontal lines that show when each task will begin and end. As you proceed to carry out the contract, shade in portions of the rectangular block formed by the double line to show the percentage of the task completed. At the end of each month, fill in actual hours worked on each

Figure 7-2. Proposed project development schedule, showing tasks and hour and cost estimates.

MONTHS AFTER AWARD OF CONTRACT

TASK	1 $50/Hr Hrs/$	2 Hrs/$	3 Hrs/$	4 Hrs/$	5 Hrs/$	6 Hrs/$	7 Hrs/$	8 Hrs/$	9 Hrs/$	10 Hrs/$	11 Hrs/$	12 Hrs/$
Development of Research Tool	20/1000											
Secondary Data Collection	10/500											
Interviewing		20/1000	20/1000	20/1000	20/1000	20/1000	20/1000					
Data Recording		2/100		5/250	5/250	5/250	5/250	3/150				
Data Analysis and Computations			5/250	5/250	5/250	5/250	5/250	10/500				
Follow-Up Interviews			2/100	3/150	2/100	1/50	1/50	5/250				
Final Report Preparation									40/2000	Report due end of ninth month after award of contract		
TOTALS 269/$13,450	30/1500	22/1100	32/1600	33/1650	32/1600	31/1550	31/1550	18/900	40/2000			

Figure 7-3. Project development schedule after project initiation.

TASK	Hours F/A* June	Hours F/A* July	Hours F/A* Aug.	Hours F/A* Sept.	Hours F/A* Oct.	Hours F/A* Nov.	Hours F/A* Dec.	Hours F/A* Jan.	Hours F/A* Feb.	Hours F/A* Mar.	Hours F/A* Apr.	Hours F/A* May
Development of Research Tool	20/18											
Secondary Data Collection	10/13								New estimated completion date			
Interviewing		20/16	20/21	20/16	20/	20/	20/					
Data Recording		2/3	5/6	5/5	5/	5/	5/	3/				
Data Analysis and Computations			5/4	5/4	5/	5/	5/	10/				
Follow-Up Interviews			2/3	3/3	2/	1/	1/	5/				
Final Report Preparation										Report due March 1		
TOTALS	30/33	22/19	32/34	33/28	32/	31/	31/	18/	40/			

*Forecast/Actual

task and compare with hours forecast. If you know that a task must be delayed for some reason, adjust your schedule by the use of a triangle and a series of dashed lines as shown in the horizontal area to the right of "Interviewing" in the figure.

Developing a PERT Chart

PERT is an acronym for Program Evaluation and Review Technique. This technique was developed by the U.S. Navy Special Projects Office working with the management consulting firm of Booz, Allen, and Hamilton back in 1958.

As you might have suspected when I mentioned the U.S. Navy, PERT was designed for use with big contracts and projects. But that doesn't stop you from using it with a small consulting proposal. Not only will it help you when you go to implement the project, it's quite impressive to your prospective client as a part of your proposal. It really shows that you've thought things through!

When you use PERT, you receive a lot of benefits. Delays, interruptions, and conflicts in developing, coordinating, and synchronizing the various parts of the overall project and in expediting completion are minimized.

PERT depends on just two elements: events and activities. An *event* is a specific task accomplishment that occurs at a recognizable point in time. An *activity* is the work required to complete an event.

Want an example? The publication of an advertisement is an event. Writing the copy, getting the artwork, preparing the layout, and submitting the advertisement for publication are all activities. As you can see, events take no time themselves. However, they do mark the beginnings and ends of the activities needed to complete the events.

Look at the graphic depiction of a PERT network shown in Figure 7-4. Events are represented by circles, and activities by arrows joining the circles. Remember, every event represents a specific point in time, and the arrow or activity

Figure 7-4.   Simple PERT network with four events and four
activities.

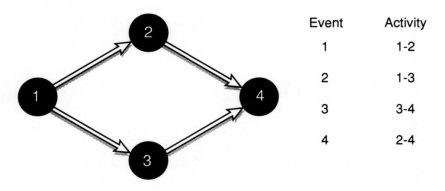

Event	Activity
1	1-2
2	1-3
3	3-4
4	2-4

connecting events represents the actual work done and the
time needed to plan and do the work.

With PERT, time is usually calculated in calendar weeks.
A *calendar week* is the number of working days required
divided by the number of working days per week. The
expected time for any activity, also known as the *expected
lapse time,* is calculated by the following equation:

$$T = \frac{a + 4b + c}{6}$$

Where T = expected lapse time, a = the most optimistic
time, b = the most likely time, and c = the most pessimistic
time.

If a = 1 week, b = 2 weeks, and c = 3 weeks, then:

$$T = \frac{1 + (4)\,2 + 3}{6} = \frac{12}{6} = 2 \text{ weeks}$$

Earliest Expected Date

The earliest expected date is represented by the letters
TE. It is the earliest possible date that a particular task can

be completed. In Figure 7-5, you can see that there are two paths through the network: One path is represented by the numbers 1, 2, 4; the second, by 1, 3, 4. Path 1, 2, 4 takes eight weeks (2 + 6); path 1, 3, 4 requires twelve weeks. Since all events have to occur before the project is completed, you must wait four additional weeks after completing path 1, 2, 4 before you can complete event 4. So the earliest expected date for the network shown in Figure 7-5 is twelve weeks.

Latest Allowable Date

Latest allowable is represented by the letters TL, the latest allowable date that an event can take place and still not interfere with the scheduled date of the entire network.

Take a look at Figure 7-6. In this network, the TE of event 6 is sixteen weeks. This is through path 1, 3, 5, 6, the longest of the three paths through the network. Path 1, 3, 5, 6 is therefore the critical path. So if any progress is to be made in reducing the time necessary to complete this project, you must reduce the activities on this path. It makes no difference whether or not you reduce the time of the activity on path 1, 2; path 1, 2 is not critical in this sense. Even if you reduce the activity on path 1, 2 to zero, the TE remains sixteen weeks. To reduce the TE of event 6, you must reduce the activities on path 1, 3, 5, 6.

Figure 7-5. Simple PERT network showing significance of TE.

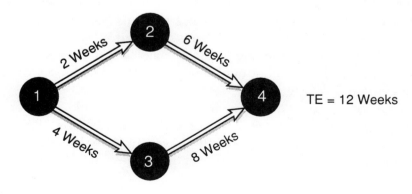

Figure 7-6. Simple PERT network showing earliest possible dates at each event.

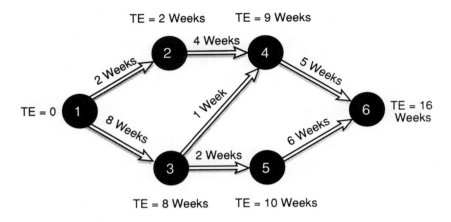

Adapted from Richard I. Levin and Charles A. Kirkpatrick, *Quantitative Approaches to Management,* 3rd ed. (New York: McGraw-Hill, 1975).

The earliest expected dates for the six various events are shown in Figure 7-6. You would expect to complete event 4 nine weeks after initiation due to the critical path 1, 3, 4. If activity begins immediately thereafter, you might expect to complete event 6 in a total of fourteen weeks after the project was initiated.

But a closer look tells you that the time is actually sixteen weeks because of other required activities. This should also tell you that event 4 really doesn't need to be completed in nine weeks; it could actually be completed in eleven weeks $(11 + 5 = 16)$ after the project was begun and still not interfere with the scheduled network time of sixteen weeks at event 6.

That is the significance of the latest allowable date. For event 4, it is eleven weeks after the project begins. This is because at that time you still have five weeks' work to complete activity 4, 6 and exactly five weeks in which to do it.

Slack

Slack is the difference between the latest allowable date and the earliest expected date. At event 4 in Figure 7-7, slack time is eleven weeks minus nine weeks, or two weeks.

You can see how a complex consulting project can be controlled fairly easily by using PERT. It shows you where you can save time and let the schedule slip and where it is critical to get a particular event done exactly on time. It shows you where to concentrate or to switch resources from noncritical paths to critical paths to effect time savings. PERT also shows you how to save money by avoiding putting resources where they will be less effective in impacting on critical dates.

The project development schedule or PERT will demonstrate to your potential client that you know what you are

Figure 7-7.   Simple PERT network with latest allowable dates and slack time added.

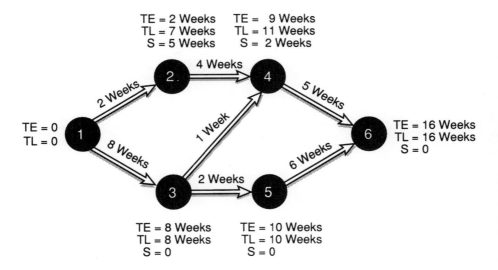

Adapted from Richard I. Levin and Charles Kirkpatrick, *Quantitative Approaches to Management,* 3rd ed. (New York: McGraw-Hill, 1975).

doing and that you have carefully thought through the entire consulting project. It will give you a much better chance of having your letter proposal accepted. Once you are under contract, these management tools will assist you in controlling and avoiding slippages and cost overruns. You will have more happy customers and fewer ulcers.

8

NEGOTIATING WITH YOUR CLIENT

Whether a consulting engagement is profitable or unprofitable has much to do with your ability to negotiate with your client. Why is this? Because even if you perform flawlessly, if you negotiate a contract that is sufficiently unfavorable, you may lose money, reputation, or both.

Robert Ringer describes an amazing negotiating incident in his best-seller, *Winning Through Intimidation*.[1] Ringer had been observing a difficult negotiation in which a businessperson he knew had ruthlessly demanded and received outrageously advantageous terms. The other party had agreed to these terms because he was clearly desperate to get the contract. Further, there were heavy penalties for failure to comply with all of the terms of the contract. When, on the way out, Ringer commented to this businessperson that it would be very difficult for the other party to live up to the terms, the businessperson smiled and said, "If you look at the contract carefully, you will see that he is already technically in violation of the contract."

Unfortunately, many consultants become so desperate for a contract that they also negotiate extremely unfavorable terms for themselves. Don't let this happen to you. Plan the negotiation of the contract before you begin.

Six Steps in Contract Negotiation as Seen by Uncle Sam

The U.S. government negotiates billions of dollars in contracts every year. Sometimes we read about the screwups in
the newspapers—the $650 toilet seats and so forth—but the
truth is, considering the fact that more than a million contracts are negotiated every year, government negotiators do
a pretty good job.

The government breaks down the process leading to
final contract negotiation into six steps:

1. Evaluation and ranking of offers (if there are more
   than one) considering evaluation criteria in the Request For Proposal
2. Identification of those offerers whose proposals are
   determined to be within a competitive range
3. Identification and elimination of unacceptable proposals due to major problems with price or technical
   merit
4. Written or oral discussions with those competitors
   remaining, permitting revision of proposals to correct
   isolated deficiencies
5. Notification of a cutoff date for receipt of a best and
   final offer
6. Selection for award or for final negotiations if appropriate

If you are bidding a contract against competitors,
whether dealing with the government or not, you can assume
that your prospective client will use a similar process. Note
that there may be several steps to the negotiating process,
but that even in the last step, final negotiations may be
necessary. It is in these final negotiations that some consultants "give away the store" and get into trouble.

**Goals and Objectives of the Party
With Whom You Are Negotiating**

In a general way, your prospective client is simply trying to
close the deal and make the final arrangements so that you

can begin work. But you may never understand the full situation, including limitations and pressures that affect the way he or she negotiates. You may be definitely interested in a win-win outcome, but there are very broad definitions of what a *win-win* is.

When I teach negotiation, one of the simulations I use is negotiation for the purchase of a computer. The computer sellers are given the following confidential instructions:

> You are the vice-president of sales of a company that designs computer systems for business. Yesterday you received an emergency notice from top management. This message told you that you must withdraw and junk one of your older models, the XC-1000 computer, immediately. This is due to the implementation of a government regulation requiring additional features to prevent tampering, which this model does not have.
>
> Unfortunately you cannot modify the XC-1000, as it was built to "last forever." You can't even use it for parts. By law you must sell or get rid of all computer systems such as the XC-1000 by April 3 (this is April 2!). After that date, you cannot offer it to the market at any price. You can't even give it away.
>
> Fortunately you have only one of the XC-1000s left in inventory. In fact you haven't sold any of these models in several years. This morning your assistant contacted the Acme Junk Company. It agreed to pick up your XC-1000 and melt it down to sell for scrap, at no charge to you.
>
> Before you can make final arrangements, you receive a call from Consolidated Unlimited. Its director of MIS would like to meet with you tomorrow about the possible immediate purchase of an XC-1000. You tell him there is one left and that the price is negotiable. You delay your arrangements with Acme and begin to prepare for your meeting with Consolidated.
>
> Do not reveal any of this information to any person not on your team. You will have thirty minutes to complete the answers to the following questions:

1. For what price do you expect to sell the XC-1000, and why?
2. What is the lowest price you will accept, and why?
3. What is your strategy for your meeting tomorrow?

Now, as the computer seller, you feel the pressure of having to sell to this potential buyer or getting nothing for the computer at all. Further, being in the business of manufacturing computers, you probably know all about the state of the art of competitive systems. From your viewpoint, you are desperate to sell, yet you don't have much of a product. You are probably wondering why in the world Consolidated Unlimited wants such a system.

I designate another group as buyers. They also receive confidential instructions. If you knew what these instructions were, you would know that Consolidated Unlimited was desperate to buy your product and would probably be willing to pay quite a bit more for it than you might expect. The instructions to the buyers are:

> Several years ago, you became director of MIS for Consolidated Unlimited, a small company manufacturing copper tubing. One of your first actions was to buy an XC-1000 computer. One of this computer's most attractive features was its lack of need of maintenance. In fact, when you bought the computer, it came with a three-year moneyback guarantee if the computer didn't perform in any way. For three years and one month, the computer performed beautifully, but this morning your XC-1000 failed completely.
>
> One of the first things you did was have your assistant look for a newer replacement model that would perform the same functions. Unfortunately, as your company grew, all functions were built around your XC-1000, so you have very limited options. As a matter of fact, the lowest-priced replacement computer other than an XC-1000 is $50,000.
>
> You made some tentative calls around the country to other companies that you knew had bought XC-1000s.

You discovered that most companies had replaced them long ago. You were also a little concerned about buying a used model, since none were less than three years old and the guarantee had expired.

You called the president to apprise her of the problem, but her response was, "Get another new XC-1000." You called the manufacturer of the XC-1000 and arranged a meeting with the vice-president of sales tomorrow for an immediate purchase of an XC-1000. When you asked her the price, she told you there was one left and the price was negotiable. You began to prepare for your meeting.

Do not reveal this information to individuals not on your team. You have thirty minutes to complete the answers to the following questions:

1. What price do you expect to pay for the XC-1000, and why?
2. What is the highest price you will pay, and why?
3. What is your strategy for your meeting tomorrow?

Now you can see that both parties to this situation have a serious problem. If the sellers do not sell the computer, they get absolutely nothing. If the buyers do not buy the computer, they must pay $50,000 to get another system elsewhere. And of course, the president of the buyer's company has flat ordered that one of these computers be purchased. Of course, at any price other than zero or $50,000, both sellers and buyers gain. It is a win-win situation.

However, if we were calculating a fair price, we would probably agree that it would be the midpoint between zero and $50,000—that is, $25,000.

But remember, neither side has the information that the other has. Both know only of their own problem, and not the main problem of the other party.

What results do I get? Interestingly, the prices vary widely between zero and $50,000 among different groups of buyers and sellers negotiating on the same day. Yet conditions are the same for all.

The last time I gave this exercise, it was to four groups of graduate students. The prices for which the computer was sold were $2,500, $12,500, $27,300, and $45,000.

This should tell you that in any situation in which you are negotiating with a client, you do not know the client's side of the story, and he or she does not know yours. Therefore, even if poor cash flow or some other situation causes you to be hungry for a job, you still want to negotiate for what you are worth.

How can you best do this? The key is preparation.

Preparation: The Key to All Contract Negotiations

For all but the simplest of contracts, you can assume that your prospective client is going to get all of the needed data together. He or she is going to do the homework, check the facts, prepare the case, anticipate your arguments, and develop responses to them. Most important, he or she will develop specific negotiation objectives related to *your* price, performance, or timing. To be prepared, you must do the same things.

Now is when all the preparation that went into your proposal really pays off. But do more than review your facts. Know the areas in which you can afford to be flexible and where you must stand fast. Know the price for your services below which you cannot go. Know the areas in which you can speed things up and where you cannot. Understand where you can increase or decrease the level of performance and what this will cost or save. And most important, write down your specific negotiating objectives.

Being Wary of Telephone Negotiations

Telephone negotiations may or may not be good for you depending on your preparation. But you should always be wary. If you are all prepared and ready to negotiate the deal, a telephone negotiation can be a quick way to close and get authority from your client to begin work. On the other hand, if you are not prepared, a telephone negotiation can be a disaster.

The problem is, unless the telephone negotiation is set up ahead of time, you may have other things on your mind. You can't think of two things at once, and trying to negotiate under these circumstances is impossible.

One day I was engaged in "fire fighting" some emergency or another. I received a call to finalize the price on an assignment I had been asked about several days earlier. I hadn't really had an opportunity to work out the pricing (in those days, I used a formula to price this type of work). Still half-thinking about the emergency, I attempted to use the formula and negotiate the price. I ended up negotiating a price only 30 percent of what I usually charge. This didn't happen because of hard negotiating tactics by my prospective client. It was due entirely to the distraction of the emergency and my own screwup.

Don't make the same mistake. After submitting a proposal, be ready for a telephone call to finalize the contract. Keep your material close to the telephone. If you get an unexpected call, as I did, ask if you can call back. Complete the project you are working on, clear your mind, review your material, and then call to negotiate the contract.

The Negotiation Plan

To reach your objectives successfully, prepare a negotiation plan. The negotiation plan should include an overall objective and a target price. Write down your limitations. As I mentioned earlier, know your bottom-line price, below which you cannot go without losing money. Then work out a strategy to achieve your objectives.

Your strategy in reaching your planned price objective might be simply to restate the price in your proposal. If this is questioned, you might show how your pricing is similar to or lower than pricing on other jobs that you or others have done. You might compare this price against the benefits that will be achieved as a result of your work. Finally, if price is still an issue, you might have a few fallback positions to show what you can accomplish for lower prices.

At every step, you should anticipate questions or objections, work out answers to the other party's questions, and counter his or her tactics to overcome objections.

Negotiation Gamesmanship

Even where both parties try to look out for each other's interests, a great deal of gamesmanship goes on in any negotiation. Some tactics are no worse than beginning at a higher price than you actually want because you know that your client always wants to negotiate you down to a lower price. However, some prospective clients, like the businessperson noted by Robert Ringer at the beginning of this chapter, see any negotiation as a competition that must be won at all costs. Such individuals may use a wide variety of tactics against you, some of which may be highly unethical.

Some people believe that lying in a negotiation is perfectly acceptable. A friend of mine who teaches negotiating says, "A lie is not a lie when the truth is not expected." He points out that when labor and management are negotiating, one or the other will make a statement something like this: "We will never, never agree to these terms. Never, never!" The next day, the contract is signed under the very terms they claimed they would *never, never* agree to. Was the statement that they would never agree a lie? You must make your own judgment about this. But in any case, you should be ready in case a prospective client uses negotiating tactics against you. Here are some of the more common ploys used:

• *Making the other party appear unreasonable.* A prospective client may point out that other consultants charge such and such or have agreed to certain terms that you won't agree to. The implication is that something is wrong with you and the way you do business. That you are being unreasonable.

Your defense against this tactic is to point out how this situation is different from the others. Of course you can always add what I consider the ultimate response: *"I am a lot better consultant than those you have mentioned."*

• *Placing the other party on the defensive.* A prospective client may ask a question for which you are unprepared— another good reason to make certain that you are as prepared as you can be.

Maybe the party you are negotiating with has a top dollar limit to his or her negotiating authority, which you both know is $100,000. During the negotiation, you agreed not to go above this amount. Just as you think you have a deal, your prospective client asks a question like this: "You aren't going to embarrass me by making your price so close to $100,000 that my supervisors will suspect what we are doing?" Being on the defensive, you could end up dropping your price several thousand dollars to protect the other party's "vanity." You may still be profitable several thousands of dollars lower, but if that is below your standard price, it is less than you are worth, and the difference comes out of your pocket. Chances are, your negotiating partner gets his or her bonuses this way.

If you are prepared for this ploy, you can say something like, "I'm sorry. I've been negotiating in good faith. This is my best offer."

• *Blaming a third party.* Here your prospective client attempts to shift the blame for unwillingness to give in on a negotiating point to someone or something over which he or she has no control: "I agree with what you are saying, but it's the policy of the company. It won't allow me to do it."

This is a difficult problem to overcome. It may mean that your prospective client absolutely will not give in on this point. If you feel strongly enough about the issue, you can test it by refusing to give in and suggesting that the negotiations be suspended while the other party checks out the situation with "the boss." Or you can explore how you might achieve the results you want while not violating this "company policy." For example, if you want money up front but company policy is not to pay until work is done, you can suggest an additional progress payment shortly after an early contract milestone.

• *The good-guy–bad-guy technique.* The good-guy–bad-guy technique began with the interrogation of prisoners. One interrogator, the "bad guy," would yell and scream and even beat the prisoner. If he didn't get the information he wanted, he would leave the room. Then the "good guy" would enter. The good guy would offer the prisoner a cigarette and commiserate with him on what a monster the other interrogator was. He might even embellish his partner's performance by describing how another prisoner had died under the bad guy's interrogation. The good guy would suggest that the prisoner give part of the information or make a reduced confession just to appease the bad guy.

This works because of the contrast between the two interrogators. Someone under the extreme pressure applied by the bad guy is in need of support, which the good guy provides. The good guy's demands seem so slight in comparison with those of the bad guy that the prisoner is likely to go along with them.

The same technique is sometimes used when you are negotiating with more than one member of the prospective client company. The "bad guy" continually puts pressure on you and rudely presses every point. While you won't get slapped around, the bad guy may actually yell and scream. The "good guy" says something like, "Gee, I think it's terrible the way he is behaving. Maybe if you can give him just a little of what he wants, he'll be satisfied. If you can do this, I'll try to help."

When you see this kind of performance, just remember that it is probably exactly that—a performance. When negotiating with someone else, the two may actually switch roles! Just remember that both are on the other side of the negotiation, and look out for your own interests.

• *Straw issues.* Straw issues are nonissues. They really aren't important to your prospective client at all. However, they may be strongly introduced as a negotiating point so that they can be given up later in exchange for a real concession from you.

The Soviets, who are quite good at negotiating, do this

all the time. They sometimes introduce positions that are completely unreasonable. They allow themselves to be negotiated out of these positions in exchange for major concessions on the other party's part. As a result, until recent years some of the treaties negotiated with the Soviets were quite lopsided in their favor. Yet when asked how it could have possibly agreed to such terms, the other negotiating team would respond, "But you should have seen the position they started with!"

When your prospective client is unreasonable or introduces straw issues, offer little or nothing in exchange for dropping them.

• *The walkout.* The walkout ploy is used infrequently because it may be difficult to get negotiations going again if the ploy fails. Your prospective clients say something like, "We can't pay any more and that's it." Then they prepare to leave. This is a supreme test, and you can either attempt to move toward their position or call their bluff and let them go. Many times, even if they leave, you can call them later and reopen negotiations. Sometimes they will even call *you* to reopen negotiations. But occasionally they are not bluffing. I am biased in favor of letting them go, unless you really have been unreasonable previously; otherwise they're going to think you're desperate and take advantage of you even more.

• *The recess.* This is almost always a good tactic because it does not break off negotiations. It allows the air to cool and may offer an opportunity for either side to rethink its position. If your prospective client calls for a recess, don't panic. It may be called simply to put pressure on you while you ask yourself why it was called. Sometimes a prospective client calls a recess when you are in a hurry, as when you must catch a plane. In that case, you can show your resolve by refusing to accept the pressure: Reschedule your flight. If necessary, stay an extra day.

• *The time squeeze.* Time is money. You know this, and so does your prospective client. Your prospective client may try to put pressure on you to come to an agreement on his or her points by using delaying tactics. The recess is one way of doing this, but there are many others. For example, your prospective employer may say, "We can't continue to negotiate past three o'clock because we have some people flying in for an important meeting."

What can you do? Tell your prospective client, "I understand, but I want to be certain that the engagement gets started right. Then we won't have problems later. If you aren't available after three o'clock, let's set a time when we can complete our negotiations."

Here are some general hints for negotiating that will help you to negotiate fairly yet competently:

Hints for Negotiating

1. When things get tense, try humor.
2. Don't ridicule or insult anyone. Don't be rude. Be courteous and considerate.
3. Don't try to make anyone look bad.
4. Be reasonable.
5. Try to find the best for both parties.
6. Negotiating means both talking and listening. Remember to do both.
7. Don't accept any statement made by the other party as 100 percent accurate. Remember, the person may be honest and trustworthy, but he or she may be "just negotiating."
8. You can give in on small points, but fight hard for the issues that are important to you.
9. Price may be only one aspect of the negotiation process. Remember that you can also manipulate time and performance. Sometimes your prospective client will give in on these to get a lower price.
10. Don't forget the computer negotiation example mentioned earlier in this chapter. You don't know your prospective client's situation. Chances are you are in at least as good a position as your prospective client.
11. If you see a good offer, take it. Don't feel that you must always knock something off a deal that is offered you.

12. Don't discuss an issue you aren't prepared for. If something comes up for which you aren't prepared, defer the issue until you are.
13. Don't assume that the other side completely understands all the advantages you are offering. Take the time to spell them out.

When you are eager to begin work, you may have a tendency to rush into negotiations ill-prepared and eager to get them over with. Negotiations are an important part of the overall consulting process. Take the time to do them right. This will pay dividends during the engagement and will do much to enhance the profitability and reputation of your practice.

Note

1. Robert J. Ringer, *Winning Through Intimidation* (New York: Fawcett Books, 1979).

9

HOW TO SOLVE YOUR CLIENT'S PROBLEMS EASILY

In this chapter, I show you a logical, step-by-step approach to problem solving as well as some important psychological problem-solving techniques. The step-by-step methodology does more than help solve problems; it also organizes your thinking process and provides an outline for presenting your analysis, conclusions, and recommendations to your client, both as a written report and as a formal, in-person presentation. I cover every step in detail and then show you a sample problem that you can work yourself, including forms to assist you. Then I go over the solution to this problem and analyze the results.

The Harvard Case Study Method

The technique I'm going to show you is commonly known as the Harvard Case Study Method of Problem Solving; it is also known in the military as the Staff Study Method. It is a structured, step-by-step process of considering and analyzing the various alternatives available to solve a problem and honing in on the one best solution. Let's take a look at the six elements of this method.

1. Central problem
2. Relevant factors
3. Alternative courses of action or solutions, with advantages and disadvantages of each
4. Discussion and analysis of alternatives
5. Conclusions
6. Recommendations

Defining the Central Problem

Defining the single central problem in a particular situation is the single most difficult, most important task in consulting problem solving. If you correctly identify the main problem in a situation, you can find many different approaches to solving it. But if the wrong problem is identified, even a brilliant solution will not correct the situation. You are well-advised to take all the time necessary; be sure you are indeed looking at the central problem.

One of the major errors that new consultants make in defining the central problem is confusing the symptoms with the problem. For example, low profits are not a central problem but a symptom of something else that is the central problem. Frequently a case has many different problems; in fact there usually is more than one. The object then is to locate the *main* problem in the situation, the one that is more important than any other and is therefore "central." If you find more than one major problem in a particular situation, you should handle each one separately.

Once you have identified the central problem, write an initial draft explaining what the problem is. Try to keep this statement as simple as possible by making it as short as you can—a one-sentence central problem is usually best. Be aware, however, that even if you have spent some time in both identifying the problem and wording it as concisely as possible, in many cases you will have to go back and modify it as you proceed through the analysis.

Also be careful not to word the problem as if it were the solution, by assuming one particular course of action is correct before you analyze it. Remember, too, that your goal is to develop as many different courses of action as possible. Try not to word your statement so that only two alternatives are possible. For example, don't ask the question, "Should a new product be introduced?" That allows for only two alternatives: yes or no. Occasionally there are some situations where only two alternatives need be analyzed. Usually, however, you can reword the problem statement in a way that opens it up to more than two courses of action.

In your statement, include important specifics about the problem. "What should be done about the possibility of introducing a new product?" is not the best problem statement. It allows for more than two alternatives, but it omits specifics about the problem that may be important to readers of your report who are not as familiar with the problem as you or the individual who hired you.

Be careful about making your problem statement too long by incorporating various additional factors. Even if these factors are relevant, they will make the problem statement unwieldy, awkward, and difficult for any reader to understand.

With these cautionary notes in mind, begin formulating your problem statement. Phrase it as a question, beginning with *who, what, when, where, how,* or *why.* Or you may start with an infinitive, as in "To determine the best source for borrowing $10,000."

Listing Relevant Factors

Note that this section of the structure speaks of "relevant factors." Both words are important. *Relevant* is critical because, even though there will be many different factors in any situation, you are to determine and list only those that are relevant to the central problem you have decided upon.

In this task, you will be listing *factors,* not just facts. You may include estimates, computations, assumptions, and even educated guesses in addition to facts. Naturally, if one of your relevant factors is not a fact, label it accurately as an assumption, an estimate, or whatever so that you won't mislead anyone.

Listing Alternatives

In this section, you list every solution or course of action that could possibly solve the central problem. Then list the advantages and the disadvantages of each one. It is frequently at this point that you must go back and modify your central problem statement. You may think of a solution that is excellent, but not a solution to the central problem as you originally wrote it. To include this course of action, you must restate your central problem so that it fits with this alternative. This is important: Each solution or course of action listed must potentially solve the central problem as you have stated it.

Although theoretically it is possible to have an alternative with all advantages and no disadvantages, this is highly unlikely. If this were the case, the solution would be self-evident, and this problem-solving procedure would be superfluous.

Analyzing the Alternatives

In this fourth section, you analyze and discuss the alternatives thoroughly in light of the relevant factors you have listed. As you proceed, additional relevant factors may come to light. If so, go back and add them to your list. However, the focus of this section should always be to compare, and discuss in detail, the relative importance of the advantages and disadvantages of each course of action. For example, the disadvantages of one course of action may be unimportant when measured against the relevant factors. Or an alternative could have advantages that are very important.

At the end of this discussion and analysis section, and even as you are doing the analysis, certain conclusions start to become obvious. Don't state these conclusions in the discussion and analysis section, however; save them for the next section. In fact, here is an accurate test of the clarity of your thinking so far: Show the entire analysis up to this point to someone who is not particularly familiar with the problem. Have him or her read your central problem, the relevant factors that you have identified, the alternative courses of action with the advantages and disadvantages, and finally your discussion and analysis. Then ask what his or her conclusions are. If they are identical to yours, you have correctly worded your discussion and analysis. If the conclusions are different, you have made an error either in the wording of the discussion and analysis or in the logic of your conclusions.

Listing Your Conclusions

In this section, you list the conclusions arrived at as a result of your discussion and analysis. Do not add any explanations; they belong in the previous section. Also don't list conclusions based on information extraneous to your analysis. Your conclusions are based solely on your discussion and analysis. Another common error here is to restate relevant factors as conclusions.

Making Recommendations

In this section, you explicitly state the results of your analysis and your recommendations on what your client should do to solve the central problem you have defined. As with your conclusions, do not include extraneous information or explanations; all such explanations go in the discussion and analysis section. If you are presenting this orally, your client can always ask additional questions; if this is a written report, your client can always contact you for additional information. However, if you have done the analysis correctly, there will be no need to explain your recommendations; your reasons will be obvious from your discussion and analysis.

Many consultants first learning this methodology ask about the difference between conclusions and recommendations. With a recommendation, you put your reputation on the line. You make it clear and unequivocal what you want your client to do. You are accepting full responsibility for the recommendations you make. A conclusion is written in the passive tense: "Marketing research should be done." Recommendations are written in the imperative: "Initiate marketing research." If a conclusion on your list reads, "A new accountant should be hired," the recommendation would be, "Hire a new accountant."

The Charles Benson Problem: A Case Study

Now we're going to work on a problem, using the methodology just discussed. Assume that the chief engineer of the Zeus Engineering Company has come to you for consulting advice. You are to analyze the chief engineer's problem, define it explicitly, and, using the methodology just described, make recommendations to him. The problem situation, forms that will help you use the structure to arrive at the solution, the solution, and a step-by-step critique follow. Do not read the critique until you work the problem in detail. Time spent now in learning to use and apply this problem-solving methodology will pay dividends later on.

A Description of the Charles Benson Problem*

Charles Benson, 35, had been employed as a design engineer for the Zeus Engineering Company for seven years. He was a reliable employee as well as a skillful and inventive engineer. Seeking to earn additional money, he decided to pursue his own business evenings and weekends. His products were similar to those made and sold by Zeus Engineering. Benson's supervisor found out about Benson's business, but took no action for several months, believing that the business probably would not amount to much and that eventually Benson would drop it. However, one afternoon Benson's supervisor found him using company time and a company telephone to order materials for his business. The

*Adapted from "Theodore Thorburn Turner," a case in *Principles of Management*, 4th ed., by George R. Terry (Homewood, Ill.: Richard D. Irwin, 1964), p. 222.

supervisor reprimanded Benson on the spot and warned him that such practices would not be tolerated. He also said that the incident would be reported to the chief engineer. A few days later Benson received written notice from the chief engineer that he must divest himself of the business within the month or resign from the company.

A month later, Benson's supervisor asked him directly for his decision. Benson stated that he had thought it over and talked with friends as well as officers of his union, and he had decided that he would not give up the business, nor would he resign. He argued that he was a good employee, and that his outside company did not interfere with his work for Zeus Engineering. The small amount of business that he did could not hurt the company, and he was neither using company resources nor soliciting its accounts. Therefore, what he did with his own time was of no concern to the company. Benson's supervisor reported the conversation to the chief engineer.

You are the chief engineer. What action should you take?

Form to Use in Solving the Charles Benson Problem

Central Problem

_____
_____
_____
_____
_____

Relevant Factors [*List*]

1. _____
2. _____

3. _____
4. _____
5. _____
6. _____
7. _____
8. _____
9. _____
10. _____
11. _____
12. _____
13. _____
14. _____
15. _____

Alternative Courses of Action

1. _____
   _____

Advantages

A. _____
B. _____
C. _____

Disadvantages

A. _____
B. _____
C. _____

2. _____
   _____

Advantages

A. _____
B. _____
C. _____

Disadvantages

A. _____
B. _____
C. _____

3. _____
_____

Advantages

A. _____
B. _____
C. _____

Disadvantages

A. _____
B. _____
C. _____

4. _____
_____

Advantages

A. _____
B. _____
C. _____

Disadvantages

A. _____
B. _____
C. _____

5. _____
_____

Advantages

A. _____
B. _____
C. _____

Disadvantages

A. _____
B. _____
C. _____

Discussion Analysis

_____
_____
_____
_____
_____
_____
_____
_____
_____
_____
_____
_____
_____
_____
_____
_____
_____
_____
_____
_____

Conclusions [*List*]

1. _____
2. _____
3. _____
4. _____
5. _____
6. _____
7. _____

8. _____

9. _____

10. _____

Recommendations or Decisions [*List*]:

1. _____
2. _____
3. _____
4. _____
5. _____
6. _____
7. _____
8. _____
9. _____
10. _____

Solution to the Charles Benson Problem

Central Problem

Begin by zeroing in on the central problem; this may require several attempts.

1. *Should Charles Benson be retained as an employee of the Zeus Engineering Company or fired?* This way of stating the problem limits the solutions to two courses of action—retaining or firing.
2. *What should be done about Charles Benson?* This statement lacks specifics about the problem that are important if the analysis is to be presented to someone else.
3. *What policy should Zeus Engineering set regarding employees establishing outside businesses?* This may be a problem that needs to be worked on, but its solution disregards specifics of Benson's case, including the earlier warning.
4. *What should be done about Charles Benson's outside business considering the fact that he was warned, that*

the union may take action, that he has been a good employee and a superior engineer? This one tries to incorporate all the relevant factors, resulting in an unwieldy and awkward statement of the central problem.

5. *How to keep Charles Benson with Zeus Engineering?* This statement assumes one alternative course of action as the solution before the analysis is done.

6. *What action should be taken regarding Charles Benson's outside business activities?* This is a simple, concise statement of the central problem.

Relevant Factors

Facts

1. Charles Benson has been a superior engineer and a reliable employee prior to the problem.
2. Benson has been with the company seven years.
3. The products that Benson makes are similar to the products made by Zeus Engineering.
4. Benson's supervisor knew about the business but took no action for several months.
5. Benson was caught by his supervisor doing business on company time, and using a company telephone.
6. Benson was ordered by the chief engineer, in writing, to drop the business or resign from the company.
7. Benson states that he will not give up the business or resign from the company.

Assumptions

1. Benson has stated that he has contacted union officers and that they support his position. This is presumed to be true.
2. Benson states that he is not soliciting company accounts. This is presumed to be true.
3. Benson's current level of business will probably not hurt the company in the sense of his being a competitor. Nor will his present product line directly compete with Zeus Engineering's product line.

4. It is assumed that Benson's business activities are no
   longer done on company time, and that his outside
   work does not currently interfere with his work at
   Zeus.
5. Current company policies do not specifically forbid an
   outside business, although conflict of interest laws,
   secrecy clauses, and the company's ownership of
   ideas resulting from company work have an impact
   on the legal aspects of the problem.
6. Benson is not a key employee, in the sense that his
   leaving the company will of itself have a major negative impact on the company.

Alternative Courses of Action

1. *Discharge Benson*

Advantages

1. Will enforce discipline, since Benson was warned that
   he must give up the business or resign.
2. Will discourage employees in the future from starting
   outside businesses.
3. Will solve any problem of conflict of interest arising
   from the nature of Benson's business.

Disadvantages

1. May lead to union problems, considering their current
   support of his position.
2. May lead to a morale problem if it is believed by other
   employees that the company has acted unfairly.
3. Will lose a superior engineer and an otherwise reliable employee.

2. *Retain Benson.*

Advantages

1. Will avoid any problem with the union.
2. Will retain a superior engineer and an otherwise reliable employee.

3. Will avoid any feeling among other employees that Benson is being treated unfairly.

Disadvantages

1. May result in a discipline problem, since Benson was ordered to give up the business or resign.
2. May eventually result in a direct conflict of interest due to the nature of the products and the customers.
3. Will effectively establish a company policy on this matter that may not be desired.
4. Will encourage other employees to start outside businesses.

3. *Discharge Benson as an employee, but retain him as a consultant. (The mechanism for the discharge should be Benson's resignation.)*

Advantages

1. May avoid any problem with the union.
2. Will reward Benson for past performance as a superior engineer and otherwise reliable employee.
3. Will maintain discipline, since Benson was warned that he must give up the business or resign.
4. Will solve any problem of conflict of interest arising from the nature of Benson's business.
5. Will avoid setting policy or precedent regarding employee businesses.

Disadvantages

1. May encourage other employees to become consultants rather than employees with the company.
2. May set policy of a different kind: that employees who start their own businesses will be retained as consultants.
3. May not solve the problem if Benson refuses to resign to accept a consultancy.

Discussion/Analysis

1. Several important issues bear on this problem:
   A. The disciplinary issue, and the fact that Benson

was told to resign or to divest himself of his business.

B. The importance of fair treatment and its potential effect on other employees. Benson has been a "superior engineer and otherwise reliable employee." There is currently no conflict of interest, and no further misuse of company time is anticipated.

C. The policy issue. If Benson is retained, this will tend to set policy and may encourage other employees to similarly start businesses on their own.

D. Potential union involvement and a legal suit.

2. All of these issues are important and must be considered in the decision. Therefore:

A. Discharging Benson should be avoided since it has considerable potential for affecting the morale of other employees (who may consider it unfair treatment of a superior and otherwise reliable employee who made one "mistake") and because it could lead to problems with the union and a legal suit.

B. Retaining Benson should also be avoided because of its potential effect on discipline and its tendency to set policy and encourage other employees to start their own businesses.

C. Discharging Benson as an employee but retaining him as a consultant is the only solution that is not negatively affected by the main issues.

3. If Benson fails to accept the solution of resigning to become a consultant, then he should be discharged. Under these circumstances there is less chance of his treatment being perceived as unfair. While the company still risks union problems and a lawsuit, discipline will be maintained, no policy on outside businesses will be set, and other employees will not be encouraged to follow in Benson's footsteps.

Conclusions

1. Discharging Benson as an employee but retaining him as a consultant is the best solution considering the major issues involved.

2. If Benson fails to resign to accept a consultancy, he should be discharged.
3. The consultancy solution must be presented to Benson as the only all-around fair solution, and not as punishment, in order to maximize his accepting it; however, it must be presented in such a fashion that other employees recognize that resigning or discharged employees are not automatically hired as consultants.
4. A policy on outside employee business should be established and publicized as soon as possible.

Recommendations

1. Discharge Benson as an employee and hire him as a consultant.
2. If Benson fails to accept this solution, discharge him immediately.
3. Establish and publicize a policy on outside employee businesses as soon as possible.

Psychological Techniques for Problem Solving

The logical, step-by-step technique to problem solving is very effective, but it is based primarily on using only the left half of the brain. Since the human brain has two halves, it makes sense to use the right brain for problem solving as well—especially since the right half of your brain is the creative half. Also, the step-by-step approach uses only your conscious mind. But you can use your unconscious mind as well.

Some consultants avoid psychological techniques like the plague. They think psychological approaches are too uncertain and smack of a "touchie-feelie" orientation. These same consultants would be surprised to learn that they have already used some of these techniques without realizing it. Have you ever awakened in the morning with the solution to a problem that had been bothering you? When your conscious mind was unsuccessful at arriving at a solution, your subconscious mind took over while you were asleep. When you woke up, it turned the solution over to your conscious mind.

Many famous and successful people use the subconscious mind to solve important problems and help in their decision making. When Thomas Edison had a problem that his conscious mind was unable to handle, he went into a darkened room and lay down. He refused to be disturbed until the solution came to him.

Builder and wheeler-dealer Donald Trump tells of an instance where his subconscious mind worked on a problem even after his conscious mind had come to what proved to be the wrong decision. "The papers were being drawn up, and then one morning I woke up and it didn't feel right." So, listening to the conclusions of his subconscious mind, Trump changed his mind. He didn't invest in a project that many experts, and his conscious mind, said was a sound investment. Several months later, the company about which Trump made his decision went bankrupt. The investors lost all of their money.[1]

After your conscious mind has collected and analyzed all the relevant factors in a situation, your subconscious mind sometimes comes to a better decision than your conscious mind. Why is this so?

1. *No pressure.* Your conscious mind may be under the pressures of time, a demanding client, or deadlines. Your subconscious mind doesn't recognize these pressures.
2. *Distractions.* Your conscious mind may be distracted by friends, family or business problems, noise, or even a lack of sleep. Not so your subconscious mind.
3. *Limited time.* Most consultants don't have the time to work on a single problem all day on a continual basis. But your subconscious mind has all night, and it will work effortlessly on a problem that needs solving.
4. *False knowledge.* For a variety of reasons, your conscious mind may be influenced by false assumptions or inaccurate facts. Your subconscious mind may know better.

How to Help Your Subconscious
Solve Your Consulting Problems

If you want to use your subconscious mind to help you solve a problem, first learn all you can about the problem. As when you use the Staff Study Method, gather all the relevant factors and spend a great deal of time arriving at the central issue in the case. You can also mull over the alternatives, talk to other people and get their opinions, do additional research. Do this until you feel slightly overloaded.

Before you go to sleep, set aside a half-hour to an hour to do nothing but think about the problem, analyze the data, and think about potential solutions.

Go to sleep in the normal way. Don't try to force a solution to your problem. Although the solution is usually ready for you sometime the next morning, it could come in the middle of the night. If it does, be ready for it by having pencil and paper nearby, and quickly scribble down the solution and any other insights.

Sometimes answers come in indirect and strange ways. In 1846, when Elias Howe was struggling to invent the sewing machine, he was stumped. Howe had invented a machine that could push and extract a needle into and out of cloth material. The problem was the thread. Since the thread went through an eye in the needle at the end opposite the point, the entire needle had to go through the material and back again in order to make a stitch. That was impossible. Howe was at an impasse. Then, for several nights in a row, Howe had identical dreams; Howe's subconscious mind was trying to tell him something. In the dreams, Howe found himself on a South Pacific island where natives armed with spears danced around him. But the spears were very strange. Each spearhead had a conspicuous hole. Only after several days did Howe realize the solution to his problem: to construct sewing needles with eyes for the thread near the point rather than at the opposite end.

If you want outstanding solutions to your client's prob-

lems, use both your right and left brains and your conscious
and subconscious minds.

Note

1. Donald J. Trump and Tony Schwartz, *The Art of the Deal* (New
York: Warner Books, 1987), pp. 27–28.

10

THE IMPORTANCE OF ETHICS IN CONSULTING

Ethics is a working concept with a real effect on your consulting practice. This chapter explains why the application of ethics to a consulting practice is so important. Ethics is not simply a matter of obeying the law; nor are ethical problems simple; you will face them frequently during your work as a consultant.

The Institute of Management Consultants (IMC) is the only body in the United States that certifies individuals as management consultants. The process to becoming a certified management consultant (CMC) includes filling out an application, preparing descriptions of client engagements, submitting to a review before a review board, and passing a test regarding IMC's Code of Ethics. This Code must be understood and adhered to by anyone who becomes a CMC.

Business Ethics: Not Clear-Cut

If ethical questions could be expressed in clear terms of black or white, decisions regarding corporate conduct would be easy. But that is seldom the case. Let me tell you about a few situations, some well-known, where decisions of business ethics were not at all straightforward.

Ethics vs. Jobs: The Lockheed Case

The Lockheed payoff scandal—Lockheed executives were found to be bribing Japanese officials to secure contracts for their aircraft in Japan—is even today pointed to as one of the most infamous examples of corporate lawbreaking and lack of corporate ethics. Without commenting on the legal aspects of this case, one could inquire into the motivation of those Lockheed executives who made the decision for these payoffs. After all, it was not simply a case of payoffs for personal profits. If the contacts had been lost, thousands of jobs would have been lost—not the jobs of the executives concerned but those of the workers and managers at lower levels. I do not suggest that eliminating jobs was necessarily the motivation for the payoffs, but it probably wasn't personal profit either. If ethics is defined as a set of moral principles for the greater good, then the bad of the payoff must be weighed against any good that results.

The Ethics of Marketing Research

Marketing research can be completely honest and aboveboard. However, marketing research is frequently competitive research, and that presents an opportunity for questionable practices. Let me tell you about my own introduction into this field.

As a newly promoted manager of research and development, I studied the possible solution to one of the problems my company faced. Because the business was heavily government-oriented, our production was a continual series of peaks and valleys. The government orders all came during one part of the year, and then we would become extremely busy, producing like mad to fulfill our contracts. Other parts of the year, we had practically no business at all, and our workers were idle. The choices in such circumstances are usually pretty limited. We could either try to manufacture our products for someone else, retain our workers and pay them for essentially doing nothing, or fire our work force every year. None of these solutions were very attractive.

Obviously, if we could find some other product to make that would fill the valleys when no government work was under contract, this would solve the problem. Our company was very much involved in fiberglass protective products such as pilot helmets. One additional fiberglass product that we considered was personal protective body armor for military and police, but we knew very little about this market. To learn more, we decided to hire a marketing research firm—that is, an independent consultant. Bids were requested from several of the leading firms in our area. The firm that won the opportunity to undertake this task had a fine proposal and a good reputation.

One aspect of the research bothered me. Since the information we required involved the total size of the market along with competing products, sales, and other proprietary information, I wondered how such information could be obtained. As I recall, I even commented to one of the executives of the research firm that I didn't know how they were going to get this information, since obviously they couldn't just call up a company and ask for it.

Two months after the contract had been initiated, I was given a final report of several hundred pages, along with a personal presentation by a representative from the marketing research firm. The information it provided was exact, precise, and explicit. It had all the information about our potential competitors, the size of the market, the sales, and even, in some cases, strategies that the competition intended to follow in the coming years. I was amazed at the detail. Innocently I asked where such information could be obtained. I was told that the gathering had been done in a very straightforward fashion. The researcher had simply called the president of every company in the business and identified himself as a student doing a report on the unusual product of body armor. In almost every case, this researcher had gotten complete information that was highly secretive and proprietary.

How do you rate that research technique? How would most people? Let's find out. Washington Researchers is a well-known consulting firm that does competitive research on companies, products, and strategies. It also conducts seminars around the country on how to accomplish various types of competitive research. Several years ago I had the good fortune to attend one. As a part of the seminar, all attendees participated in a survey of company information techniques. This survey was developed originally because participants had asked Washington Researchers for judgments about the ethics of various means of company information gathering. Washington Researchers decided that the issues were too complex to allow for easy answers. So they decided to conduct this survey as a simple measurement of individual and company practices.

Please stop at this point and take this questionnaire,* which asks your opinion about several research techniques or strategies. Results from more than five hundred professional marketing, planning, and business researchers at seminars around the country are contained in Figure 10-1.

Washington Researchers Survey
of Company Information Techniques

During past seminars, participants have asked Washington Researchers for judgments regarding the ethics of company information-gathering. There are too many complex issues involved to allow easy answers, but we have decided to attempt a simple measurement of individual and company practices. For the purposes of this questionnaire, *assume that you are asked to find out everything you can about the finances, products, marketing strategies, etc. of your company's closest competitor.* Several research techniques or strategies are listed below. Please respond to each by indicating the following:

1. Would your company encourage or condone the use of the technique?
2. Aside from your company's policies, would you (personally) feel comfortable using the technique?
3. Do you believe that other companies in your industry would use the technique in trying to find information about your company?

Note: If unemployed, answer question 1 in each series about a company you would like to work for.

*Used with permission of Washington Researchers, Ltd., Washington, D.C. 20007 (202/333-3499).

Research Strategy Alternatives

A. Researcher poses as graduate student working on thesis. Researcher tells source that dorm phones are very busy, so researcher will call back rather than having phone calls returned. In this way, researcher's real identity is protected.

   1. Would your company use this technique?   Yes _____ No _____

   2. Would you personally use this technique?   Yes _____ No _____

   3. Do other companies use this technique?   Yes _____ No _____

B. Researcher calls the V.P. while s/he is at lunch, hoping to find the secretary who may have some information but is likely to be less suspicious about researcher's motives.

   1. Would your company use this technique?   Yes _____ No _____

   2. Would you personally use this technique?   Yes _____ No _____

   3. Do other companies use this technique?   Yes _____ No _____

C. Researcher calls competitor's suppliers and distributors, pretending to do a study of the entire industry. Researcher poses as a representative of a private research firm and works at home during the project so that the company's identity is protected.

   1. Would your company use this technique?   Yes _____ No _____

   2. Would you personally use this technique?   Yes _____ No _____

   3. Do other companies use this technique?   Yes _____ No _____

D. The competitor's representative is coming to a local college to recruit employees. Researcher poses as a student job-seeker in order to learn recruiting practices and some other general information about the competitor.

   1. Would your company use this technique?   Yes _____ No _____

2. Would you personally use this
   technique?　　　　　　　　　　Yes _____　No _____

3. Do other companies use this
   technique?　　　　　　　　　　Yes _____　No _____

E.　The researcher is asked to verify rumors that the competitor
　　is planning to open a new plant in a small southern town.
　　The researcher poses as an agent from a manufacturer
　　looking for a site similar to the one that the competitor
　　supposedly would need. Researcher uses this cover to
　　become friendly with local representatives of the Chamber of
　　Commerce, newspapers, realtors, etc.

1. Would your company use this
   technique?　　　　　　　　　　Yes _____　No _____

2. Would you personally use this
   technique?　　　　　　　　　　Yes _____　No _____

3. Do other companies use this
   technique?　　　　　　　　　　Yes _____　No _____

F.　Researcher corners a competitor employee at a national
　　conference, such as the one sponsored by the American
　　Marketing Association, and offers to buy drinks at the hotel
　　bar. Several drinks later, the researcher asks the hard
　　questions.

1. Would your company use this
   technique?　　　　　　　　　　Yes _____　No _____

2. Would you personally use this
   technique?　　　　　　　　　　Yes _____　No _____

3. Do other companies use this
   technique?　　　　　　　　　　Yes _____　No _____

G.　Researcher finds an individual who works for the competitor
　　to serve as informant to researcher's company.

1. Would your company use this
   technique?　　　　　　　　　　Yes _____　No _____

2. Would you personally use this
   technique?　　　　　　　　　　Yes _____　No _____

3. Do other companies use this
   technique?　　　　　　　　　　Yes _____　No _____

Figure 10-1. Washington Researchers survey: typical results.

Percentage of "Yes" Responses

Question A	1. 39%	Question E	1. 36%
	2. 46%		2. 36%
	3. 86%		3. 80%
Question B	2. 63%	Question F	1. 63%
	2. 65%		2. 60%
	3. 86%		3. 91%
Question C	1. 41%	Question G	1. 35%
	2. 47%		2. 36%
	3. 88%		3. 80%
Question D	1. 33%		
	2. 38%		
	3. 71%		

Used with permission of Washington Researchers, Ltd., Washington, D.C. 20007 (202/333-3499).

An Executive Recruiting Story

Along the same lines, I would like to tell you this story about executive recruiting. The neophyte executive recruiter (headhunter) has two tasks. One is to cold-call companies, as described in Chapter 2, in order to obtain what are known as job orders—the authority to do a search. The other task is to identify candidates with the qualities specified by companies and to recruit for the position. Both components of this task are challenging.

This particular neophyte headhunter was told to cold-call a list of potential clients and get as many job orders as he could and then to start recruiting candidates for these jobs. Naturally not all the companies called were in need of a headhunter's services, and some of the contacts were not particularly polite. One of the companies this neophyte called was the "Dynamic Petroleum Company," whose vice-president of engineering gave a most memorable response. He began to yell and shout and curse at the headhunter, saying that he never dealt with headhunters, that no one in his company was permitted to talk to headhunters, that he fired any of his engineers or even his secretary for talking to headhunters, and that furthermore, if he was ever called again, he would institute legal action. With that he hung up. This unnerved the neophyte, who was observed by the president of the search firm. The president said, "Let me show you how to handle this. A guy like this isn't a client; he is the source of our product. These are the people that we recruit from."

Five minutes later, the president phoned that same vice-president at Dynamic Petroleum. He said that he was a college student whose professor had told him to contact one of the petroleum engineers at Dynamic, that he had forgotten this engineer's name, and that he was afraid to call his professor back. Over the next half-hour, this vice-president of engineering proceeded to read off the names of over 150 different petroleum engineers in his organization, describing them by specialty, background, and years of experience. He gave away an immense amount of intelligence, which was ultimately used against him, for now his engineers could be contacted by name for recruiting purposes.

I once told this story to a group of approximately fifty middle to senior managers. Several commented on the lack of ethics of the search firm president. But one individual present was himself president of a search firm. He protested, "But that's the business. That's how its done. You can't be a headhunter if you don't operate in this way."

Again, I don't want you to draw any conclusions about my personal feelings regarding these matters one way or the other. I want you merely to consider that at least some headhunters consider this practice common, if not ethical.

A Japanese View of Duty

Peter Drucker tells the story of a large Japanese company that wanted to open an American plant. After an investigation of many locations in several different states, a suitable site was located. So important was this operation that a special ceremony was scheduled that included the governor, many senior state officials, and the CEO from Japan.

The Japanese CEO spoke fairly good English; however, to ensure that everything he said would be absolutely correct, the company hired an American of Japanese descent to translate his speech into English. With dignity and measured tones, the Japanese CEO began to speak, noting the great honor it was for his company to be able to locate in the United States with mutual benefits to his company and to the surrounding citizens. He also discussed the benefits to the local economy and to Japanese-American friendship. And then, nodding in the direction of the governor and other state officials, he added, still in Japanese, "And furthermore, Mr. Governor and senior officials, please understand that we know our duty, and when the time comes that you retire from your honored positions, my corporation will not forget and will repay you for the efforts which you have expended in our behalf in giving us this opportunity."

The Japanese-American translator was horrified. Instantly she made a decision to omit these remarks in her English translation. The Japanese CEO, who understood enough English to realize what she had done but not why, continued his speech as if nothing had happened. Later, when the two were alone, the executive asked the translator, "How could you exclude my reassurances to the governor and officials? Why did you leave this important part out of my speech?" Only then could it be explained that what is ethical, even a duty, in Japan is considered unethical and corrupt in the United States.

General Electric, Westinghouse, and Allis-Chalmers

Some years ago, when jet turbine engines were first being developed, General Electric, Westinghouse, and Allis-Chalmers formed what would technically be considered a cartel. Cartels, of course, are illegal under the antitrust laws of this country, and this one was eliminated. This is another instance where the law and ethics might be considered at odds, because when the cartel broke up, prices went up, with a resulting drop in demand, bringing a considerable loss of jobs and the eventual bankruptcy of Allis-Chalmers.

Again, a question here: I don't recommend either breaking the law or establishing cartels, but which was the more ethical conduct?

Typical Problems Pertaining to Ethics in Consulting

In the practice of consulting, you will eventually be involved in numerous ethical questions. Fortunately, some of them can be anticipated. Consider the following example from my own seminars and courses on consulting. Usually there is no simple solution, although some problems are easier to resolve than others.

1. *Client already knows the solution that he or she wants to a problem.* This typically occurs when a client requires an outsider to confirm information that he or she already knows. For example, you may run into a situation such as the one I described in Chapter 1. Suppose a division of a company has already done a very thorough internal study that suggests the division get into the such and such business. However, because this study was done by the division itself, it is suspect. Top management may wish to have an independent study by a consultant. You may be engaged by that division of the company, and yet the client makes it very clear to you what answer is expected. Do you accept such a consulting engagement or not?

Some consultants say it doesn't make any difference. You're getting paid to do the study even if the answer is known. If the client makes it very clear at the beginning that what he expects is a yes answer, that's what he's paying for and that's what he'll get. Other consultants take the position that they will do the job and provide whatever answer results from their analysis. If the client insists upon having a yes answer and nothing else (usually this insistence is not stated explicitly but is very subtle), they will refuse to undertake the study.

There are many different issues to consider. It will be difficult to escape your need for cash and possible additional business from this client later. But there is no right answer. You have to consider it yourself, and my only advice is to think about the alternatives now, because you will almost certainly encounter this situation sooner or later.

2. *Client wants you to omit information from your written report.* This generally occurs when you have included information in your report that your client feels will hurt him with others, either inside or outside his company. After reviewing your report in draft form, he may ask you to delete certain information. Some consultants take the position that they will decide how to handle this based on relevance to the central issue. If the information is not relevant, they will exclude it. Otherwise they will refuse. However, other consultants feel that since the client is paying and since "the customer is always right," if the customer wants this information left out, it will be left out. Still others stand on their professionalism and refuse to change so much as a comma. You pay your money and you take your choice.

3. *Client wants proprietary information that you learned while employed with someone else.* This situation usually arises when you first become a consultant. A former competitor immediately contacts you about a potential engagement. It soon becomes clear, however, that he is hiring you not for what you can do but rather for what you know about your former employer. This situation can also come up when a potential client realizes that you have completed a consulting job for a competitor.

If it becomes clear that all the potential client wants is proprietary information, most consultants will refuse to get involved. You should also realize that unless you are a professional industrial spy—which, by the way, is illegal—a client who hires you for information you learned working for a competitor has every right to expect that you will give his proprietary information to someone else in the future. As a result, he will probably not hire you for any other purpose.

If a competitor wants to hire you for a job similar to one you did as a consultant in another company, it may be completely acceptable. "I heard about the great job that you did with the ABC Company; we'd like you to do the same thing for us," he may say. One fully ethical approach is to tell your potential client something like this: "I'd be happy to do this for you if I can get permission from the ABC Company. I don't think that I would be giving away any of their secrets if I did the same job for you. However, since you two are competitors, I would rather have their concurrence. Is that okay with you?"

A question that sometimes comes up is, Who owns proprietary data or information that you develop as a consultant? Usually this is more of a legal question than an ethical one. Many companies, as well as the U.S. government, are well-aware of this issue. Your contract may specify that your client owns all data developed unless you negotiate the contract otherwise. Anything that you develop as part of a consulting engagement but consider your own might possibly be challenged in a court of law in the future. Therefore, if you think something that comes out of an engagement may be useful to you in the future, it's better to agree what will belong to whom up front. For some types of information, this may not be a problem. It's just too difficult to prove that techniques or methodologies that you developed came out of one specific assignment, or out of many. However, some results from marketing research done for a company, or information about a company, clearly belong to the company for which you developed it. But in all cases, it's better to make it contractual. Then you'll know where you stand from the start. Most companies could care less about who owns consulting methods or techniques. But they rightfully feel that the information developed from these techniques— which they pay for—belongs to them.

4. *Client wants you to lie to his boss.* This usually involves a lower-level manager who wants you to lie to a manager at a higher level, or it could be the president of a company who wants you to lie to the board of directors or someone else outside the company. Some consultants have stated that it depends on the lie. They might go along with a harmless "white lie" to protect someone's feelings. Others

would not. Let's say that you are on assignment for the vice-president of a company that is owned by the president, and as a part of this job you have to analyze the efficiency and effectiveness of all managers working for this vice-president, one of whom happens to be the president's son. You rate the son as a very poor executive. When the vice-president sees this report, he says something like this: "Look, the president of our company has a heart condition. If you report that his son is a very poor executive, it could easily upset him and may actually bring on a heart attack. How about toning this down a bit and saying that this executive is unsuited to his present position?" Many consultants would consider this a "white lie" and would go along with this request. Other consultants might take the position that this executive was very poor and that this is what they intended to put in their report, heart attack or no.

Other lies are far more questionable in both their motives and the net result on the company officials, the company's well-being, or even the general public. Some would say that agreeing to lie would depend on the effect that the lie would cause. Others say simply that they would refuse to lie under any circumstances.

5. *You are a headhunter, and a member of a client's company wants you to recruit him.* This situation again demonstrates that what might be ethical under some circumstances is totally unethical under others. To honor this request is unethical for any headhunter. Under no conditions can a headhunter recruit from his client's company, and no ethical headhunter would even consider it. If a member of a client's organization wants you to recruit him, the only ethical thing that you can do is first seek approval from this individual's boss.

One question that comes up, however, is, For how long a period after you complete a search for a company is it still considered a client? Few would still term a company a client after five years with no new assignments. For a lesser period, you have to make your own decisions. Many headhunters indicate that clientage lasts something less than three years after a search is completed.

6. *Client wants you to bill for more or for less than the actual amount.* This can involve the law as well as ethics. And you can be certain that the IRS would take a very dim view of this suggestion. But, aside from its possible legal connotations, it is also a lie. Would you do it or would you not?

All these are typical problems, and you will see many more in your practice. In all cases, only you can decide on the action to take. Some otherwise unethical practices are often considered ethical because of the nature of the work accomplished. These would probably include the marketing research and headhunting situations noted earlier which are acceptable in their professions but certainly considered unethical for anyone else. The only analogy that I can think of is military spying. The professional soldier is prohibited from spying. Spying is illegal. A person caught spying may be hanged. Yet for a spy, spying would probably be considered ethical behavior.

More than twenty years ago, a young air force lieutenant was ordered by a superior officer to falsify a report in order to make a score from a simulated aircraft attack appear better than it actually was. This lieutenant faced a serious moral and ethical dilemma; it appeared that his future career in the air force hinged on an outright lie. Despite considerable pressure, this lieutenant resisted and refused to lie. The threat of punitive action was never carried out, and he had an outstanding career right up until the time he left the air force. Today this lieutenant has major responsibilities outside of the government that have little to do with flying. He rates his success in entirely different activities in no small part to this instance when he decided who he was and how he would live his life.

Ethical questions are rarely simple and rarely easy to resolve. Frequently it's a question not of lying, cheating, or stealing but of doing either the greater good or the lesser evil. Whatever you do, you must be able to respect yourself in the future. Otherwise you will be useless to your clients and to yourself.

11

MAKING PROFESSIONAL PRESENTATIONS

The success of a consultant engagement is based not only on actually doing the assignment professionally but on your ability to present the results of your work to your client. Presenting is crucial. Yet one survey of company presidents showed that more were afraid of public speaking and presenting than of dying! In this chapter I cover the important skills and techniques of presentations and show you five keys to presentation success.

Objectives of Presentations

With a presentation, you want to inform your client of the results of the assignment, make recommendations that will benefit your client, and confirm that you have done a good job so that you will be retained in the future. Each of these objectives is, in its own way, important.

If you don't take the time to build a case for your recommendations, explaining what has happened during the engagement, your client is less likely to accept your recommendations. Your client wants to know how you arrived at the conclusions that led to these recommendations, and why you used one methodology over others. If you've run into problems, your client also wants to know what these problems have been and what assumptions you have had to make. If there were changes to the original contract, even though prior approval has already been given, you should restate them, both to remind your client of these changes and to inform others.

Either the quality of the work that you have done or the recommendations you have made for action are the bottom line of the consulting engagement. It's results that you are actually getting paid for. Without them the engagement, although it might make an interesting case study, would be of no benefit to your client.

Confirming that you have done a good job so that you will be retained in the future is also important. If you've done a good job, you deserve recognition for it. You can do this only by convincing your client through your presentation. If you do it properly, your client will come away from the consulting engagement looking good, and you will be retained again; futhermore, you will get referrals to additional clients who would like you to duplicate your success for them.

Five Keys to a Successful Presentation

Every successful presentation has five essential components. These are: (1) professionalism; (2) enthusiasm; (3) organization; (4) practice; (5) visual aids.

Let's look at each in turn.

Professionalism

The quality of professionalism must be evident throughout your presentation. It is demonstrated by your dress and personal appearance, the quality of the visual aids you use, your demeanor, your preparation, and your delivery.

If you show up for a presentation wearing a suit that

needs pressing or clothes that are not appropriate for the occasion, you will not be perceived as a professional.

If there are typographical or grammatical mistakes in your visual aids, or if the lettering is sloppy, this also will not be perceived as professional.

If the way you handle yourself during the presentation indicates that you are unsure of yourself or defensive, or that you do not know what you are talking about, you will not be perceived as a professional.

If things go wrong during your presentation because of an obvious lack of preparation, again, you will not be perceived as a professional.

But if your presentation is clear and well-organized, if it goes like clockwork and you are prepared to answer all questions asked, if your appearance matches your performance—then your professionalism will be obvious.

Enthusiasm

Enthusiasm is absolutely crucial. If you do nothing else, be enthusiastic. If you are not enthusiastic about what you did, I guarantee you that your client will not be enthusiastic either. In my opinion, enthusiasm is the most important secret of making a good presentation.

What should you do if you really are not enthusiastic? First of all, it is very difficult for me to believe that you could ever become a good consultant and *not* be enthusiastic about what you are doing. But if, for whatever reason, you really are not enthusiastic about a particular assignment, there is only one thing you can do: *Pretend.* Whenever I talk with my senior students about the absolute necessity of enthusiasm, I always tell them the story of General George S. Patton, Jr., one of the most successful generals of World War II. He won battles *and* saved the lives of his men by motivating them to do their very best. And he did this by becoming a consummate actor.

I have read Patton's published diaries, which go back as far as the turn of the century, when Patton was a cadet at West Point. During World War I, when still in his twenties, he was a colonel in command of the U.S. Army's first tank corps. Patton wrote his wife regularly, and these letters were published with the diaries. In one letter, Patton says, "Every day I practice in front of a mirror looking mean." Can you imagine that? A hard-boiled colonel of the U.S. Army practicing in front of a mirror looking mean? But Patton did this for a reason. He knew that his ability to motivate his men— sometimes by joking, sometimes by intimidation—could win battles and save lives. So he made himself become a great actor.

If Patton could act to save lives and win battles, then you can act, and act enthusiastically, to make a successful consultant presentation. Remember, you *must* do this. It is not an option. It is the most important secret of success in presenting. You must be enthusiastic, and you must show this enthusiasm to your client audience. I promise you that the enthusiasm, even though self-generated, will come through, and it will help make your presentation successful.

Organization

You can't just stand up and speak without having thought ahead of time about what you are going to say. Even a terrific off-the-cuff speaker would get into trouble making consultant presentations that way. If you try it, invariably certain facts will be left out, and then your presentation will not be as clear and logical as it must be. If you are questioned because of this lack of clarity, the pressure on you will increase, and your difficulties will become even greater.

Proper organization of your presentation ahead of time will prevent many problems once you are face-to-face with your client. Fortunately you already have the ingredients of your presentation from the work you did in earlier chapters, including material from the contract, the proposal, and even your initial interview. So you can organize the facts of the engagement and present them to the client in a clear and logical manner using this outline:

1. Background of the consulting assignment and the problem to be solved

2. Statement of the project objectives
3. Methodologies used to do the assignment, along with alternative methodologies and reasons why they were rejected
4. Problems encountered during the engagement and how each was handled
5. The results or conclusions stemming from this engagement
6. Specific recommendations to the client on what he or she should do as a result of the work you have done, not excluding additional work that you or someone else must do in the future

Frequently you can incorporate the problem-solving methodology explained in Chapter 9. This is especially useful in presenting your analysis of alternative solutions to a problem, which will lead logically to your recommendations.

Practice

Practice does not mean that you must read your report aloud or that you must memorize anything. In fact the contrary is true. Reading will make the presentation boring and stilted. It is not natural. The same is true of memorization. Even if you have the ability to memorize quickly, I do not recommend using it in a consulting presentation. First, the time spent in memorization can be better used in getting your presentation together. Second, there is always a chance that, under the pressures of the situation, your timing and memory may be thrown off by a question asked out of turn or a discussion initiated by your client.

I learned this lesson the hard way. As a young air force officer flying B-52s out of Altus, Oklahoma, I was extremely interested in navigation. On one occasion, the Texas Math and Science Teachers Association contacted my wing commander to ask if there was someone who could travel to its annual meeting in Wichita Falls, Kansas, and speak for about an hour on a subject of interest to the members. The wing commander asked me, and, since I had waited for a chance to do research in space navigation, I jumped at the chance. Using notes collected over several months, I wrote a terrific one-hour presentation (at least I thought it was terrific, and it must have been reasonably good, because it was later published by a national magazine). I was also given the opportunity to have excellent artwork prepared as 35mm slides. I felt that I had the very best support possible. But I made one mistake: I memorized every single word in that one-hour presentation. I even knew where to pause for the commas! When the time came, I went down to Wichita Falls and, in full uniform, looked out at nearly three hundred math and science teachers. I had been a junior high school student in that very same city, and seeing so many teachers looking at me immediately had its effect. I forgot parts of my presentation, became flustered, and eventually had to read it word for word. What a failure! But it taught me a valuable lesson, and never since then have I memorized anything, even though I am frequently a guest speaker for many different organizations. Do not repeat my mistake. Do not memorize, and do not read anything.

If you don't read and you don't memorize, how are you supposed to make your presentation? Very easily. Once you have your material organized, you can use either 3- by 5-inch file cards or visual aids to help you discuss each point. You might have one card that says "background of the consulting assignment and the problem." You would then simply look up and talk to your audience about this background. If there are any important statistics that you do not wish to leave out, you would put them sequentially on other cards. Other main ideas are also on sequential cards. But you should write no more than one sentence on each card. The idea is not to read what is written on each card but rather to talk about that one sentence. If you are using visual aids, they could display the key sentence or statistics to remind you of what you are going to talk about at that particular time.

Controlling Time. It is extremely important as a part of your practice to control the time available for your presentation. If your client wants a one-hour presentation, make it a one-hour presentation. If your client wants thirty minutes, make it that. Do not under any circumstances extend your presentation unless requested to do so. That is disaster. Let me tell you three stories to prove my point.

I was once associated with a major aerospace company that was bidding on a multibillion-dollar contract for the government. On one of the reviews, representatives of the government visited our organization for a four-hour briefing by our engineers. These engineers lost control of the time and went well over the limit requested by the customer. Despite frantic signals from company employees, they completed their presentation more than an hour and a half late. The customers remained the extra hour and a half without complaint, but they missed their return flights. And while I would not say this was the only reason that the large contract was lost, it was certainly a factor.

Some years ago, I was on a search committee to find a new professor for our department at the university. The procedure in academia is somewhat different than in industry, and in many hirings the professor must be voted on and accepted by the department before the university can make an offer. Usually a candidate for faculty membership must not only interview with many department members but make a formal presentation to the department sitting as a group. On this occasion, the candidate, who had only recently obtained his Ph.D., was asked to make a twenty-minute presentation about the research for his dissertation. The time limit was necessary because many faculty members had other meetings to attend. The candidate had graduated from an excellent university, and prior to his visit most of the department members had decided to vote for his hiring based solely on his background and experience. During the visit, the individual interviews seemed to be going fairly well. The presentation was the final obstacle before the department voted on his hiring. He began his presentation. Five minutes passed. Ten minutes passed. Fifteen minutes passed. Twenty minutes came and went. The presentation continued on and on. The entire department was restless; all of us were late for other meetings. Individuals slipped out one after the other. Finally, after forty-five minutes, the candidate concluded. By then a receptive faculty eager to hire him no longer existed. The faculty did eventually vote to hire, but only for a one-year appointment. In fact it was two years before this individual was finally granted the permanent position that he all but had even before his visit. It is no exaggeration to say that failure to control time for twenty-five additional minutes cost two years of promotion, pay, and other benefits.

While attending the Industrial College of the Armed Forces in 1989, I saw an otherwise excellent course go awry because the professor failed to have the students control the time of their required presentations. The result was lack of attention and problems with car pools, and the professor himself received a poor course evaluation.

Never think that time control is a small item—it is essential.

The Practice Sequence. Here's the practice sequence I use: First, I note the time available and outline the presentation using the organization structure indicated earlier in this chapter. I write this information on 3- by 5-inch file cards. I then go through the presentation once, using the cards. In this run-through, I change the cards, add facts if required, and delete or change others if they don't seem to fit. I watch my time closely as I make this presentation to myself, and I make adjustments, through insertion or deletion of material, so that my presentation is several minutes less than the time I have been allotted.

If there are several presenters, I insist that we practice together. Some consultants simply divide the available time and develop separate presentations, but I have found that such a presentation doesn't quite fit together when done before the client. Further, frequently one or more of the presenters will exceed the amount of time allotted, and the total presentation runs much longer than anticipated.

I practice at first very informally—perhaps in a room by myself, perhaps sitting around a table with the other presenters. I do this several times until I am confident of the overall structure and the time. Now I also know what visual aids I will need, and I can have them made.

The Formal Practice Presentation. The formal practice presentation is done as if it were real. In fact I insist upon doing it in front of someone who can give me feedback. Usually this is my wife, but it has also been a colleague or someone else who was not involved in the presentation itself. You must present it to an outsider who is not part of the consultant presentation team.

The Live Demonstration. If there is some demonstration to be done as a part of the presentation, I insist upon a practice live demonstration. This is essential to make sure that it fits into the time and that the results of the demonstration are as anticipated. You will find that at actual presentations everything that can go wrong will go wrong. Therefore, you must anticipate and eliminate potential problems before they actually happen.

Let me give you an example of how important this can be. Some years ago, I attended an annual meeting of the Survival and Flight Equipment Association, an organization of industry, military, and civilian-airline personnel who develop and manufacture life-support equipment for people who fly. A project manager from the navy made a very interesting presentation on a very important piece of equipment.

A navy flier has special problems because he flies over the sea. If he must eject from the aircraft, he hits the water. He must climb into a small life raft while weighted down with equipment such as survival gear, boots, and helmet. This is difficult enough even on a calm sea, but it is almost impossible if the parachute is still attached to him, since even the slightest wind will drag the chute. If the open chute fills with water, it can drag the aviator straight to the bottom. So the approved procedure is to use a quick-release, attached to the harness, to get rid of the parachute just as the aviator's boots touch the water. The problem with this procedure is that it is very difficult to judge height over a flat surface like the ocean, and it's even more difficult in the dark under the pressure of emergency conditions. As a result, some aviators who think they are just about to touch the water are actually one hundred feet or more in the air. Jettisoning the chute at that height is clearly not recommended. The navy's solution was highly innovative as well as effective. A small explosive squib in the parachute harness separates the chute from the harness on contact with water; the water completes an electrical contact. Thus, when the aviator enters the water, the parachute is blown away from him automatically.

Now you may be thinking, *That's just fine for the ocean water, but what if a pilot must eject through a rain shower? Does this mean the apparatus will become wet and the aviator will be dropped thousands of feet?* The navy has anticipated this problem. The device works only in sea water, which has a high salt content.

The navy project manager explained all this in a most interesting fashion and finally came to the most dramatic point of the presentation. He himself donned a parachute. While he could not submerge his whole body, he had two live wires leading to the squib and had a glass of sea water before him. He then described in vivid terms exactly what would happen. He would take the two wires and thrust them into the sea water. We would see a flash and hear a loud bang, he said, and the parachute would be separated from the harness instantly. The entire audience waited in great anticipation; several people stuck their fingers in their ears. Knowing that he had everyone's attention, the presenter, with the parachute strapped tight to his body, took the two wires and jammed them into the sea watrer. Nothing happened. At first there were smirks; then scattered laughter spread throughout the room. This presenter—who had otherwise made a perfect presentation—took the harness off and discovered that someone had failed to replace the electrical batteries.

Let this teach you the lesson that it taught me: Always prepare for any live demonstrations by actually doing them yourself. Don't assume that something will work as planned. Actually do the demonstration as a part of your practice.

Visual Aids

Visual aids are also essential to a good presentation. In general you have five options for good visual aids: (1) flip charts; (2) overhead transparencies; (3) 35mm slides; (4) handouts; and (5) blackboards.

Flip Charts. Flip charts are large charts connected at the top that are flipped over as each one is used. The main advantage of flip charts is that they don't require any type of projector. However, since they are large, they are sometimes difficult to transport. And depending on the size of your audience, you may not be able to make the lettering large enough to be seen by everyone in the room.

Overhead Transparencies. Overhead transparencies require the use of an overhead projector. Transparencies themselves usually have a viewing area of approximately 8½ by 11 inches. Machines are available today to make these transparencies instantly without the use of photographic equipment. If you have a typewriter with large letters and have access to a transparency reproduction machine, you can make visuals fairly rapidly. If not, they can be prepared at many printing and art shops. Transparencies themselves are fairly easy to carry around. They are not as small as 35mm slides, but they are easier to use than slides, and much easier to transport than flip charts. They can, however, be expensive—as much as several dollars each. And, of course, they require the use of the special projector already mentioned.

35mm Slides. Slides are very easy to transport. They do require the use of a slide projector, however, and they can be expensive. As is sometimes the case with transparencies, slides require additional lead time, usually a week or so.

Handouts. Handouts can be typed on a piece of paper and reproduced through one of the many photographic reproduction processes at a few cents per page. They can be used for either small or large groups, and the expense depends on the number that must be reproduced. You can make the handouts yourself, and they can be prepared at the last minute without a long lead time, both of which factors are important. For smaller groups, it is fairly easy to carry around the handouts with you. However, for a large group and a large handout, this visual aid becomes cumbersome and expensive. One additional disadvantage is that your audience may tend to read ahead of you; if you have some dramatic point to make, it could be spoiled by your audience's getting there first.

Blackboards. I say *blackboards*, even though the boards used may be green or some other color. Also, there are now smooth white boards available on which you can write in washable pastel colors. I like the latter: no more scratching sound as you write, and no more chalk dust on your hands and clothes.

Still, the advantages and disadvantages of all types of boards on which you write for group consulting presentations are the same. One advantage is flexibility. Until you actually touch chalk to board, you are not committed to revealing anything. Even after you use the board, changes are easy to make on the spot. Along with flexibility is the timing of what you display. You don't write anything down until you need it. Cost is another advantage. There is no cost in preparing for a chalk presentation as long as you don't have to buy a board. Also, as long as you have something to write with and some means of erasure, there isn't much that can go wrong as with electronic gadgetry.

Disadvantages? You can't reproduce a chalk presentation the way you can with overhead or 35mm transparencies. Also, if you have a lot to write down, what is your audience doing while you are writing?

I once started a presentation while my partner tried to write extensive material on a blackboard. Talk about distractions! I don't recommend it.

If you can't print clearly, the professionalism of your presentation will suffer—yet another disadvantage.

Whatever option you select in visual aids, make sure you keep these points in mind:

1. *Use big type.* The print must be large enough to be visible. If your visual aids cannot be read, you may as well not use them.

2. *Keep it simple.* Don't put too much information on a single slide, transparency, chart, or page of a handout. The information should only be keys to remind you of your major points and to reinforce these major points with your audience. Entire explanations, facts, figures, and so forth can be included as an appendix to your written report. If you put too much information on a single visual, you will only confuse your audience.

3. *Allow lots of lead time.* While handouts can be changed fairly easily, flip charts, transparencies, and slides take longer. Plan to have them completed a couple of days before the presentation itself. Typographical errors are common, and they must be corrected before the presentation. Even a simple spelling error leaves the thought in your client's mind, *If this consultant has made this error and allowed it to pass, what else has been screwed up?*

Overcoming Stage Fright

Every great presenter is a little apprehensive about making a presentation. If you weren't apprehensive, you would be indifferent, and the presentation would be boring. So a little bit of stage fright is fine. On the other hand, you do not want to be so apprehensive that you cannot make a smooth, forceful, and motivating presentation.

In order to overcome stage fright, I do two things. First, I accomplish at least two live rehearsals before other people. These are formal demonstrations to people not familiar with the presentation so that I can receive feedback and criticism on what I say. This criticism allows me to polish my presentation and often uncovers rough points I never thought about.

The second thing I do is something called *creative visualization*. Somehow I stumbled into this technique, and because it is a little strange, for many years I didn't tell too many people about it. Then, in the January 13, 1982, issue of *The Wall Street Journal*, I read an article about it. A performance psychologist, Charles Garfield, had found one reason why some people were superior performers. It was the trick of mental rehearsal, something top athletes had done for a long time. Top chief executives would visualize every aspect of what it would be like to have a successful presentation—sort of a deliberate daydreaming. In contrast, Garfield said, run-of-the-mill executives would organize their facts but not their psyches.

Thus, my creative visualization got official blessing from a performance psychologist and *The Wall Street Journal*. Believe me when I tell you the technique is simple. I like to do it the night before I make the presentation, just before I go to sleep. I'm lying there with nothing else to do; I go through my entire presentation, not memorizing it but going through it in my mind from start to finish, from the time I first enter the room until my conclusion. I visualize everything that happens, including standing up and shaking hands and describing the background of the assignment, the objectives of the project, the methods I used and why I chose them, the problems and how they were handled, the resulting conclusions, and the recommendations to my client. I even visualize questions that are asked and my answering them forcefully and correctly. I visualize smiles all the way around, knowing that I have made an excellent presentation and that everyone, including and especially the client who hired me, is happy with the excellent job I have done. I don't stop at doing this once; I repeat the visualization episode several times. You can visualize an entire hour presentation in a few minutes.

To my way of thinking, this creative visualization technique offers several outstanding features. First, when you actually go to make the presentation, it doesn't feel new. You've done it dozens of times before. This takes the sting out of stage fright. Second, I believe that visualizing my presentation in a presentation in a positive fashion, as a success, prepares me positively. I believe that my presentation will be successful, and therefore it is. I sense that my audience will be friendly to me, and therefore it is. I have confidence in my ability to answer questions because I have already seen myself doing these things.

In my years of using this creative visualization technique, it has never failed me. I strongly recommend that you try it too. The results will amaze you.

One variation I have heard about is called *the split-focus technique,* where you visualize the presentation while you physically do something else, such as working in the garden or taking a shower.

Answering Questions

Many presenters fear answering questions more than anything else; yet research has shown that 85 percent of the questions asked during a presentation can actually be anticipated. Therefore, when I prepare myself for a presentation, I sit down and try to anticipate questions that members of my client's company are likely to ask me. I actually write them down. Some of the questions bring up items I feel should be included in my presentation, so I modify it accordingly. Others I just think I should be ready for, so I simply think them through and write out the answers. If additional statistics or information is necessary to give a complete answer, I make sure I have this information available. In some cases, I even go so far as to make up a special visual aid with the information, which I hold in readiness to use only if I am asked this question.

When I am actually asked a question, I always repeat it. This gives me additional time to think about the answer, and at the same time it ensures that other members of the audience hear the question too. After repeating the question, I state first my answer, and then why my answer is what it is, giving supporting facts. I try never to be defensive about a question, even if it is asked in a belligerent tone of voice.

In fact, remembering that the customer is always right, I try never to get into an argument with a client. This does not mean I agree that the client is right if that's not the case. It simply means that I state the facts as I know them, and if the client insists on arguing, I explain my position as tactfully as possible and move on to something else.

One important key to answering questions—in fact for your whole presentation—is to view members of the audience as friends, not adversaries. Do this even if the climate is political and some members of the audience can be expected to snipe at you. You can at least treat them as friendly snipers, not as enemies out to demolish you.

The other point to watch out for is not to give long-winded answers. Try to make your answers short and to the point. Long-winded answers only fuzz up the issue and may lead to more in-depth questioning.

If you follow this advice, you cannot fail to have an outstanding presentation. Not only will you receive accolades for it, but your advice will be respected and followed and will lead to further consulting assignments.

12

HOW TO RUN YOUR CONSULTING BUSINESS

No matter how excellent you are technically as a consultant, unless you are a good business manager you will not realize your full business potential. Your business can even go bankrupt because of your failure to sustain a profit. Therefore, don't skip this chapter. I explain the various forms of business organization including proprietorships, partnerships, and corporations. I include information on business licenses, resale permits, fictitious name registration, use of credit cards, stationery, business cards, insurance, and personal liability. I also tell you about other important topics, such as how to keep your overhead low, what expenses to anticipate, and what records you should maintain.

Selecting the Legal Structure for Your Consulting Firm

There are several different structures recognized by law from which you can choose for your consulting practice. These are the sole proprietorship, the partnership, and the corporation. Each structure has its own advantages and disadvantages, and you should select the one that is most suitable for you.

The Sole Proprietorship

The sole proprietorship is a business structure for a company that is owned by only one person. All you need to do to establish a sole proprietorship is obtain whatever business licenses are required in your local area. This makes it the easiest of legal structures to set up. It is also the one most frequently used for many types of small businesses and certainly one that you should consider for your practice.

Advantages

1. *Ease and speed of formation.* With the sole proprietorship, there are fewer formalities and legal requirements. Sometimes you need only visit your county clerk, fill out a simple form, and pay the license fee, which is generally $200 or less. In most cases, there is no waiting period; you can satisfy all legal requirements the same day you make your visit.

2. *Reduced expense.* Because of the minimal legal requirements, the sole proprietorship can be set up without an attorney, so it is much less expensive than either a partnership or a corporation.

3. *Total control.* Since you have no partners and your business is not a corporation, complete control of its management is yours; as long as you fulfill the legal requirements, you run your business as you see fit. Except for your clients, you have no boss. You and the marketplace make all the decisions. This has the additional advantage of responsiveness: You can usually respond much more quickly to changes in the marketplace.

4. *Sole claim to profits.* Since you are the sole owner, you are not required to share your profits with anyone. The profits are yours, as are all the assets of the business.

Disadvantages

1. *Unlimited liability.* While you own all assets and can make all decisions in a sole proprietorship, you are also held

to unlimited personal liability. This means that you are responsible for the full amount of business debts and judgments
against your business. This could amount to more money
than you have invested in your business. If your business
fails with you owing money to various creditors, those debts
could be collected from your personal assets. Of course there
are various methods of reducing this risk—for example,
through proper insurance coverage, which I discuss later in
this chapter.

   2. *No one to consult with.* Since in a sole proprietorship
you are probably a one-person show, you are limited by your
own skills, education, background, and capabilities. You may
be able to get advice and counsel from friends, relatives, or
business acquaintances, but no one is motivated by personal
investment to give you this advice, nor will the giver suffer
the consequences if the advice proves to be poor.

   3. *Difficulty in absences.* Again, since there is only you,
you will have to find someone to cover for you when you are
sick or on vacation. Of course there are various ways around
this limitation. You could agree to watch over the practice of
some other consultant who works in the same area with the
understanding that he or she will do the same for you when
required. You could also pay someone to cover for you during
your periods of absence. But no matter what solution you
select, until you have employees working for you who can
perform certain services for clients, it is a limitation that must
be considered.

   4. *Difficulties in raising capital.* Potential lenders see
the sole proprietorship as represented essentially by one
person. As a result, they feel the risk is greater than if there
were more people involved, as in a partnership, or if you had
a permanent legal identity, as in a corporation.

The Partnership

   Legally a partnership can be entered into by simply
acquiring a business license from your county clerk. However, unlike the sole proprietorship, I don't recommend that

you attempt to do this by yourself; use the assistance of an attorney. Partnership definitions may vary in different states, and it is extremely important to document such obligations of each of the partners as investments and profits with a partnership agreement. Such an agreement should typically cover the following aspects of the practice:

- Absence and disability
- Arbitration
- Authority of individual partners in the conduct of the business
- Character of partners, including whether general or limited, active or silent
- Contributions by partners, both now and at a later time
- Dissolution of the practice if necessary
- Division of profits and losses
- Salary, including draws from the business during its growth state or at any period thereafter
- Duration of the agreement
- Managerial assignment within the firm
- Expenses and how they will be handled by each partner
- Name, purpose, and domicile of the partnership
- Performance by partners
- Records and methods of accounting
- Release of debts
- Required and prohibited acts
- Rights of continuing partner
- Sale of partnership interest
- Separate debts
- Settlement of disputes

How a Partnership Differs From a Sole Proprietorship. It is important to understand the elements that differentiate a partnership from a sole proprietorship. A partnership features:

1. Co-ownership of the assets
2. Limited life of the partnership

3. Mutual agency
4. Share in management
5. Share in partnership profits
6. Unlimited liability of at least one partner

Advantages

1. *Ease and speed of formation.* As with the sole proprietorship, it is fairly easy and quick to establish a consulting business using the partnership structure.

2. *Access to additional capital.* In a sole proprietorship, the initial capital must come from your personal funds or loans from other sources. In the case of a partnership, you have at least one other source of additional capital for your consulting practice.

3. *Assistance in decision making.* It is said that two heads are better than one. With a partnership, you have at least one other person to help you analyze the various situations that you may come across in the management of the business, and to conduct the consulting work itself.

4. *Vacation and sickness stability.* When you have a partner, it's much easier to take a vacation or to have someone else handle clients when you are ill. Partners can cover for each other.

Like all other structures of business, partnerships have disadvantages too, and some of them are severe. In fact many attorneys recommend against a partnership because of potential problems later on. However, it should also be noted that many law firms themselves are organized as partnerships.

Disadvantages

1. *Liability for actions of partners.* All partners are bound by the actions of any one partner, and under normal circumstances you are liable for the actions and commitments of any partner. Thus, a single partner can expend

resources or make business commitments, and all partners are liable whether or not they agree.

2. *Potential organizational disputes.* Organizations are made up of human beings. As a result, partners, especially equal partners, disagree. Even friends may find themselves at loggerheads if it is not clearly decided ahead of time, and in writing, who is the president, who the chief executive officer, who the vice-president, and so on. It has been said that for this reason, partnerships have all the disadvantages of a marriage with none of the advantages.

3. *Difficulty in obtaining capital.* Like a sole proprietorship, a partnership may be viewed as less stable than a corporation. As a result, in comparison to corporations, partnerships find it relatively more difficult to raise capital when and if needed.

The Corporation

Unlike a sole proprietorship or a partnership, a corporation is a legal entity separate and distinct from its owner. Also unlike the other two, a corporation cannot be viewed as a simple organizational structure. It is possible to set up a corporation without the aid of an attorney, but I don't recommend it. The reason is that state laws on corporations differ, and there are many trade-offs for the state you operate in that should be explained by an attorney. Also corporations that do business in more than one state must comply with the federal laws on interstate commerce and with the laws of the various states, which vary considerably. Further, you can limit yourself severely and may actually be in violation of the law if you deviate from the purpose of the corporation as set forth when you incorporate. Again, attorneys can be of great help here; in my experience, the basic forms found in books telling you how to form your own corporation often lead to problems later on down the road.

Advantages

1. *Limited liability.* In a corporation, your liability is limited to the amount of your investment in the business.

This protects you from creditors or judgments against you, since you can lose only what you have invested and not your personal holdings outside of the business. However, the limited liability concept does *not* apply to corporations that offer professional services, and it is entirely possible that some consultancies may fall into that category.

2. *Relative ease in obtaining capital.* Many consulting firms need capital at one time or another for expansion or other purposes. Lenders of all types are usually more willing to make loans to an organization with a more permanent legal structure, such as a corporation, than to either of the other two basic types of structures. However, note that many banks may require the officer or officers of a small corporation to personally cosign loans.

3. *Additional human resources.* A board of directors is required for a corporation. As long as qualified board members are appointed, more help is available to you as an integral part of the business than is the case with either a partnership or a sole proprietorship. It should also be noted, however, that a one-person corporation is in the same boat as a sole proprietorship—should the owner be absent, no one will be there to cover.

4. *Credibility to clients and the industry.* A corporation, because of its permanent legal status, generally has more credibility with potential clients. Admittedly, at some point in the lifetime of your firm this becomes a very minor advantage, since your firm's reputation, whether you've incorporated or not, will be the primary factor. But at the start, incorporation can be of some importance.

Disadvantages

1. *Additional paperwork and government regulations.* There is a fair amount of paperwork and many more regulations associated with the corporation than with either of the other two structures.

2. *Reduced control.* A corporation must have a board of directors. There are additional local, state, and federal gov-

ernment regulations to contend with. Business activities thus tend to be much more restricted than in the simpler types of business structures. Also, the corporation cannot diverge from its mission statement without an amendment to its corporate charter.

3. *Expense in formation.* The corporate structure is the most expensive to form, because of the need to use an attorney. It is also slower to set up.

4. *Inability to take losses as deductions.* If you lose money in your business with either a partnership or a sole proprietorship, you can take these losses as deductions for personal income tax purposes. With a corporation, losses sustained in the current year cannot be used to reduce other personal income. However, a corporation's loss may be carried forward or back to reduce another year's income. There is an exception in dealing with corporation losses; it involves setting up a special type of corporation, a possibility you should discuss with your accountant or attorney.

5. *Income taxes.* A few years ago, favorable income tax treatment would have been considered an advantage of incorporating. But that was when the maximum rate of federal income tax on corporations was 46 percent of net profits, while maximum personal income tax was 50 percent. Earlier yet, personal income tax was as high as 90 percent. Because tax laws change frequently, always check with an accountant.

Currently, income taxes are usually a disadvantage of the corporate form because of double taxation. Corporate profits are taxed once through the corporation itself as a legal entity. However, Uncle Sam gets a second bite through your salary or when profits are distributed to you as a shareholder. If profits are high enough, this may not be an important factor to you. You could be building your practice and then taking your money out when you sell the practice. However, if profits are not that high, you'll be losing money through taxation instead of saving it.

Also, since 1988, corporate taxes have been higher than individual income taxes. A corporation currently pays taxes to a maximum of 34 percent, unless it is in the 5 percent surtax range of $100,001 to $335,000. Then it is taxed at 39 percent while it phases out its lower bracket. The individual rate is currently only 28 percent except for those in the 5 percent surcharge range, which begins at $71,900.

The S Corporation

The S corporation is a particular type of corporation created especially by Congress to benefit small companies. At the option of the corporation, it can have its income taxed to the shareholders as if it were a partnership. Why is this a good deal? First, it permits you to avoid the double tax disadvantage of taxing corporate income. Second, it lets you offset business losses incurred by the corporation against your personal income. The net result is that you have the advantages of incorporating without the taxation disadvantages.

To qualify as an S corporation, you must meet certain requirements. These are:

1. There may be no more than ten shareholders, all of whom are individuals or estates.
2. You cannot have any nonresident alien shareholders.
3. You must have only one class of outstanding stock.
4. All shareholders must consent to the election of S corporation treatment.
5. A specified portion of the corporation's receipts must be derived from actual business activity rather than passive investments.

Because of higher corporate taxes under the new tax laws, it may be better not to incorporate at all if your practice is enjoying high profits. So be sure to consult with your accountant before making the decision to be treated as an S corporation.

Other Legal Necessities

Once you decide on a form of business structure, you still have a few other legal details to take care of.

Obtaining a Business License

As noted earlier, unless you incorporate, you generally need only local business licenses, either municipal or county or both. The licenses may require that you conform to certain zoning laws, building codes, and other regulations set forth by local health, fire, or police departments. However, usually these restrictions are minimal and fairly easily met in the case of a consulting practice. Certain permits may be required for certain types of consultancies or activities that are considered hazardous or in some other way detrimental to the community. But if you are required to obtain such a permit, you will be so informed when you purchase the business license. Again, for a consulting practice, usually this is not required.

Some states require licensing for certain occupations, which may affect certain types of consulting practices. Again, if that is the case, you will be so informed when you get your local business license. For example, most states require personnel recruiters who place job applicants to be licensed. For complete information, contact your state department of commerce.

There are also federal licensing requirements for some businesses that could affect certain types of consulting, such as an investment advisory service. Again, you will usually be informed if you need an additional license when you get your local business license. But to be absolutely certain, contact the U.S. Department of Commerce, which can be found under the "U.S. Government" listing in your local telephone directory.

The Resale Permit

If your state has a sales tax, it also has a state board to control and collect the tax. Usually this board will allow you to secure a resale permit.

The resale permit has two purposes. First, it assigns you duties as an agent of the state in the collection of taxes for products subject to sales tax. Second, it allows you to purchase items you intend to resell to someone else without paying the tax yourself. In purchasing such products from a vendor, you must give your resale permit number; otherwise you must pay the tax. If a fee is required to obtain a resale permit, the agency involved will inform you at the time you apply for it. Frequently this agency requires security from you in the form of a cash deposit against the payment of future state tax on the products that you will sell. This amount can be sizable, as much as several thousand dollars in some states. If you fail to pay any sales tax due, the state can deduct this amount from your deposit. Thus, it is protected even if you go bankrupt. Bear in mind that in most states, there is no sales tax on professional services, only on the sale, rental, and repair of tangible personal property. Check your local state regulations.

It is definitely not to your advantage to tie up several thousand dollars of your hard-earned cash merely to satisfy a security deposit for a resale permit. In some cases, where the deposit is high, installment payment arrangements can be made. However, the amount of money required—if any—depends on the information you provide at the time you obtain the resale permit. Minimum requirements are usually determined when certain conditions are met. These situations include: if you own your home and have substantial equity in it; if the estimated monthly expenses of your consulting practice are low; if your estimated monthly sales are low; if you are presently employed and your business activities are part-time; if you have no employees other than yourself; and if you have only one place of business. As I said before, services are usually not taxed, only products. But if products are part of your business or an adjunct to your consulting practice, you should obtain a resale permit if there is a state tax in your state.

Fictitious Name Registration

Fictitious name registration is required if you use any name in your practice other than your own. If you use a business name that includes names other than yours or your partners', implies the existence of additional partners, or indeed implies anything that your practice is not, you will need fictitious name registration. Thus "James A. Smith" is a perfectly acceptable business name that does not require fictitious name registration as long as your name is actually James A. Smith. However, "James A. Smith and Associates" requires fictitious name registration. There are some fictitious names that you usually cannot use at all. You cannot, for example, call yourself a university or research center, or use other descriptions that imply a nonprofit corporation unless you are one. Most states will prohibit you from using the title Doctor, Reverend, or Professor unless you meet certain legal requirements. But other than those types of restrictions, most "doing business as" names are acceptable as long as you obtain the proper registration. Interestingly, consulting firms may take advantage of fictitious name registration; law and CPA firms may not.

Fictitious name registration is usually very easy; it should not be considered a major problem in setting up your consulting practice. First, find out the law in your state by contacting someone such as the country clerk. Typically there is a small registration fee of less than fifty dollars and another small fee, perhaps thirty to fifty dollars, for publication of your registration in a general circulation newspaper distributed in the area in which you intend to do business. Once publication is accomplished, you file the affidavit with your county clerk's office. In many cases, the newspapers can handle the entire matter for you. The form is simple, and filling it out takes only a few minutes. Many states allow you to obtain more than one fictitious name on the form. For some types of consulting practices, this could be useful; it allows you to test certain products under names other than your client's or the regular business name of your practice. Then, if the product fails in the marketplace, it will have no effect on either your or your client's image.

Fictitious name registration is in force for a predetermined fixed period, which varies by state; five years is typical. In many cases, newspapers will write you ahead of time offering to handle the whole renewal business for you. In this way, they secure publication of the form in their newspaper.

Clients' Use of Credit Cards

Credit cards, such as Visa and MasterCard, are becoming increasingly useful for the professional consulting practice. In fact many other professionals, such as doctors and dentists, now accept credit cards from their patients or clients. Accepting credit cards has two major benefits for you. First, it adds additional credibility. Companies or individuals that have not done business with you before will recognize the Visa or MasterCard name and will realize that those agencies investigated you before allowing you to use their services. Second, the consumer credit company will provide credit to your clients and will collect the money for you. Thus, several thousand dollars in consulting fees can be billed and paid over a period of time without your being the collection agency. Of course there is a disadvantage to using consumer credit companies: You pay the company a certain percentage of each billing. Usually the higher your credit card sales, the lower the percentage the consumer credit company charges. The percentage involved is generally about 4 percent of the sale.

Stationery and Business Cards

It's extremely important that you get the highest-quality business cards and stationery that you possibly can. These items represent you to your clientele and communicate a message about the type of firm you are. Get the most expensive you can afford. Your stationery should have at least 25 percent rag content, and your name should be engraved. The raised print has a classic appearance. (A less expensive way to achieve this raised look is a process known as thermography.) The same is true of your business cards. If a logo is used, it should be simple and representative of the type of consulting you do. "High-class professional" is what you want your stationery and business cards to say.

Insurance and Personal Liability

As a consultant, you face certain risks, some of which you can insure against and some of which you cannot. For example, changes in economic and business conditions, the marketplace, or technology cannot be insured against. Any of these can change and hurt your business. However, other types of risks can be transferred through insurance. These include bad debts caused when subcontractors or clients go bankrupt, disasters caused by weather or fire, theft, liabilities from negligence and other actions, and death or disability of key company executives. You should think of insurance as a form of risk management. Do your risk managing in a four-step process.

1. *Identify* the risks to which your consulting practice will be subjected.
2. *Evaluate* the probability of occurrence of each risk. Also list the cost to you should this event occur and the cost of insurance protecting you against the risk.
3. *Choose* the best way to allow for each risk, whether to accept all or part of the risk or to transfer the risk through insurance.
4. *Control* the risk by implementing what you select as the best method.

The services of direct writers or agents are helpful in the risk-assessment process. A direct writer is a commissioned employee of the insurer; the business that he or she writes belongs to the insurance company. An agent, on the other hand, is an independent businessperson like you who has negotiated with the insurer to represent it for a given territory. The agent is also compensated on a commission basis.

There are advantages in both cases. An independent agent may represent many different insurers and so would be able to offer you a wider choice of coverage. Also, because the independent agent deals with these many different types, he or she may have greater knowledge in the overall field than a direct writer whose experience is limited to the employer company. However, direct writers may cost less, as their commission is less than that of the independent agent. Also, direct writers become specialists in their line, with in-depth knowledge and experience. This means that for a certain type of insurance of particular importance to you, this seller may know the finer details of the risk you are attempting to manage.

To locate direct writers or agents, consult your phone book or friends or acquaintances in business.

Insurance Checklist

A valuable checklist on insurance for small businesses was developed by Mark R. Greene, distinguished professor of insurance at the University of Georgia.[1] It will help you establish your risk-management program; if you already have insurance, it can help you discover areas in your insurance program that can be improved with reduced cost and increased effectiveness. It also serves as a guide to whom to talk with when dealing with your insurance agent, broker, or other insurance contacts.

The points covered in the checklist are grouped under three general classes of insurance: (1) coverages that are essential for most businesses, (2) coverages that are desirable for many companies but not absolutely necessary, and (3) coverages for employee benefits. For each of the statements, put a check in the first answer column if you understand the statement and how it affects your insurance program. Otherwise, check the second column. Then study your policies with these points in mind and discuss any questions you still have with your agent or direct writer.

Essential Coverages.   Four kinds of insurance are essential: fire insurance, liability insurance, automobile insurance, and workers compensation insurance. In some areas and in some kinds of businesses, crime insurance, which is discussed under "Desirable Coverages," is also essential.

Fire Insurance

	No Action Needed	To Look Into
1. You can add other perils—such as windstorm, hail, smoke, explosion, vandalism, and malicious mischief—to your basic fire insurance at a relatively small additional cost.	___	___
2. If you need comprehensive coverage, your best buy may be one of the all-risk contracts that offer the broadest available protection for the money.	___	___
3. The insurance company may indemnify you—that is, compensate you for your losses—in any one of several ways: (a) It may pay actual cash value of the property at the time of loss; (b) it may repair or replace the property with material of like kind and quality; (c) it may take *all* the property at the agreed or appraised value and reimburse you for your loss.	___	___
4. You can insure property you don't own. You must have an insurable interest—a financial interest—in the property *when a loss occurs* but not necessarily at the time the insurance contract is made. For instance, a repair shop or dry-cleaning plant may carry insurance on customer's property in the shop, or a person holding a mortgage on a building may insure the building although he or she doesn't own it.	___	___

5. When you sell property, you cannot assign the insurance policy along with the property unless you have permission from the insurance company.   ——   ——

6. Even if you have several policies on your property, you can still collect only the amount of your actual cash loss. All the insurers share the payment proportionately. Suppose, for example, that you are carrying two policies—one for $20,000 and one for $30,000—on a $40,000 building, and fire causes damage to the building amounting to $12,000. The $20,000 policy will pay $4,800; that is, $\frac{20,000}{50,000}$, or $\frac{2}{5}$, of $12,000. The $30,000 policy will pay $7,200, which is $\frac{30,000}{50,000}$, or $\frac{3}{5}$, of $12,000.   ——   ——

7. Special protection other than the standard fire policy is needed to cover the loss by fire of accounts, bills, currency, deeds, evidence of debt, and money and securities.   ——   ——

8. If an insured building is vacant or unoccupied for more than sixty consecutive days, coverage is suspended unless you have a special endorsement to your policy canceling this provision.   ——   ——

9. If, either before or after a loss, you conceal or misrepresent to the insurer any material fact or circumstance concerning your insurance or the interest of the insured, the policy may be voided.   ——   ——

10. If you increase the hazard of fire, the insurance company may suspend your coverage even for losses not originating from the increased hazard. (An example of such a hazard might be renting part of your building to a dry-cleaning plant.)   ___   ___

11. After a loss, you must use all reasonable means to protect the property from further loss or run the risk of having your coverage canceled.   ___   ___

12. To recover your loss, you must furnish within sixty days (unless an extension is granted by the insurance company) a complete inventory of the damaged, destroyed, and undamaged property showing in detail quantities, cost, actual cash value, and amount of loss claimed.   ___   ___

13. If you and the insurer disagree on the amount of loss, the question may be resolved through special appraisal procedures provided for in the fire insurance policy.   ___   ___

14. You may cancel your policy without notice at any time and get part of the premium returned. The insurance company also may cancel at any time with a five-day written notice to you   ___   ___

15. By accepting a coinsurance clause in your policy, you get a substantial reduction in premiums. A coinsurance clause states that you must carry insurance equal to 80 or 90 percent of the value of the insured property. If you carry less than this, you cannot collect the full amount of your loss, even if the loss is small. What percentage of

your loss you can collect will depend on
what percentage of the full value of the
property you have insured it for.   ——   ——

16. If your loss is caused by someone
else's negligence, the insurer has the right
to sue this negligent third party for the
amount it has paid you under the policy.
This is known as the insurer's right of subrogation. However, the insurer will usually
waive this right upon request. For example,
if you have leased your insured building to
someone and have waived your right to recover from the tenant for any insured damages to your property, you should have your
agent request the insurer to waive the subrogation clause in the fire policy on your
leased building.   ——   ——

17. A building under construction can
be insured for fire, lightning, extended cov-
erage, vandalism, and malicious mischief.   ——   ——

Liability Insurance

1. Legal liability limits of $1 million are
no longer considered high or unreasonable
even for a small business.   ——   ——

2. Most liability policies require you to
notify the insurer immediately after an incident on your property that might cause a
future claim. This holds true no matter how
unimportant the incident may seem at the
time it happens.   ——   ——

3. Most liability policies, in addition to
bodily injuries, may now cover *personal* injuries (libel, slander, and so on) *if* these are
specifically insured.   ——   ——

	No Action Needed	*To Look Into*

4. Under certain conditions, your business may be subject to damage claims even from trespassers.

5. You may be legally liable for damages even in cases where you used "reasonable care."

6. Even if the suit against you is false or fraudulent, the liability insurer pays court costs, legal fees, and interest on judgments *in addition to* the liability judgments themselves.

7. You can be liable for the acts of others under contracts you have signed with them. This liability is insurable.

8. In some cases, you may be held liable for fire loss to property of others that is in your care. Yet this property would normally not be covered by your fire or general liability insurance. This risk can be covered by fire legal liability insurance or through requesting subrogation waivers from insurers of owners of the property.

Automobile Insurance

1. When an employee or a subcontractor uses his or her own car on your behalf, you can be legally liable even if you don't own a car or truck yourself.

2. Five or more automobiles or motorcycles under one ownership and operated as a fleet for business purposes can generally be insured under a low-cost fleet policy against both material damage to your vehicle and liability to others for property damage or personal injury.

3. You can often get deductibles of almost any amount—say $250 or $500—and thereby reduce your premiums.   ——   ——

4. Automobile medical payments insurance pays for medical claims, including your own, arising from automobile accidents regardless of the question of negligence.   ——   ——

5. In most states, you must carry liability insurance or be prepared to provide other proof (surety bond) of financial responsibility when you are involved in an accident.   ——   ——

6. You can purchase uninsured motorist protection to cover your own bodily injury claims from someone who has no insurance.   ——   ——

7. Personal property stored in an automobile and not attached to it (for example, merchandise being delivered) is not covered under an automobile policy.   ——   ——

Workers Compensation Insurance

1. Common law requires that an employer (a) provide employees a safe place to work, (b) hire competent fellow employees, (c) provide safe tools, and (d) warn employees of an existing danger.   ——   ——

2. If an employer fails to provide the above, under both common law and workers compensation laws he or she is liable for damage suits brought by an employee.   ——   ——

3. State law determines the level or type of benefits payable under workers compensation policies.   ——   ——

	No Action Needed	To Look Into

4. Not all employees are covered by workers compensation laws. The exceptions are determined by state law and therefore vary from state to state.

5. In nearly all states, you are now legally *required* to cover your workers under workers compensation.

6. You can save money on workers compensation insurance by seeing that your employees are properly classified.

7. Rates for workers compensation insurance vary from 0.1 percent of the payroll for "safe" occupations to about 25 percent or more of the payroll for very hazardous occupations.

8. Most employers in most states can reduce their workers compensation premium cost by reducing their accident rates below the average. They do this by using safety and loss-prevention measures.

Desirable Coverages. Some types of insurance coverage, while not absolutely essential, add greatly to the security of your business. These coverages include business interruption insurance, crime insurance, glass insurance, and rent insurance.

Business Interruption Insurance

	No Action Needed	Look Into This

1. You can purchase insurance to cover fixed expenses that would continue if a fire shut down your business—such as salaries to key employees, taxes, interest, depreciation, and utilities—as well as the profits you would lose.

2. Under properly written contingent business interruption insurance, you can also collect if fire or other peril closes down the business of a supplier or customer and this interrupts your business.   ——   ——

3. The business interruption policy provides payments for amounts you spend to hasten the reopening of your business after a fire or other insured peril.   ——   ——

4. You can get coverage for the extra expenses you suffer if an insured peril, while not actually closing your business down, seriously disrupts it.   ——   ——

5. When the policy is properly endorsed, you can get business interruption insurance to indemnify you if your operations are suspended because of failure or interruption of the supply of power, light, heat, gas, or water furnished by a public utility company.   ——   ——

Crime Insurance

1. Burglary insurance excludes such property as accounts, fur articles in a showcase window, and manuscripts.   ——   ——

2. Coverage is granted under burglary insurance only if there are visible marks of the burglar's forced entry.   ——   ——

3. Burglary insurance can be written to cover inventoried merchandise and damage incurred in the course of a burglary in addition to money in a safe.   ——   ——

4. Robbery insurance protects you from loss of property, money, and securities by force, trickery, or threat of violence on *or off* your premises.   ——   ——

	No Action Needed	Look Into This

5. A comprehensive crime policy written just for small businesspeople is available. In addition to burglary and robbery, it covers other types of loss by theft, destruction, and disappearance of money and securities. It also covers thefts by your employees.   ___   ___

6. If you are in a high-risk area and cannot get insurance through normal channels without paying excessive rates, you may be able to get help through the federal crime insurance plan. Your agent or state insurance commissioner can tell you where to get information about this plan.   ___   ___

Glass Insurance

1. You can purchase a special glass insurance policy that covers all risk to plate-glass windows, glass signs, motion picture screens, glass brick, glass doors, showcases, countertops, and insulated glass panels.   ___   ___

2. The glass insurance policy covers not only the glass itself, but also its lettering and ornamentation, if these are specifically insured, and the costs of temporary plates or boarding up when necessary.   ___   ___

3. After the glass has been replaced, full coverage is continued without any additional premium for the period covered.   ___   ___

Rent Insurance

1. You can buy rent insurance that will pay your rent if the property you lease becomes unusable because of fire or other insured perils and your lease calls for continued payments in such a situation.   ___   ___

2. If you own property and lease it to others, you can insure against loss if the lease is canceled because of fire and you have to rent the property again at a reduced rental.   —   —

Employee Benefits Coverages. Insurance coverages that can be used to provide employee benefits include group life insurance, group health insurance, disability insurance, and retirement income. Key-man insurance protects the company against financial loss caused by the death of a valuable employee or partner.

Group Life Insurance

1. If you pay group insurance premiums and cover all employees up to $50,000, the cost to you is deductible for federal income tax purposes, and yet the value of the benefit is not taxable income to your employees.   —   —

2. Most insurers will provide group coverages at low rates even if there are ten or fewer employees in your group.   —   —

3. If the employees pay part of the cost of the group insurance, state laws require that 75 percent of the employees must elect coverage for the plan to qualify as group insurance.   —   —

4. Group plans permit employees leaving the company to convert their group insurance coverage to a private plan, at the rate for their age, without a medical exam if

they do so within thirty days after leaving
their job.   ___   ___

Group Health Insurance

1. Group health insurance costs much
less and provides more generous benefits
for the worker than individual contracts
would.   ___   ___

2. If you pay the entire cost, individual
employees cannot be dropped from a group
plan unless the entire group policy is can-
celed.   ___   ___

3. Generous programs of employee
benefits, such as group health insurance,
tend to reduce labor turnover.   ___   ___

Disability Insurance

1. Workers compensation insurance
pays an employee only for time lost because
of work injuries and work-related sickness—
not for time lost because of disabilities incurred off the job. But you can purchase, at
a low premium, insurance to replace the lost
income of workers who suffer short-term or
long-term disability not related to their work.   ___   ___

2. You can get coverage that provides
employees with an income for life in case of
permanent disability resulting from work-
related sickness or accident.   ___   ___

Retirement Income

1. If you are self-employed, you can get
an income tax deduction for funds used for

	No Action Needed	Look Into This

retirement for you and your employees through plans of insurance or annuities approved for use under the Employee Retirement Income Security Act of 1974 (ERISA).   ___   ___

2. Annuity contracts may provide for variable payments in the hope of giving the annuitants some protection against the effects of inflation. Whether fixed or variable, an annuity can provide retirement income that is guaranteed for life.   ___   ___

Key-Man Insurance

1. One of the most serious setbacks that can come to a small company is the loss of a key employee or partner. But such a person can be insured with life insurance and disability insurance owned by and payable to your company.   ___   ___

2. Proceeds of a key-man policy are not subject to income tax, but premiums are not a deductible business expense.   ___   ___

3. The cash value of key-man insurance, which accumulates as an asset of the business, can be borrowed against, and the interest and dividends are not subject to income tax as long as the policy remains in force.   ___   ___

Keeping Overhead Low

One of the most important pieces of advice that I can give to you for managing your consulting practice is to maintain a low overhead. This means keeping costs that do not directly contribute to each and every project or to marketing to the absolute minimum. Many new consultants feel, for example, that they must have a fancy office at a prestigious address. If an address is indeed necessary to your success, you can usually rent a mail drop in an esteemed neighborhood. But usually this is not really an important factor in your being hired as a consultant. The fact is, most clients won't come to your office; usually you'll go to theirs.

Many years ago, when I was working for another company as director of research and development, I interviewed an individual who told me the following sad tale. He and several other senior executives in a major aerospace company resigned to form their own consulting practice. Each invested enough money to last many months—they thought. Coming from a large company in which each had had an expensive office, elegant furniture, and a personal secretary, these new consultants found it impossible to control spending for what they considered minimum requirements. They acquired expensive offices in a high-rent area and outfitted them with rich mahogany paneling and thick, luxurious rugs. But that rich image didn't save this fledgling consulting firm from bankruptcy; in a few weeks, their money was depleted. On the other hand, I am acquainted with a wealthy search consultant who did half a million dollars in billing his first year out of his home. As his partner told me, he did hundreds of thousands of dollars in billings in his pajamas, but neither his clients nor the executives he placed ever knew.

Remember, at first you don't even need a secretary, only typing services. What you definitely don't need is a secretary sitting around with nothing to do except contribute to your ego.

For most consulting practices, it is better to consider a home office to start with, especially if you are beginning part-time. In my many years of consulting, I can count on one hand the number of times a client has visited the office that I maintain in my home. It happens usually if the client is in a start-up situation and thus has no office for me to go to. Occasionally the pressure of time will prevent you from traveling, and your client will come to you. One multimillion-dollar accountant calculated that since my billing rates were higher than his, it was less expensive for him to travel to my office than the other way around.

The Telephone

To keep overhead low and yet maintain a business telephone without a secretary, you have two alternatives. One is a telephone answering service; the second is to buy or rent a telephone answering machine. Again there are trade-offs to be made, advantages and disadvantages to both. The telephone answering machine is very inexpensive; a good, professional-quality machine can be had for between $100 and $200. The disadvantage is that some potential clients simply will not leave a message on an answering machine. However, I believe that if your answering message is tactfully worded and if you promise to get back with the caller soon, you have the greatest probability of getting the message that you need to continue the business relationship.

Even though an answering service may cost more, it may not be as good. Some answering service operators are rude and inconsiderate and will leave your caller on hold for long periods of time. This can be worse than a machine, where at least you control the friendliness and professionalism of the voice doing the answering. If you do use an answering service, I recommend that you check on it periodically to ensure that the operator has the highest standards of professionalism and is not losing clients through rudeness or incompetence.

Should you have a special business phone for the home? Maybe not. Business telephones are usually more expensive than personal telephones. It's true that the business telephone does entitle you to a special listing in the Yellow Pages, and if you want a special advertisement, as discussed in Chapter 2, you need a business telephone in order to get one. However, another quirk in many telephone systems is that they will charge you more to connect a business telephone than a personal telephone. Yet you can have a personal telephone converted to the business telephone at little or no extra charge. If your practice is listed under your real name, and you don't need the Yellow Pages listing as a consultant, it makes little sense to obtain a special business telephone—as defined by telephone companies. There is nothing wrong with having a telephone company install an additional personal phone that you call a "business tele- phone." As long as you use it totally for business purposes, it should be deductible for tax purposes. If it is listed on your business card and your stationery, as far as your clients know, it is your business telephone.

Fax Machines

Fax machines are definitely in. With a fax machine, you can send or receive photographs, reports, or other docu- ments. When you want to get or send something instantly, a fax machine is really handy. Now don't get the wrong idea. You can still operate with great efficiency without owning or using a fax machine. But after you begin to see a positive cash flow, it is a handy item to have. Fax machines are quicker than the mail. Because the information is transmit- ted superfast over your telephone lines, you can save a lot of money over using overnight couriers.

Fax machine prices currently range from $800 on up to about $4,000 depending on features. However, if you have a computer and either a dot matrix or a laser printer, you can utilize your computer as a fax machine. The device and software go from $200 to $400. If you don't have a source, try DAK Industries, Inc., 8200 Remmet Avenue, Canoga Park, Calif. 91304 (1-800/325-0800).

Anticipating Expenses

One of the biggest mistakes new consultants make is failure to anticipate expenses. Recognize ahead of time that certain expenses will be necessary to set up and run your consulting practice as a business. Plan ahead for these ex- penses when you estimate what being in business will cost. Typical consulting expenses may include:

- Water, electricity, and gas
- Office supplies
- Postage
- Automobile expenses
- Telephone
- Travel other than by automobile
- Promotional material, including brochures
- Entertainment
- Income taxes
- Subscriptions to professional journals
- Memberships in professional and other associations

There will undoubtedly be additional expenses depending upon the type of consulting you do. Make sure that you forget nothing; anticipate them *before* you establish your practice.

Necessary Records and Their Maintenance

Good records are necessary for several reasons. You'll need them for preparing tax returns, measuring management effectiveness and efficiency, reducing material waste, and even obtaining loans. These are the essential records you should maintain:

1. Daily summary of income received. Figure 12-1 shows a sample form.
2. An expense journal (see the example in Figure 12-2) that lists your expense payments in chronological order.
3. An expense ledger summary (see Figure 12-3) in which cash and check payments are totaled by category—for example, rent, wages, and advertising.
4. An inventory purchase journal (if product is in any way a part of your practice) that notes shipments received, accounts payable, and cash available for future purchases, as shown in Figure 12-4.
5. An employee compensation record, listing hours

(*text continues on page 215*)

Figure 12-1. Daily summary of income received.

Day/Date Item Sold or Service Performed	Amount	
Total amount received today		
Total amount received through yesterday		
Total amount received to date		

Figure 12-2. Expense journal.

Date	To Whom Paid	Purpose	Check Number	Amount	
			Total expenditures		

Figure 12-3. Expense journal summary.

Purpose	Total This Period		Total Up to This Period		Total to Date	
Advertising						
Car and truck expense						
Commissions						
Contributions						
Delivery expense						
Dues and publications						
Employee benefit program						
Freight						
Insurance						
Interest						
Laundry and cleaning						
Legal and professional services						
Licenses						
Miscellaneous expense						
Office supplies						
Pension and profit sharing plan						
Postage						
Rent						
Repairs						
Selling expense						
Supplies						
Tax						
Telephone						
Traveling and entertainment						
Utilities						
Wages						
Totals						

Figure 12-4.   Inventory purchase journal.

Date	Inventory Ordered Carried Forward	Shipment Received/Date	Accounts Payable	Cash Available for Future Purchases
		Totals		

worked, pay rate, and deductions withheld for both part-time and full-time employees, as shown in Figure 12-5.

6. An accounts receivable ledger for outstanding invoices, as shown in Figure 12-6.

Tax Obligations

As the owner of a consulting practice, you are responsible for payment of federal, state, and local taxes. Because the federal taxes tend to be the most complex for new consultants, we'll look at them first. There are four basic types of federal taxes that you may run into: income taxes, Social Security taxes, excise taxes, and unemployment taxes. Let's look at each in more detail.

(*text continues on page 218*)

Figure 12-5. Employee compensation record.

Name _____ Social Security No. _____

Date	Period Worked (hours, days, weeks, or months)	Wage Rate	Total Wages		Deductions					Net Paid	
					Soc. Sec.	Fed. Inc. Tax	State Inc. Tax				
			Totals								

Figure 12-6.   Accounts receivable ledger (for consulting services billed but not yet paid).

Date	Customer/Client Name	Products/Services	Amount Owed	Payments Made/Date

Income Taxes

The amount of federal taxes you owe depends on the earnings of your company and on your company's legal structure, as I discussed earlier in this chapter.

If you have a sole proprietorship or partnership, your other income exemptions and nonbusiness deductions and credits are also important factors. The tax formula used is generally the same as that for the individual taxpayer. The only difference is that you file an additional form (Schedule C of Form 1040, Profit or Loss From Business or Profession) that identifies items of expense and income connected with your consulting business. If your business is a partnership, the partnership files a business return (Form 1065), and you report only your share of the profit or loss on your personal return.

However, there is an important difference between being a sole proprietor or a partner and being a salaried employee working for someone else. As a sole proprietor or a partner, you are required by law to pay federal income taxes and self-employment taxes *as the income is received*. You do this by completing Estimated Tax for Individuals Form 1040-ES. This is an estimate of the income and self-employment taxes you expect to owe on the basis of anticipated income and exemptions. Payment of tax is made quarterly—April 16, June 15, September 17, and January 15.

If you have a corporation, you must also pay income tax on its net profits separate from the amount taken out for salary, which is considered part of your personal income.

Since the 1988 tax year, every corporation whose tax is expected to be $500 or more is required to make estimated tax payments. These must be deposited with an authorized financial institution or a Federal Reserve Bank. Each deposit is made with a federal tax deposit coupon and done in accordance with the instructions on the coupon. A corporation's estimated tax should be deposited on or before the 15th day of the fourth, sixth, ninth, and twelfth months of the corporation's tax year.

In order to operate your practice, it is extremely impor-tant that you have the necessary funds to pay your income taxes on time. Your accountant can help you work out a budget to allow for this. You can also use the work sheet in Figure 12-7 developed by the Small Business Administration.

Withholding Income Taxes

According to the law, you must withhold federal income tax payments for your employees. These payments are passed on to the government periodically. The process be-gins when you hire a new employee. He or she must sign a Form W-4, Employee's Withholding Allowance Certificate, listing any exemptions and additional withholding allowances claimed. The completed W-4 is your authority to withhold income tax in accordance with the current withholding tables issued by the IRS. If an employee fails to furnish a certificate, you are required to withhold taxes as if he or she were a single person with no exemptions. Before December 1 of each year, you should ask your employees to file new exemp-tion certificates for the following year if there has been a change in their exemption status. At the end of each year, you must furnish each employee copies of Form W-2, Wage and Tax Statement. As you are aware if you have worked for someone else, the employees must file a copy of this with their income tax return. You, as the employer, must also furnish a copy of this Form W-2 to the IRS on or before February 28 of each year. For complete details, contact the office of the IRS in your area.

And don't forget to check with your state office to find out if you are responsible for withholding your employees' state income taxes as well.

Withholding Social Security Taxes

For Social Security taxes, you must deduct 7.51 percent from each employee's wages. As an employer, you must match that sum. Currently, the wages subject to these taxes are the first $48,000 earned. The first $48,000 of your own

Figure 12-7. Worksheet for meeting tax obligations.

Kind of Taxes	Due Date	Amount Due	Pay to	Date for Writing the Check
Federal Taxes				
Employee income taxes and Social Security taxes	____	____	____	____
	____	____	____	____
	____	____	____	____
	____	____	____	____
Excise Taxes	____	____	____	____
Owner–manager's and/or corporation's income taxes	____	____	____	____
	____	____	____	____
	____	____	____	____
	____	____	____	____
Unemployment taxes	____	____	____	____
	____	____	____	____
	____	____	____	____
State Taxes				
Unemployment taxes	____	____	____	____
	____	____	____	____
	____	____	____	____
	____	____	____	____
Income taxes	____	____	____	____
Sales taxes	____	____	____	____
	____	____	____	____
	____	____	____	____
	____	____	____	____
Franchise taxes	____	____	____	____
Other	____	____	____	____
	____	____	____	____
Local Taxes				
Sales taxes	____	____	____	____
	____	____	____	____
	____	____	____	____
	____	____	____	____
Real estate taxes	____	____	____	____
Personal property taxes	____	____	____	____
Licenses (retail, vending machine, etc.)	____	____	____	____
Other	____	____	____	____
	____	____	____	____
	____	____	____	____

income is subject to self-employment tax. However, your net tax rate is 13.02 percent.

The following kinds of payments are not subject to Social Security taxes:

1. Payments made more than six months after the last calendar month in which the employee worked.
2. Payments made under a workers compensation law.
3. Payments or portions of payments attributable to the employee's contribution to a sick-pay plan.
4. Most payments made to a state or local government employee. The third-party payer should contact the state or local government employer for instructions.
5. Payments made for medical care.
6. Payments (generally for injury) that are not related to absence from work.[2]

Remitting Federal Taxes

Remitting federal taxes involves three steps: You must *report* the income and Social Security taxes you have withheld from the employee's pay, and you must *deposit* the funds you withheld. In the third step you *match* your employees' contributions. Reporting withheld income and Social Security taxes is done on Form 941. These withheld taxes are paid together. A return for each quarter is due on the last day of the following months—April 30, July 31, October 31, and January 31. In many cases, remittance of these taxes is required before the return date is due; these dates depend on your situation. To make deposits, you complete Form 8109, Federal Tax Deposit Coupon Book. This form, with a check, is sent to the Federal Reserve Bank that serves your district or to a commercial bank that is authorized to accept such tax deposits. Your local bank or Federal Reserve Bank can give you the names of such commerical banks. In general, the smaller the amount of your tax liability, the less frequently you are required to make a deposit. The third step, matching the contribution, is done on Form 940. Any additional details are available from your local IRS office.

Excise Taxes

Federal excise taxes are due on the sale or use of certain items or transactions and on certain occupations. Normally, a consultant is not involved in excise tax. However, to be absolutely certain, again check with your local IRS office.

Unemployment Taxes

If you pay wages of $1,500 or more in any calendar quarter, or if you have one or more employees on at least some portion of one day in each of twenty or more calendar weeks, either consecutive or nonconsecutive, your consulting practice is liable for federal unemployment (FUTA) taxes.[3] It doesn't need to be the same employee, and individuals on sick leave or vacation are counted as employees.

Currently, you figure this tax at a rate of 6.2 percent on the first $7,000 in wages you pay to each employee. Further, it's your tax. You can't collect it or deduct it from the wages of your employees.

There is one good deal, however. You are given a credit of up to 5.4 percent for the state unemployment tax you may pay. This means that the net tax rate can be as low as 0.8 percent (6.2% − 5.4%) if your state is not subject to a credit reduction. If your state tax rate is less than 5.4 percent, you are still allowed the full 5.4 percent credit. However, you cannot take this credit if for any reason you are exempt from or do not pay the state tax.

You pay the FUTA tax on Form 940, Employer's Annual Federal Unemployment (FUTA) Tax Return. This form covers one calendar year and is generally due one month after the calendar year ends—even if you file on a fiscal-year basis. But beware. You may have to make deposits of the tax before filing the return.

Here's what you must look at. If at the end of any calendar quarter, you owe but haven't deposited more than $100 in FUTA tax for the year, you must make a deposit— accompanied by a preinscribed Form 508, Federal Unemployment Tax Deposit—by the end of the next month in an authorized commercial bank or Federal Reserve Bank. If the tax is $100 or less at the end of a quarter, you don't have to deposit it. However, you must add it to the tax for the next quarter. If total undeposited FUTA tax is more than $100, you make the deposit.

Your due dates are as follows:

Undeposited FUTA tax more than $100 on:	Deposit full amount by:
March 31	April 30
June 30	July 31
September 30	October 31
December 31	January 31

Copies of Form 508 are furnished to you automatically once you have applied for an employer identification number, which I discuss shortly. The IRS usually mails copies of Form 940 to you as well. Of course both forms may be obtained from your local IRS office.

Obtaining an Employer Identification Number

An employer identification number is required for all employment tax returns filed with the federal government. You obtain this number by filing a Form SS-4 with your regional Internal Revenue Service Center. At the same time, you can ask for your business tax kit, IRS 454; it has additional information on taxes pertinent to each particular business or consulting practice with which you may be involved.

State and Local Taxes

State and local taxes vary by area. Three major types of state taxes are unemployment taxes, income taxes, and sales taxes (see the discussion of The Resale Permit under "Other Legal Necessities" earlier in this chapter). Every state has unemployment taxes; the rules vary by state and may not be the same as those of the federal government. Local taxes from counties, towns, and cities may include real estate, personal property taxes, taxes on receipt of businesses, and so forth. For more information on all these types of taxes, contact your local and state governments.

Minimizing Tax Paperwork

As you can see, many of the required taxes concern employees. If you have no employees, the amount of paperwork is significantly reduced. Instead of hiring permanent staff for your company, try to retain individuals and pay them as consultants. There are some restrictions on how many hours or days someone may work for you and still be considered a consultant, so be sure to check on the current regulations if you do this.

For remitting all types of taxes, be certain to consult a good tax accountant. You will pay for the service, but this expert will save you far more in the long run.

Notes

1. Mark R. Greene, *Insurance Checklist for Small Business* (Washington, D.C.: Small Business Administration, 1979).
2. *Tax Guide for Small Business* (Washington, D.C.: Department of the Internal Revenue Service, 1988), p. 120.
3. Ibid., pp. 123–124.

13

WHAT A COMPUTER CAN DO FOR YOU IN CONSULTING

Computers suitable for consultants didn't exist when I first "hung up my shingle." Today a computer can do more to raise your consulting productivity than any other single tool I can think of.

It took me a long time to become fully aware of all the things a computer could accomplish. For several years after computers became available, I could think of no reason to buy one. What could I do with a computer that I couldn't do with pencil, paper, or typewriter?

Friends told me I should get a computer to use in writing my books. I told them that if I got a computer to write with, it would probably cause my productivity to decline. This was because I dictated much of my books onto audiotape. My typist would type out a draft from the tape, and I would correct it and return it to my typist. I couldn't see how I could beat that method unless computers that would type out my dictation as I spoke came on the market. I was wrong.

How the Computer Revolutionized My Writing and Consulting Practice

It was my wife, Nurit, who got me to use a computer. Nurit was working on her doctoral dissertation in clinical psychology and insisted that a computer could save her lots of time. As I had completed my own doctoral dissertation some years earlier without a computer, I wasn't really convinced. Whenever I needed computing done for research, I had it done on the big mainframe at the university. True, each draft of my dissertation had to be more or less completely retyped—that cost me a bundle—but when you are that close to completing your doctorate, you tend not to worry about the cost of typing.

Anyway, Nurit made her case and got one of the IBM PC "clones." The clone was completely compatible with the IBM PC and could do everything an IBM PC could do. However, it cost a good deal less.

I was amazed by how easily Nurit mastered the computer. The advantages of using it were obvious. She could quickly revise entire chapters of her dissertation without having to retype them. When I reviewed her work, I was also surprised at the complete lack of typographical errors and the neatness of the printout. Unlike many typewritten pages, the right side of the page was as even as the left (this process is as easy as the stroke of a key and is called justifiction). Further, the entire document could be stored on a floppy disk. Any time she wanted to work on it, she simply put the disk in the computer. That made it a space saver.

It wasn't long before I got her to teach me how to use the word processing program for my correspondence. The time I saved was just incredible. If I misspelled a word, it was easy to correct before I printed the letter. I no longer faced the terrible choice between a messy erasure or correction fluid and retyping an entire letter; there were no more typos. There was a spelling program on another disk. I just loaded that up and my spelling mistakes disappeared. If I had to write a similar letter to someone else, it was easy just to modify the old letter on the disk.

Not too long afterward, I went on contract for a college textbook. A textbook is different from a regular book in that not only must you write the basic text but your publisher usually wants ancillary materials. In my case, I had to furnish a five-hundred-page instructor's manual and another manual with 2,100 multiple-choice and true-or-false questions. Further, the publisher wanted these additional materials as "camera ready copy." This means that instead of typesetting, the publisher simply takes a picture of each page that you furnish and reproduces it. Consequently your manuscript has to be letter-perfect and error-free, because it is not reset in type later.

I made an audiotape that I sent to my typist. But instead of sending me a corrected manuscript, my typist worked with her computer, using the same word processing program I used. She sent me a disk that I put in my computer. I made the corrections I wanted, and I printed the final "camera ready copy" myself. Now that was fast!

How the Computer Can Double or Triple Your Productivity

The word processing by itself allowed me to double the work I turned out in a given amount of time—and the quality of work was better too. But I soon discovered that my computer could do other things that saved me time and money and made my consulting operations more efficient.

Proposals and Desktop Publishing

In the "bad old days," I used to pay a graphic artist to do my layout and typesetting for proposals, brochures, fliers, or other booklets. This typically cost a minimum of $100 or more per job and took at least a week before I even had the material to proofread. Now, using a software program costing a couple of hundred dollars, I do everything myself. I have a full choice of dozens of different type styles (fonts) and sizes. As a bonus, I don't have to wait; except for my own time constraints, or the time constraints of people I hire to help me out from time to time, I get the work done immediately. I don't mean that I no longer use a graphic artist, but much of the routine work I can do myself. And I can do it better and faster. The same is true of overhead transparencies, which I use for consulting presentations or

seminars. It once took at least a week to have these done.
Further, there were always typographical errors, some of
which I caught too late to have corrected. With word processing and a graphics program, all that is past. I do all my own
stuff, with incredible savings in time and cost.

Another bonus is that I am able to save all of my material
so that if I ever want it again, or want it with minor changes,
it's easy to make the changes and print out the new material.
All of this material is filed on computer disks. The material is
together where I want it, takes up little space, and is easily
retrieved.

Managing Your Practice

If you are concerned with managing the financial side of
your practice, or if finances have been a drag in the past,
worry no more. There are hundreds of programs around to
help you with your financial decision making and record
keeping. There are programs that track your income, accounts receivable, payroll, inventory. Programs can help you
make loan decisions and decide whether to make or buy
equipment. There are complex accounting programs, and
there are very simple ones.

There are even programs that help you prepare your
own state and federal income taxes. They are fantastic and
will cut the time for tax preparation (if you do your own) by
50 percent or more. They save you time even if you use an
accountant.

Direct Marketing

Certain programs allow you to merge a list of current or
potential clients with one of your sales letters. This means
that every letter is personalized to that individual customer.
What once had to be done by someone else can now be done
by you at home. This is especially valuable for relatively
small mailings that aren't cost-effective to have done by
someone else.

You can do these mailings almost on a moment's notice.

If the list is already available, it is actually possible to mail an advertisment or announcement to thousands of people the same day you make the decision to do it.

Fixing Your Writing

In addition to programs that correct your spelling, there are also programs that will correct your grammar, give you choices of the words you may want to use (a thesaurus program), help you make your writing more readable, and so forth. A computer software program probably can't turn you into an instant professional writer, but it certainly can turn you instantly into a more competent one. If you want help with copywriting for your ads, there are programs for this also. One program, called Headliner, even creates headlines, theme lines, slogans, and jingles.

Naming Products and Services

Another program can help you select names for products or services. Many consultants work with their clients on the crucial decision of naming. This program, called The Namer, was developed by the Salinon Corporation of Dallas, Texas. It is designed to generate as many reasonable names as possible. It analyzes the statistical properties of letter combinations while using special filters for rejecting poor name formations. It even checks names for hidden or embedded profanities in several different languages, and it has the "smarts" to review a trillion permutations of a fifteen-letter word. Try doing that for a client over the weekend.

Making Forecasts and Plans

One of the most common computer uses for business is that of the spreadsheet. A spreadsheet program can be used to do sophisticated calculations, provide data for graphs, do forecasts, view results by changing various "what if" variables, estimate costs, and so forth. Basically, a spreadsheet is simply a chart with rows and columns filled with numbers.

But the beauty of this type of program is that you can do the formula calculations to fill in these rows and columns with hundreds of accurate numerical results almost instantly. You just plug in the basic numbers that the formula calls for.

There are also software programs around to assist you in developing plans of all types incorporating the spreadsheet concept. Let's say you are developing a marketing plan for a client. Can you imagine the time you'll save when all you have to do is plug in numbers? From those numbers, the program develops charts, alternative strategies, financial ratios, balance sheets, cash flow analyses, income statements, sales projections, and a lot more for you simply by your pressing a few basic keys.

Evaluating Potential Employees

Big companies pay big fees to consultants to obtain complete psychological evaluations of potential key employees. Even this has been computerized: You can obtain programs in which you input data based on questions answered by the candidate. The output can tell you how the individual is likely to behave in different situations. Or the information can be used for vocational counseling. One such program intended for use by both mental health and vocational professionals is The Professional Analyst, published by Neutralytic Systems of San Mateo, California.

In Europe especially, handwriting analysis is popular for prehiring evaluation of executives. Handwriting analysis computer programs are also available.

Simplifying Marketing Research

There are probably hundreds of marketing research programs. They not only help you to design your research tool but analyze your data and interpret the results. Much of the time-consuming drudgery of manipulating the results from research is eliminated. The computer prints all the backup analysis for you, as well as the bottom-line results you need for your client.

Gaining Access to Electronic Information
The World Over Without Leaving Your Office

Modems, which are simple devices that attach to your computer, can gain you access to immense databases and a lot more—all through your telephone lines. The potential of this device for multiplying for effectiveness and efficiency in consulting is almost unbelievable. One electronic information service lets you exchange messages with clients and other consultants through an electronic mail system. In seconds you can call up product ratings from consumer reports, or access key articles in leading magazines. You can research just about any topic you want; you can even do comparative shopping and make travel arrangements.

Here's a precise example of how you can make your operation more efficient through the use of a modem. Let's say that you need census tract data, demographics, and market potential for a client. Normally, you might need to go to a specialized business library and the chamber of commerce or consult various other sources, which may take you hours or even days. Through use of a modem and an electronic information service, you can reach hundreds of databases and complete the job in minutes.

I hope I've said enough to show you what a computer may be able to do for you. Your local computer software store can show you most of the programs I've described and a lot more (new programs are being developed every day). If you live in a town that doesn't have a software store, get a copy of one of the many computer magazines that are now being published. Not only will you see many programs advertised and described right in the magazine, you can obtain catalogs from companies that publish hundreds of other programs to help you run and build your business.

What You Need to Know About Computers

Before I begin, let me say that you really don't need to know much. But if you are unfamiliar with computers, the topic may seem confusing. I'm going to clear up that confusion right now. When you buy a computer, you need a keyboard, the computer proper, one or more disk drives, a visual indicator (called a monitor), and a printer. If you can use a typewriter, you can run a computer. You do not have to learn a special computer language. You do not need to learn how to "program." All that has been done for you by a programmer. All you need to do is turn the computer on. Just start up the program and follow the simple directions right on the program.

The keyboard attaches to the computer and is very similar to the one on a typewriter. It has a few more keys than most typewriters, but nothing overly complicated. The instructions that come with any program you buy tell you what keys to press to get the computer to do what you want. Through the keyboard, you tell the computer what you want it to do. What is called *typing* on a typewriter is called *word processing* on a computer. Each time you push a key, you're telling the computer to make a letter on the screen of your monitor. A monochrome screen is single-colored, usually green or amber, and is fine for most purposes. However, some programs require the use of color.

The disk drives work like a record player. You play your computer programs on them. The programs themselves are on disks and are known as *software*. These disks may be 3½ or 5¼ inches in diameter. The industry is tending toward high-density disks today. The old standard was the 5¼-inch disk, which held 360,000 (360K) bits of data. The high-density 5¼-inch disks hold 1.2 million bits of data, read as *1.2 megabytes* or *1.2MB*. The 3½-inch disk holds 1.44 million bits of data, read as *1.44 megabytes,* or *1.44MB*. A 5¼-inch high-density disk drive will read 360K disks. However, the reverse is not true. A 360K disk drive cannot read a high-density disk.

One important software program that comes on a disk is the Disk Operating System (DOS). My Microsoft DOS program is currently in version 3.10. As with all software programs, when a new version comes out, the number increases. Thus, the previous version of Microsoft DOS was

2.11. The DOS runs your computer system. It manages the communications among such devices as the computer itself, keyboard, monitor, and printer, and it helps other programs to run.

I strongly recommend that you get one of the many computers that come with a built-in hard disk. In addition to containing software programs that you may want to run, disks are also used for storing data such as your advertising brochure, customer lists, and sales letters. Even the regular-density disk allows you to store 375,000 bits of almost 0.4 megabytes of information. That may be a hundred typewritten pages or so. Now I know that this sounds like a lot, but you will soon discover that it's not. The beauty of a hard disk is that depending on what hard disk you buy, it will store ten, twenty, forty, sixty, or even more megabytes of data. What this means is that programs and data you want stored can all go on the hard disk. You'll find accessing these data from a hard disk *much* faster and more convenient than retrieving them from a floppy disk; the difference will amaze you.

Now, one way or another, you're going to need two disk drives. My recommendation is to start right off with one hard disk and one regular disk drive to input the new programs that you buy. How many megabytes for your hard disk? Once again, my general advice is to buy more than you think you need. Once you start using a computer, and you see more potential in using it in your practice, your needs will grow exponentially.

What Kind of Computer Should You Buy?

Whatever computer you buy, make certain that it has at least 640Kb RAM. RAM stands for random access memory. This is a description of your computer's power. Less than 640Kb of RAM denies you access to many business software programs that you may want to use.

The two biggest personal computer types on the market today are the IBM and IBM compatibles and Apple's Macintosh. The biggest advantage of the IBM and its clones is the amount of software available; everybody and his brother develops software for the IBM. The advantage of the Macintosh is its ease of use. With the Macintosh, use of a "mouse" is standard. A mouse is a pointing device. You point to a symbol on the screen and click a button on your mouse, and the computer reacts to a command. For many operations, this is faster and easier than using the conventional keyboard. However, you can also buy a mouse for an IBM or IBM compatible.

I do not recommend buying a computer by mail until you get more experience. There are always a few things that just don't seem to go right. Sure, most companies have telephone numbers that you can call, even toll-free numbers. But spending valuable time and running up a large telephone bill while someone walks you through the problem is not my idea of fun. Buy your computer locally, and your initial problems with setup are much diminished, even though you can probably buy more cheaply through the mail.

What Kind of Printer Should You Buy?

There are three basic kinds of printers: dot matrix, letter-quality, and laser. The *dot matrix* is fast, but every letter is formed from little dots. The old ninepin models were not much good for letters or advertisements or communicating with a client. However, there are newer models now with more pins. They are advertised as "near letter quality." They aren't bad, but they still don't produce work that looks as good as letter-quality printers or laser printers. *Letter-quality* printers use daisy wheels with letters on them very much like those used on some typewriters. The printing looks great. The problems are speed (you may think this isn't important, but wait until you spend several hours printing out a lengthy document) and lack of graphic capability. *Laser printers* solve all of the above. Their problem is that they'll currently set you back a minimum of $1,500. However, there are some printers out now for under $1,000 that use a process similar to the laser printers. The Hewlett-Packard Deskjet is one. I've used all of these printers and feel that what kind of printer to buy really depends on the kind of work you want your computer to do and how much you can afford. You can get good advice at your local computer store.

I hope I have convinced you that use of a computer in a consultancy today is essential. No matter what your expertise or how fast you work, you just aren't going to be very competitive without one.

EPILOGUE

There is no question in my mind that you can become a successful consultant (either full- or part-time) and make a valuable contribution to your clients and to society at the same time. Everything you need to know in order to market and put into practice your own expertise in any particular field has already been given to you in the pages of this book. The questions that remain unanswered are those that will arise as you begin actual work as a consultant. This is as it should be, for certain aspects of your consulting work are unique not only to your category of consulting, type of industry, or geographic area but, more important, to your personality, style, and way of doing business. All totaled, the answers to these questions constitute your differential advantage over all the others doing identical work, and a sustained differential advantage over your competition will be the primary factor in your success.

A great adventure awaits you with many challenges, some disappointments, and the thrill of victory along the way. Further, your journey will involve not only monetary rewards but also the satisfaction of doing what you want and doing it well.

But no book, regardless of how complete or thorough it may be, can begin this journey for you. This you must do for yourself. Without your beginning, your action, your taking the steps toward starting your consultancy, there can be nothing. Therefore, the rest is up to you. I wish you the great success that only you yourself can achieve.

Appendix A

References Useful to Consultants

General Consulting

Albert, Kenneth J. *How to Be Your Own Management Consultant*. New York: McGraw-Hill, 1978.

The Consultant's Library—a collection of books for consultants published by Bermont Books, P.O. Box 309, Glenelg, Md. 21737.

Fuchs, Jerome H. *Making the Most of Management Consulting Services*. New York: AMACOM, 1975.

———. *Management Consultants in Action*. New York: Hawthorne Books, 1975.

Greiner, Larry E., and Robert O. Metzger. *Consulting to Management*. Englewood Cliffs, N.J.: Prentice-Hall, 1983.

Holtz, Herman. *How to Succeed as an Independent Consultant*. 2nd ed. New York: Wiley, 1983.

Kelley, Robert E. *Consulting*. 2nd ed. New York: Scribner, 1987.

Klein, Howard M. *Other People's Business—A Primer on Management Consultants*. New York: Mason/Charter, 1977.

Kubr, Milan. *Management Consulting—A Guide to the Profession*. Geneva, Switzerland: International Labor Office, 1976.

Tepper, Ron. *How to Become a Top Consultant*. New York: Wiley, 1986.

Consulting for the Government

Bevers, Charles, Linda Christie, and Lynn Price. *The Entrepreneur's Guide to Doing Business With the Federal Government*. Englewood Cliffs, N.J.: Prentice-Hall, 1989.

Cohen, William A. *How to Sell to the Government*. New York: Wiley, 1981.

Holtz, Herman. *The $100 Billion Market: How to Do Business With the U.S. Government.* New York: AMACOM, 1980.

Marketing for Small Businesses and Consultants

Cohen, William A. *Building a Mail Order Business.* 2nd ed. New York: Wiley, 1985.

Cohen, William A., and Marshall E. Reddick. *Successful Marketing for Small Business.* New York: AMACOM, 1981.

Connor, Richard A., and Jeffrey P. Davidson. *Marketing Your Consulting and Professional Services.* New York: Wiley, 1986.

Holtz, Herman. *Expanding Your Consulting and Professional Services.* New York: Wiley, 1986.

Kotler, Philip, and Paul N. Bloom. *Marketing Professional Services.* Englewood Cliffs, N.J.: Prentice-Hall, 1984.

Wilson, Aubrey. *The Marketing of Professional Services.* Maidenhead, UK: McGraw-Hill, 1972.

Problem Solving for Consultants

Albert, Kenneth J., ed. *Handbook of Business Problem Solving.* New York: McGraw-Hill, 1980.

Blake, Robert R., and Jane S. Mouton. *Consultations.* 2nd ed. Reading, Mass.: Addison-Wesley, 1976.

Chase, Cochrane, and Kenneth L. Barasch. *Marketing Problem Solver.* 2nd ed. Radnor, Pa.: Chilton, 1977.

Cohen, William A. *The Entrepreneur and Small Business Problem Solver.* New York: Wiley, 1983.

Weinrauch, J. Donald. *The Marketing Problem Solver.* New York: Wiley, 1987.

Executive Search/Executive Job Finding

Boll, Carl R. *Executive Jobs Unlimited: Updated Edition.* New York: Macmillan, 1980.

Cohen, William A. *The Executive's Guide to Finding a Superior Job.* Rev. ed. New York: AMACOM, 1983.

Conarroe, Richard R. *Executive Search.* New York: Van Nostrand Reinhold, 1976.

Cox, Allan J. *Confessions of a Corporate Headhunter.* New York: Trident Press, 1973.

Djeddah, Eli. *Moving Up*. Berkeley, Calif.: Ten Speed Press, 1978.
Wareham, John. *Secrets of a Corporate Headhunter*. New York: Atheneum, 1980.

Newsletters/Journals

Consultants News, Templeton Road, Fitzwilliam, N.H. 03447.
Consulting Opportunities Journal, 1629 K Street, NW, Suite 520, Washington, D.C. 20006.
Journal of Consulting, St. Louis University, 3674 Lindell Boulevard, St. Louis, Mo. 63108.
Journal of Management Consulting, Elsevier Science Publishers, 52 Vanderbilt Avenue, New York, N.Y. 10017.
The Professional Consultant and Seminar Business Report, 20750 Ventura Boulevard, Suite 206, Woodland Hills, Calif. 91364.

Appendix B

Sample Consultant's Brochure

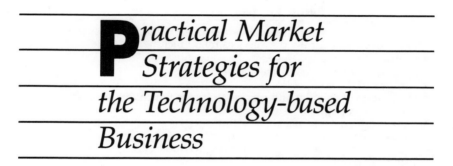

Practical Market Strategies for the Technology-based Business

ROSENAU CONSULTING COMPANY

The Company

Rosenau Consulting Company was founded in 1978 to assist clients with marketing, new product development, and other aspects of technology management. Simply stated, we can assist management to define the main elements of a profitable business strategy, by analyzing:

- What markets the company should pursue;
- What products and services the company should provide;
- Why, how, and to what extent customers will buy;
- How to best introduce the new product or service.

What We Do

While the uniqueness of each client dictates the exact services needed, typically our services might include:

- Identification of market needs;
- Determination of market size and structure;
- Analysis of the competition;
- Delineation of product and service attributes which differentiate them from the competition;
- Market research and sales forecasting;
- Venture analysis and business planning;
- Evaluation and forecasting of changing technology;
- Technical audits;
- Facilitation of the development and introduction of the new product or service.

Clients

We have been involved with a wide variety of technologies and industries, but most of our clients manufacture or provide technology-based products or services for industrial and commercial markets. These have included:

- Corporations in the Fortune 500 list;
- Foreign corporations;
- Smaller companies;
- Service businesses;
- Individual investors and entrepreneurs.

Qualifications

Milton D. Rosenau, Jr., is a Certified Management Consultant (CMC). Before founding Rosenau Consulting Company in 1978, he was Vice President for Science and Technology at Avery International. Preceding that he had been Vice President and General Manager at Optigon Research and Development Corporation, now, a division of Vivitar. And for seventeen years before that he worked for The Perkin-Elmer Corporation in management, marketing and engineering.

His major accomplishments in these industrial positions include successful commercial product diversification from technology developed on government contract programs as well as new product development for consumer and industrial markets.

He recently authored *Innovation: Managing the Development of Profitable New Products* which has been variously reviewed as "excellent reading for both entrepreneurs and managers" and "an outstanding practical guide...for developing the new product from the original idea through the stages of strategic planning, business organization, production, and marketing the finished product." His previous book was *Successful Project Management*.

Mr. Rosenau's degree in Engineering Physics from Cornell University was followed by management programs at MIT, Cornell, and UCLA. He is a member of several professional groups, has lectured frequently, and has authored numerous articles in addition to the above mentioned books.

ROSENAU CONSULTING COMPANY

Recent Assignments

Marketing

- Corporate market and product strategy formulation
- Marketing and licensing direction for proprietary technology
- Market and technology analysis for corporate five-year plan
- Market planning for software mail-order business
- Market analysis of product concept to establish appropriate R&D program
- Advice on consumer product importation and distribution
- Survey of threats to and viability of new retail service concept

New Product Development

- Market studies: automated inspection of printed circuit boards, fiber optic transducers, and video display microscopes
- Critical path network for new product introduction
- New product strategy and idea brainstorming
- Technical and market analysis of photogrammetric instrument
- Radiation curing market study to identify unfilled requirements
- Development of market-based product qualification standard
- Appraisal of solar energy venture
- Systems and business analysis of lasers for a product application
- Review of major retroreflective product development program
- Guidance on establishing a procedure for new product development

Technology Management

- Recommendation on how to introduce project management capability
- Guidance on the proposed use of computers in a laboratory
- Specification of experiments to evaluate electron-beam curing process
- Assistance to research laboratory director to help increase productivity
- Attitude survey of R&D department personnel
- Training seminars

General

- Business strategy guidance
- Specification of position to be filled by an executive recruiter
- Counselling on career development options
- Time management assistance

ROSENAU CONSULTING COMPANY

Our *Code of Professional Responsibility*

The basic responsibility of every *Certified Management Consultant* (CMC) is to put the interests of clients ahead of his or her own, and to serve them with integrity and competence.

As a CMC, Mr. Rosenau and his company agree to abide with all the professional ethics implied by that title.

We know that we are being hired for independent judgement and objectivity, technical expertise, analytical skill and concentrated attention to the solution of a problem. We will provide those skills. We will be impartial.

We will guard the confidentiality of all client information. We will not take financial gain or any other kind of advantage based on inside information. We will not serve two or more competing clients on sensitive problems without obtaining the approval of each client to do so. We will inform the client of any circumstances which might influence our judgement or objectivity.

Before accepting an assignment, we will confer with the client in sufficient detail to understand the problem and the scope of study needed to solve it. Such preliminary consultations are conducted confidentially, on terms agreed to by the client.

We will accept only those assignments we are qualified to perform which will provide real benefit to the client. But we cannot guarantee any specific results, such as the amount of cost reduction or profit increase. We present our qualifications on the basis of competence and experience. We perform each assignment on an individualized basis, and develop recommendations specifically for the practical solution of each client problem.

Whenever feasible, we agree with the client in advance on the fee basis for an assignment. We do not accept commissions or pay them to others for client referrals. Nor may we accept fees or commissions from others for recommending equipment, supplies, or services to his or her clients, as this would affect our impartiality.

ROSENAU CONSULTING COMPANY

Contractual Terms and Conditions

Professional time of M.D. Rosenau will be billed as either a fixed fee (if the required result can be precisely defined) or at an hourly rate quoted upon agreement of the scope of the effort.

In addition, the client will reimburse all expenses, plus a 20% handling charge added to these expenses. These expenses will be estimated upon agreement of the project's scope; if the actual expenses exceed the agreed estimate, the client will reimburse such excess expenses, but will not be charged any further handling charge on the additional amount.

Expenses include all out of pocket costs such as travel, telephone, printing and copying, postage, user fees for on-line information retrieval, publications, independent contractor assistance, and similar items. Other costs such as word processing, and mileage will be treated as expenses at rates approximating local commercial charges. Detailed expense records are maintained in our office and may be inspected if desired.

If travel costs are incurred on a trip that serves two or more clients, common travel costs will be allocated to each client in proportion to costs that would have been incurred for travel dedicated solely to each client alone.

Bills will be submitted twice a month, normally on the first and fifteenth. Bills are due and payable when submitted. A late payment charge of 1-1/2% per month (18% annually) may be applied to amounts outstanding ten (10) days after the date of the statement.

The client always has the right to terminate the assignment upon written notice. In such a case the client has no liability for charges beyond those incurred on their behalf through the date when notice of termination is received by us.

Because we cannot serve a client under terms or conditions that might impair our objectivity, independence, or integrity, Rosenau Consulting Company reserves the right to withdraw from the assignment if conditions develop to interfere with the successful completion of the assignment (except where our efforts are integral with the client's efforts).

It is understood that Rosenau Consulting Company and its contractors, if any, shall be in the relation of independent contractors with the client, and nothing herein shall be construed as designating us as employees or agents of the client for any purpose.

Rosenau Consulting Company will guard as confidential all information concerning the affairs of the client that is gathered during the course of the assignment. We agree to hold such information in strict confidence, and not to disclose it to others for a period of five years or until such information is otherwise released by the client.

Rosenau Consulting Company will not serve two or more competing clients in areas of vital interest without first informing each client.

The rights to any inventions that result from our work will be assigned to the client without any further charge for professional time. The client is responsible for all legal fees and similar expenses necessary to obtain patents that the client may desire to register.

ROSENAU CONSULTING COMPANY

Case History

Client Problem A small direct response advertiser sold microcomputer software by mail and wanted to grow. The industry was very competitive with sales volume obtained primarily by low discounted prices. They wanted to develop a strategic market plan which would permit them to outperform their industry competition.

What We Did Rosenau Consulting Company first examined their sales records and segmented their existing market. We obtained industry data to establish their market share and industry trend. We then interviewed industry experts, past customers, and a few prospective customers. This gave us enough information to help the client conduct economical mail surveys of customers and potential customers.

Result The client was able to selectively raise prices by providing other value to buyers. A new advertising and public relations campaign was initiated to convey this.

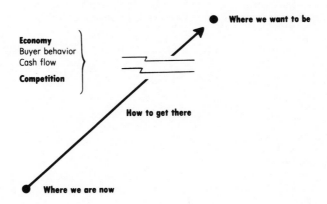

ROSENAU CONSULTING COMPANY

Case History

Client Problem A prior client received two recent inquiries about using one of their standard products or modifications of it to scan printed circuit boards. The purpose of the intended scanning was to rapidly and reliably locate defects on the printed circuit boards.

Because the client was not then serving that market, they retained us to estimate the market need and determine whether there was significant competition.

What We Did Rosenau Consulting Company quickly surveyed the available secondary market data using our on-line information retrieval system. We also conducted telephone interviews with potential users, industry experts, and providers of other test equipment. Simultaneously, we used an associate consultant to conduct field interviews.

Result In just a few months we were able to tell the client the approximate size of the market, to identify the nature of the competition, and, most importantly, to indicate the key product attributes that the design engineers would have to provide in a viable product. The client then initiated a joint venture development program.

ROSENAU CONSULTING COMPANY

How We Work

We cannot begin solving your specific problem until we first gain a solid basic understanding of it. In our initial contact we try to learn:

- Specific needs and background;
- Origins of the problem;
- Scope of the investigation;
- Key issues to be examined.

At this time we try to determine:

- A broad definition of the assignment and expected results;
- The information gathering methodology;
- Logical phases (if practical);
- Approximate time and cost.

At this initial point there is no obligation on either side. Once gathered, the above information helps the client decide whether we are the best people to handle the assignment, and helps us determine if we can do the job and whether we can do it properly in the time available.

When appropriate, the details and results of this discussion are confirmed in a written proposal outlining:

- Our understanding of the assignment;
- Suggested approach;
- Type and extent of client involvement;
- Organization of the work;
- Expected results;
- Estimated time and cost.

The client has no obligation until our proposal is accepted.

During each assignment, periodic updates are given. These are augmented by at least one interim review to summarize our findings to date and discuss any modifications in the direction for the balance of the project. Upon completion of our work, we report our findings and recommendations to client management, normally in the form of a briefing presentation. While structured, this presentation encourages the questioning and discussion of our findings. Our goal is to provide clients with recommendations which are practical for them to implement. The presentation is then documented with a written report.

Fees are based on the time needed plus expenses actually incurred in carrying out the assignment. More detail may be found on the "Contractual Terms and Conditions" insert.

W*hy Retain Rosenau Consulting Company?*

1. *Expertise* We are not trying to be all things to all people. We offer a specialized service in management consulting concerning the development of profitable new products and services. We have great experience and expertise in our chosen specialization. Milton D. Rosenau, Jr., founder, has extensive functional and general management experience in this area. Associate consultants are also utilized when their experience is relevant and helpful to the client.

2. *Efficiency* Because we are specialized, we have files and tools that often allow us to perform an assignment better, faster, and cheaper than clients can on their own. We can interrogate on-line information data bases. This offers two benefits: It decreases the amount of time we need to spend in the field, and it makes our fieldwork yield better results because it is well focused.

3. *Concentration* Because we can concentrate on accomplishing a critical assignment quickly, our clients are freed to operate the on-going business without diversion.

4. *Anonymity* Because we are an independent firm, we need not reveal the identity or purpose of our clients, within normal legal and ethical bounds. And we will not reveal critical information without prior approval.

5. *Objectivity* We bring a fresh viewpoint, unencumbered by hierarchical pressure or bias. If we cannot help our client, we will say so and refer them to other appropriate sources. We will never be used simply as an outside stamp of approval on an executive's pet project.

C*lient Relationships*

Work is carried out in a manner which best satisfies the client in accordance with the Code of Professional Practice of the Association of Management Consultants (of which Rosenau Consulting Company is a member). This can be arranged by either a retainer for a stipulated period or, more commonly, as a single project assignment. Milton D. Rosenau, Jr., CMC, directs all assignments and client relations. Specialist associate consultants are called upon as needed.

Appendix C

The Consultant's Questionnaire and Audit

Part I: Organization

Company: _____

Division: _____

Address: _____

City, State, and Zip Code: _____

Other Division Locations: _____

_____

_____

_____

Company Officers and Other Key Executives: _____

_____

_____

_____

Primary Contact for This Engagement: _____

Title: _____

Address: _____

City, State, and Zip Code: _____

Phone Number: _____

Backup Contact for This Engagement: _____
Title: _____
Address: _____
City, State, and Zip Code: _____
Phone Number: _____

Note: Obtain relevant company organization charts.

Part II: Production

What percentage of production is:

_____ %   Job-order (custom) manufacture?

_____ %   Repetitive (standard) manufacture?

100 %   Total

What percentage of production is:

_____ %   Private label for someone else?

_____ %   Sold under your own name?

100%   Total

Do you subcontract? _____
_____ %   If yes, what percentage of your total work?

Who are your major subcontractors? _____

_____

_____

_____

Are you satisfied with their work? _____

_____ %   What percentage of your production do you export?

What countries do you export to? What is the percentage of export to each country?

_____   _____ %

_____   _____ %

_____   _____ %

_____ %   At what current percentage of production capacity are you now operating?

_____ %   What additional percentage could you add to total capacity (100%) in order to accommodate additional sales?

How many months would it take to reach this figure? _____ months

_____ %   What is the minimum percentage of capacity at which you must operate in order to break even?

How seasonal is your production?

☐ Not at all   ☐ Highly
☐ Slightly   ☐ Totally
☐ Fairly

At which season(s) is production at its peak? _____

At which season(s) is production at its minimum? _____

To what extent are your production operations regulated by governmental controls?

_____ % Federal   _____ % Local
_____ % State

Who are your major suppliers? Are you satisfied with them?

_____   _____ %
_____   _____ %
_____   _____ %

Part III: Markets Served

If accurate figures are unavailable, give estimates for the following:

	Last Year	Three Years Ago
Total industry sales	$_____	$_____
Your sales	$_____	$_____
Your market share	$_____	$_____

	Last Year	Three Years Ago
Major competitor's share	$_____	$_____
Second-ranking competitor's share	$_____	$_____
Third-ranking competitor's share	$_____	$_____

_____ % Consumer market
_____ % Industrial market

Describe each consumer market or industrial market by SIC code.* List your products, or services, the channels used to distribute them, and your approximate percentage share of each market.

Market	Products	Channel(s)	Market Share

List your major competitors.

	Name	Strongest markets	Why strong in these markets?	Strongest products	Why strong with these products?
1.	_____	_____	_____	_____	_____
	Address: _____				
2.	_____	_____	_____	_____	_____
	Address: _____				
3.	_____	_____	_____	_____	_____
	Address: _____				

*This is a code developed by the federal government to describe products and services and the companies that offer them.

What new competitors have entered the marketplace in the past three years? _____

_____

Have any done unusually well? If so, in what markets, with what products, and why? _____

_____
_____
_____

Part IV: Products

Approximately how many different individual products do you manufacture? _____

$_____ What is the dollar amount of your average sale (to your end customer)?

How many times is your average product purchased by the same customer in a single year? _____

_____% Approximately what percentage of your customers are repeat customers?

What is the average purchase life of your customers? _____

Why do they stop buying from you? _____

_____

Which of your products have the highest margins? _____

_____
_____

Do you sell any "loss leaders"? List them below:

_____
_____
_____
_____

Has their effectiveness ever been tested against that of other items? If so, which items, and how?

_____   _____
_____   _____
_____   _____
_____   _____
_____   _____
_____   _____

List your products below by sales and profits:

Product	Annual Sales	Annual Profits
_____	$_____	$_____
_____	$_____	$_____
_____	$_____	$_____
_____	$_____	$_____
_____	$_____	$_____
_____	$_____	$_____

Have you considered dropping those products that account for low profits? If low-sales/low-profit products are being retained, indicate why:

_____
_____
_____
_____
_____
_____
_____
_____

Do you have an ongoing new-product research and development program? _____

When was your last new product introduced? _____

When was your last major product modification introduced? _____

How do you do new-product research and development?
☐ In-house
☐ Subcontract

Why do you do new-product research and development?
☐ Meet the competition
☐ Counter product obsolescence
☐ Reduce production costs
☐ Reduce material costs
☐ Enter new markets
☐ Increase sales
☐ Other _____

How do you screen potential products for development? _____
_____

Part V: Marketing Research

Do you have an ongoing market research program? _____

Do you have correct information on:
☐ Who's buying your products?
☐ Why they're buying?
☐ Where your products are being bought?
☐ Who's making the purchase decision?
☐ How to best reach your customers through advertising?
☐ The effectiveness of advertising programs?
☐ Your competitors' products?
☐ Your competitors' strategies?
☐ Potential markets?
☐ Relative effectiveness of different channels of distribution?
☐ New applications of your products?
☐ Export potential?
☐ Related products demanded by your customers?
☐ Relative effectiveness and efficiency of salespeople?
☐ Packaging effectiveness?
☐ Pricing sensitivity?
☐ Image and positioning of your product relative to others?
☐ Publicity possibilities?
☐ Operating ratios in your industry?

What trade associations do you belong to? _____
_____
_____

What trade magazines or journals do you subscribe to? _____
_____
_____
_____

Do you use the market research available from associations and magazines? _____

If you make use of internally generated market research, which organizations within your company provide this research, and what research do they provide? _____
_____
_____
_____

What outside organizations have assisted you in doing research? _____
_____
_____
_____

Part VI: Market Segments

Consumer Market

What segments of the market do your present customers represent? _____
_____
_____
_____

Are your products more:
- [ ] Habitual purchase?
- [ ] Impulse?
- [ ] Planned purchase?

In your market, which are the most important factors for buying?
- [ ] Price
- [ ] Quality
- [ ] Features
- [ ] Performance
- [ ] Appearance

- [ ] Other _____

Who influences the decision to buy your products?
☐ Men   ☐ Lawyers
☐ Women   ☐ Religious leaders
☐ Children   ☐ Mechanics
☐ Doctors   ☐ Contractors
☐ Dentists   ☐ Tradespeople
☐ Educators   ☐ Fraternal or social groups
☐ Beauticians   ☐ High-income or influential people
☐ Barbers

☐ Others _____

Industrial Market

Who makes the purchase decision for your product? If more than one
individual, indicate all.

_____
_____
_____
_____

Outline the sequence of events as to how this decision is made. Include
other factors or individuals influencing this decision.

_____
_____
_____
_____
_____
_____

Part VII: Pricing

How do you decide on the price for your products? _____
_____
_____
_____

What's your warranty policy? _____
_____
_____
_____

What's your service policy? _____
_____
_____
_____
_____

Any other special policies of importance? _____
_____
_____
_____
_____

Pricing Checklist

   Examining Costs, Sales Volume, and Profits. The questions in this part should be helpful when you look at prices from the viewpoint of costs, sales volume, and profits.*

   Pricing and Costs. The company that sets the price for an item by applying a standard markup may be overlooking certain cost factors that are connected with that item. The following questions are designed to help you gather information that should be helpful when you are determining prices on specific types of items.

		Yes	No
1.	Do you know which of your operating costs remain the same regardless of sales volume?	___	___
2.	Do you know which of your operating costs decrease percentagewise as your sales volume increases?	___	___
3.	Have you ever figured out the breakeven point for your items selling at varying price levels?	___	___
4.	Do you look behind high gross margin percentages? (For example, a product with a high gross margin may also be a slow turnover item with high handling costs. Thus it may be less profitable than lower-margin items that turn over fast.)	___	___

*This section (which continues until the beginning of Part VIII) is adapted from Joseph D. O'Brien, "A Pricing Checklist for Managers" (Small Business Administration, 1972).

Yes   *No*

5.   When you select items for price reductions, do you
     project the effects on profits? (For example, if a
     food marketer considers whether to run canned
     ham or rump steak on sale, an important cost
     factor is labor. Practically none is involved in fea-
     turing canned ham; however, a rump steak sale
     requires the skill of a meat cutter, and this labor
     cost might mean little or no profits.)   _____   _____

Pricing and Sales Volume. An effective pricing program should also
consider sales volume. For example, high prices may limit your sales
volume, while low prices may result in a large but unprofitable volume.
The following questions should be helpful in determining what is right
for your situation.

Yes   *No*

6.   Have you considered setting a sales volume goal
     and then studying it to see if your prices will help
     you reach it?   _____   _____
7.   Have you set a target of a certain number of new
     customers for next year?   _____   _____
     If so, how can pricing help to get them? _____

     _____

8.   Should you limit the quantities of low-margin
     items that any one customer can buy when such
     items are on sale?   _____   _____
     If so, will you advertise this policy? _____

     _____

9.   What is your policy when a sale item is sold out
     before the end of the advertised period? Do you
     allow disappointed customers to buy the item later
     at the sale price? _____

     _____

Pricing and Profits. Prices should help bring in sales that are profitable
over the long pull. The following questions are designed to help you think
about pricing policies and their effect on your annual profits.

Yes   *No*

10. Do you have all the facts on costs, sales, and
     competitive behavior?   _____   _____

		Yes	*No*
11.	Do you set prices with the hope of accomplishing definite objectives, such as a 1 percent profit increase over last year?	___	___
12.	Have you set a given level of profits in dollars and in percentage of sales?	___	___
13.	Do you keep records to give you the needed facts on profits, losses, and prices?	___	___
14.	Do you review your pricing practices periodically to make sure that they are helping to achieve your profit goals?	___	___

Judging the Buyer, Timing, and Competitors. The questions in this part are designed to help you check your practices for judging the buyer (your customer), your timing, and your competitors.

The Buyer and Pricing. After you have your facts on costs, the next point must be the *customer*—whether you are changing a price, putting in a new item, or checking out your present price practices. Knowledge of your customers helps you determine how to vary prices in order to get the average gross margin you need for making a profit. (For example, to get an average gross margin of 35 percent, some retailers put a low markup—10 percent, for instance—on items that they promote as traffic builders and use high markup, sometimes as much as 60 percent, on slow-moving items.) The following questions should be helpful in checking your knowledge about your customers.

		Yes	*No*
15.	Do you know whether your customers shop around and for what items?	___	___
16.	Do you know how your customers make their comparisons?	___	___
	☐ By reading newspaper ads?		
	☐ Store shopping?		
	☐ Hearsay?		
17.	Are you trying to appeal to customers who:		
	☐ Buy on price alone?		
	☐ Buy on quality alone?		
	☐ Combine the two?		
18.	Do any of your customers tell you that your prices are in line with those of your competitors?	___	___
	☐ Higher?		
	☐ Lower?		

Yes   *No*

19. Do you know which items (or types of items) your customers call for even though you raise the price? _____ _____

20. Do you know which items (or types of items) your customers leave on your shelves when you raise the price? _____ _____

21. Do certain items seem to appeal to customers more than others when you run weekend, clearance, or special-day sales? _____ _____

22. Have you used your individual sales records to classify your present customers according to the volume of their purchases? _____ _____

23. Will your customers buy more if you use multiple pricing (for example, three for thirty-nine cents for products with rapid turnover)? _____ _____

24. Do your customers respond to odd prices more readily than to even prices, for example, ninety-nine cents rather than one dollar? _____ _____

25. Have you decided on a pricing strategy to create a favorable price image with your customers? (For example, a retailer with eight thousand different items might decide to make a full margin on all medium or slow movers while featuring—at low price levels—the remaining fast movers.) _____ _____

26. If you are trying to build a quality price image, do your individual customer records, such as charge account statements, show that you are selling a larger number of higher-priced items than you were twelve months ago? _____ _____

27. Do your records of individual customer accounts and your observations of customer behavior in the store show price as the important factor in their:
    - [ ] Buying?
    - [ ] Service?
    - [ ] Assortments?
    - [ ] Some other consideration? _____

Time and Pricing. Effective merchandising means that you have the right product at the right place, at the right price, and at the right time. All are important, but timing is the critical element for the smaller retailer. The following questions should be helpful in determining what is the right time for you to adjust prices.

	Yes	*No*
28. Are you a "leader" (rather than a "follower") in announcing your price reductions? (Followers, even though they match their competitors, create a negative impression on their customers.)	___	___
29. Have you studied your competitors to see whether they follow any sort of pattern when making price changes? (For example, do some of them run clearance sales earlier than others?)	___	___
30. Is there a pattern to the kinds of items that competitors promote at lower prices at certain times of the month or year?	___	___
31. Have you decided whether it is better to take early markdowns on seasonal or style goods or to run a clearance sale at the end of the season?	___	___
32. Have you made regular annual sales—such as anniversary sales, fall clearance, or holiday cleanup—so popular that many customers wait for them rather than buying in season?	___	___
33. When you change a price, do you make sure that all customers know about it through price tags and so on?	___	___
34. Do you try to time reductions so they can be promoted in your advertising?	___	___

Competition and Pricing. When you set prices, you have to consider how your competitors might react to your prices. The starting place is learning as much as you can about their price structures. The following questions are designed to help you check out this phase of pricing.

	Yes	*No*
35. Do you use all the available channels of information to keep you up-to-date on your competitors' price policies? (Some useful sources of information are: things your customers tell you; competitors' price lists and catalogs, if used; competitors' advertising; reports from your suppliers; trade paper studies; and shoppers employed by you.)	___	___
36. Should your policy be always to: ☐ Try to sell above or below competition? ☐ Or only to meet the competition?		
37. Is there a pattern to the way your competitors respond to your price cuts?	___	___

		Yes	No
38.	Is the leader pricing of your competitors affecting your sales volume to such an extent that you must alter your pricing policy on individual items (or types of items) or merchandise?	____	____
39.	Do you realize that no two competitors have identical cost curves? (This difference in costs means that certain price levels may be profitable for you but unprofitable for your competitor or vice versa.)	____	____

Practices That Can Help Offset Price. Some companies take advantage of the fact that price is not always the determining factor in making a sale. They supply customer services and offer other inducements to offset the effect of competitors' lower prices. Delivery service is an example. Providing a comfortable shoppers' meeting place is another. The following questions are designed to help you take a look at some of these practices.

		Yes	No
40.	Do the items or services you sell have advantages for which customers are willing to pay a little more?	____	____
41.	From personal observation of customer behavior in your store, can you estimate about how much more customers will pay for such advantages?	____	____
42.	Should you change your services so as to create an advantage for which your customers will be willing to pay?	____	____
43.	Does your advertising emphasize customer benefits rather than price?	____	____
44.	Are you using the most common nonprice competitive tools? (For example, have you tried to alter your product or service to the existing market? Have you tried stamps, bonus purchase gifts, or other plans for building repeat business?)	____	____
45.	Should policies on returned goods be changed so as to better impress your customers?	____	____
46.	If you sell repair services, have you checked out your guarantee policy?	____	____
47.	Should you alter assortments of merchandise to increase sales?	____	____

Part VIII: Distribution

How much of your product line is:
_____ %   Manufactured by you?
_____ %   Manufactured for you by someone else?
   100%   Total

Is your distribution:
☐ Regional? In what areas? _____
_____
☐ National? What are your strongest areas? _____
_____
☐ International? What are your strongest foreign countries? _____
_____

What systems of distribution do you use? _____
_____
_____
_____

How do you subdivide your product lines in your sales organization?
☐ Geographic territories   ☐ Type of customer
                                     ☐ Type of product
☐ Other _____

How do you decide on methods of distribution and which distributors to use? _____
_____

Part IX: Selling

Do your salespeople, agents, or distributors have exclusive territories?
_____
_____
_____

How many people do you have selling your product, and what are their responsibilities?
_____
_____
_____

How do you compensate your salespeople?

_____

_____

_____

Do you offer any special sales incentives?

_____

_____

_____

Who prepares your product catalogs?

_____

_____

_____

_____

_____

What aids to selling do you, *your distributor, or your agent* provide to people selling your product?

_____

_____

_____

_____

Do you provide any type of formal sales training? Explain type, subjects, length of programs, etc.

_____

_____

_____

_____

_____

How frequently do you hold sales meetings or conferences? What subjects are covered?

_____

_____

_____

_____

What branch offices do you maintain?

_____

_____

_____

_____

How do you select or recruit your agents and salespeople?

_____
_____
_____
_____

How do you set sales quotas?

_____
_____
_____
_____

What trade discounts do you offer?

_____
_____
_____
_____

What terms of sale do you use?

_____
_____
_____

Do you grant any special concessions or offers to stimulate sales?

_____
_____
_____

_____ %   What is your percentage of returned goods?

_____ %   What is your percentage of goods returned due to damage?

_____ %   What is your percentage of bad debts?

What is the average time for collection of amounts owed to you? _____

How frequently do your salespeople send in reports? _____

How do you maintain your sales records?

_____
_____
_____

What is your ratio of sales made to number of calls made? _____

Are your "cold calls" supplemented by any other type of communication such as direct mail? _____

_____

_____

_____

How do you control your salespeople's activities? _____

_____

_____

_____

_____

What percentage of your salespeople's time is spent on:
_____ %   Planning?
_____ %   Preparation?
_____ %   Travel?
_____ %   Calls on prospects?
_____ %   Calls on established customers?
_____ %   Other?
   100%   Total

What are the following yearly gross sales figures of your salespeople?
$ _____   Average gross
$ _____   Lowest gross
$ _____   Highest gross

$ _____   What is the average amount spent on promotion activities that back up sales per salesperson per year (total spent yearly on sales promotion, advertising, and publicity divided by number of salespeople)?

$ _____   What is the average amount spent on sales activities per salesperson per year (total spent on recruiting, training, expense accounts, and compensation divided by number of salespeople)?

Part X: Advertising

What media do you use to promote to your customers? _____

_____

_____

_____

What advertising (including direct mail and telephone) have you done, and what were the costs over the last year? What were the results? _____

_____
_____
_____
_____
_____
_____

How were results measured for these ads? _____

_____
_____
_____
_____

Do you have an advertising agency? _____
    Name: _____
    Contact: _____
    Address: _____
    Phone number: _____

Part XI: Promotion

What types of sales promotion have you done (discounts, coupons, contests, etc.), and what were the costs? What were the results? _____

_____
_____
_____
_____
_____
_____

Part XII: Publicity and Public Relations

What type of public relations program did you engage in over the previous year, and what were the costs? What were the results? _____

_____
_____
_____
_____
_____
_____

Part XIII: Management Operations

What type of planning does the organization do? _____

_____

_____

_____

_____

How is budgetary control of operations planned and maintained? _____

_____

_____

_____

Part XIV: Financial Checklist

Are You Making a Profit?

Analysis of Revenues and Expenses. Since profit is revenues less expenses, you must first identify all revenues and expenses for the period under study to determine what your profit is.*

		Yes	*No*
1.	Have you chosen an appropriate period for profit determination?	____	____

For accounting purposes, businesses generally use a twelve-month period, such as January 1 to December 31 or July 1 to June 30. The accounting year you select doesn't have to be a calendar year (January to December); a seasonal business, for example, might close its year after the end of the season. The selection depends upon the nature of your business, your personal preference, or possible tax considerations.

2.	Have you determined your total revenues for the accounting period?	____	____

*This section (which continues until the beginning of Part XV) is adapted from Narendra C. Bhandari and Charles S. McCubbin, Jr., "Checklist for Profit Watching" (Small Business Administration, 1980).

In order to answer this question, consider the following questions.

$ _____ What is the amount of gross revenue from sales of your goods or service (*gross sales*)?

$ _____ What is the amount of goods returned by your customers and credited (*returns and rejects*)?

$ _____ What is the amount of discounts given to your customers and employees (*discounts*)?

$ _____ What is the amount of net sales from goods and services (*net sales = gross sales [returns and rejects + discounts]*)?

$ _____ What is the amount of income from other sources, such as interest on bank deposits, dividends from securities, and rent on property leased to others (*nonoperating income*)?

$ _____ What is the amount of total revenue (*total revenue = net sales + nonoperating income*)?

3. Do you know what your total expenses are?   _____   _____

Expenses are the cost of goods sold and services used in the process of selling goods or services. Some common expenses for all businesses are:

$ _____ Cost of goods sold (cost of goods sold = beginning inventory + purchases − ending inventory)

$ _____ Wages and salaries (don't forget to include your own—at the actual rate you'd have to pay someone else to do your job)

$ _____ Rent

$ _____ Utilities (electricity, gas, telephone, water, etc.)

$ _____ Supplies (office, cleaning, and the like)

$ _____ Delivery expenses

$ _____ Insurance

$ _____ Advertising and promotion costs

Yes   No

$ _____ Maintenance and upkeep
$ _____ Depreciation (here you need to make sure your depreciation policies are realistic and that all depreciable items are included)
$ _____ Taxes and licenses
$ _____ Interest
$ _____ Bed debts
$ _____ Professional assistance (accountant, attorney, etc.)

There are, of course, many other types of expenses, but the point is that every expense must be recorded and deducted from your revenues before you know what your profit is. Understanding your expenses is the first step toward *controlling them* and *increasing your profits*.

Financial Ratios

A *financial ratio* is an expression of the relationship between two items selected from the income statement or the balance sheet. Ratio analysis helps you evaluate the weak and strong points in your financial and managerial performance.

Yes   No

4. Do you know your *current ratio*?   ____ ____

The *current ratio* (current assets divided by current debts) is a measure of the cash or near cash position (liquidity) of the company. It tells you if you have enough cash to pay your company's current creditors. The higher the ratio, the more liquid the company's position, and hence the higher the credibility of the company. Cash, receivables, marketable securities, and inventory are current assets. Naturally you need to be realistic in valuing receivables and inventory for a true picture of your liquidity, since some debts may be uncollectible and some stock obsolete. Current liabilities are those that must be paid in one year.

Yes   No

5.   Do you know your *quick ratio*?   ____   ____

      Quick assets are current assets minus inventory. The *quick ratio* (or acid-test ratio) is found by dividing quick assets by current liabilities. The purpose, again, is to test the company's ability to meet its current obligations. Because it doesn't include inventory, *quick ratio* is a stiffer test of the company's liquidity. It tells you if the business could meet its current obligations with quickly convertible assets should sales revenues suddenly cease.

6.   Do you know your total debt to net worth ratio?   ____   ____

      This ratio (the result of total debt divided by net worth, then multiplied by 100) is a measure of how the company can meet its total obligations from equity. The lower the ratio, the higher the proportion of equity relative to debt, and the better the company's credit rating will be.

7.   Do you know your average collection period?   ____   ____

      You find this ratio by dividing accounts receivable by daily credit sales. (Daily credit sales = annual credit sales divided by 360.) This ratio tells you the length of time it takes the company to get its cash after making a sale on credit. The shorter this period, the quicker the cash inflow is. A longer than normal period may mean overdue and uncollectible bills. If you extend credit for a specific period (say, thirty days), this ratio should be very close to the same number of days. If it's much longer than the established period, you may need to alter your credit policies. It's wise to develop an aging schedule to gauge the trend of collections and identify slow payers. Slow collections (without adequate financing charges) hurt your profit, since you could be doing something much more useful with your money, such as taking advantage of discounts on your own payables.

8.   Do you know your ratio of net sales to total assets?   ____   ____

      This ratio (net sales divided by total assets) measures the efficiency with which you are using your assets. A higher than normal ratio indicates that the company is able to generate sales from its assets faster (and better) than the average concern.

9. Do you know your operating profit to net sales ratio?

     This ratio (the result of dividing operating profit by net sales and multiplying by 100) is most often used to determine the profit position relative to sales. A higher than normal ratio indicates that your sales are good, that your expenses are low, or both. Interest income and interest expense should not be included in calculating this ratio.

10. Do you know your net profit to total assets ratio?

     This ratio (the result of dividing net profit by total assets and multiplying by 100) is often called return on investment, or ROI. It focuses on the profitability of the overall operation of the company. Thus it allows management to measure the effects of its policies on the company's profitability. The ROI is the single most important measure of a company's financial position. You might say it's the bottom line for the bottom line.

11. Do you know your net profit to net worth ratio?

     This ratio is found by dividing net profit by net worth and multiplying the result by 100. It provides information on the productivity of the resources the owners have committed to the company's operations.

     All ratios measuring profitability can be computed either before or after taxes, depending on the purpose of the computations. Ratios have limitations. Since the information used to derive ratios is itself based on accounting rules and personal judgments as well as facts, the ratios cannot be considered absolute indicators of a company's financial position. Ratios are only one means of assessing the performance of the company and must be considered in perspective with many other measures. They should be used as a point of departure for further analysis and not as an end in themselves.

Sufficiency of Profit

The following questions are designed to help you measure the adequacy of the profit your company is making. Making a profit is only the first step; making enough profit to survive and *grow* is really what business is all about.

		Yes	*No*
12.	Have you compared your profit with your profit goals?	____	____
13.	Is it possible your goals are too high or too low?	____	____
14.	Have you compared your present profits (absolute and ratios) with the profits made in the last one to three years?	____	____
15.	Have you compared your profits (absolute and ratios) with profits made by similar companies in your line?	____	____

A number of organizations publish financial ratios for various businesses, among them Dun & Bradstreet, Robert Morris Associates, the Accounting Corporation of America, NCR Corporation, and Bank of America. Your own trade association may also publish such studies. Remember, these published ratios are only averages. You probably want to be better than average.

Trend of Profit

		Yes	*No*
16.	Have you analyzed the direction your profits have been taking?	____	____

The preceding analyses, with all their merits, report on a company only at a single time in the past. It is not possible to use these isolated moments to indicate the trend of your company's performance. To do a trend analysis, you should compute performance indicators (absolute amounts or ratios) for several time periods (yearly for several years, for example) and lay out the results in columns side by side for easy comparison. You can then evaluate your performance, see the direction it's taking, and make initial forecasts of where it will go.

Mix of Profit

Yes   No

17. Does your company sell more than one major product line or provide several distinct services? ____ ____

    If it does, a separate profit and ratio analysis of each should be made: to show the relative contribution of each product line or service; to show the relative burden of expenses of each product or service; to show which items are most profitable, which are less so, and which are losing money; and to show which are slow and fast moving.

    The profit and ratio analyses of each major item help you uncover the strong and weak areas of your operations. They can help you to make profit-increasing decisions to drop a product line or service or to place particular emphasis behind one or another.

Records

Good records are essential. Without them a company doesn't know where it's been, where it is, or where it's heading. Keeping records that are accurate, up-to-date, and easy to use is one of the most important functions of the owner-manager, his or her staff, and his or her outside counselors (lawyer, accountant, banker).

Basic Records

Yes   No

18. Do you have a general journal and/or special journals, such as one for cash receipts and disbursements? ____ ____

    A general journal is the basic record of the company. Every monetary event in the life of the company is entered in the general journal or in one of the special journals.

19. Do you prepare a sales report or analysis? ____ ____

    a. Do you have sales goals by product, department, and accounting period (month, quarter, year)? ____ ____

	Yes	*No*
b. Are your goals reasonable?	____	____
c. Are you meeting your goals?	____	____

     If you aren't meeting your goals, try to list the likely reasons on a sheet of paper. Such a study might include areas such as general business climate, competition, pricing, advertising, sales promotion, credit policies, and the like. Once you've identified the apparent causes, you can take steps to increase sales (and profits).

Buying and Inventory Systems

		Yes	*No*
20.	Do you have buying and inventory systems?	____	____
	The buying and inventory systems are two critical areas of a company's operation that can affect profitability.		
21.	Do you keep records on the quality, service, price, and promptness of delivery of your sources of supply?	____	____
22.	Have you analyzed the advantages and disadvantages of:		
	a. Buying from suppliers?	____	____
	b. Buying from a minimum number of suppliers?	____	____
23.	Have you analyzed the advantages and disadvantages of buying through cooperatives or other such systems?	____	____
24.	Do you know:		
	a. How long it usually takes to receive each order?	____	____
	b. How much inventory cushion (usually called safety stock) to have so you can maintain normal sales while you wait for the order to arrive?	____	____
25.	Have you ever suffered because you were out of stock?	____	____
26.	Do you know the optimum order quantity for each item you need?	____	____
27.	Do you (or can you) take advantage of quantity discounts for large-size single purchases?	____	____
28.	Do you know your costs of ordering inventory and carrying inventory?	____	____

     The more frequently you buy (smaller quantities per order), the higher your average ordering costs are (clerical costs, postage, telephone costs, etc.), and the lower the average carrying costs are (storage, loss through pilferage, obsolescence, etc.). On the other hand, the larger the quantity per order, the lower the average ordering costs, and the higher the carrying costs. A balance should be struck so that the minimum cost overall for ordering and carrying inventory can be achieved.

29.   Do you keep records of inventory for each item?   _____   _____

These records should be kept current by making entries whenever items are added to or removed from inventory. Simple records on 3- by 5- inch or 5- by 7-inch cards can be used, with each item being listed on a separate card. Proper records will show, for each item, quantity in stock, quantity on order, date of order, slow or fast seller, and valuations (which are important for taxes and your own analyses).

Other Financial Records

30.   Do you have an accounts payable ledger?   _____   _____

This ledger shows what, whom, and why you owe. Such records should help you make your payments on schedule; any expense not paid on time could adversely affect your credit. But even more importantly, such records should help you take advantage of discounts that can help boost your profits.

31.   Do you have an accounts receivable ledger?   _____   _____

This ledger shows who owes money to your company. It shows how much is owed, how long it has been outstanding, and why the money is owed. Overdue accounts could indicate that your credit-granting policy needs to be reviewed and that you may not be getting the cash into the company quickly enough to pay your own bills at the optimum time.

32.   Do you have a cash receipts journal?   _____   _____

This journal records the cash received by source, day, and amount.

| | |
Yes	No

33. Do you have a cash payments journal? ____ ____
    This journal is similar to the cash receipts journal but shows cash paid out instead of cash received. The two cash journals can be combined if convenient.

34. Do you prepare an income (profit and loss, or P&L) statement and a balance sheet? ____ ____
    These are statements about the condition of your company at a specific time; they show the income, expenses, assets, and liabilities of the company. They are absolutely essential.

35. Do you prepare a budget? ____ ____
    You could think of a budget as a "record in advance," projecting future inflows and outflows for your business. A budget is usually prepared for a single year, generally to correspond with the accounting year. It is then, however, broken down into quarterly and monthly projections.
    There are different kinds of budgets: cash, production, sales, and the like. A cash budget, for example, shows the estimate of sales and expenses for a particular period of time. The cash budget forces the company to think ahead by estimating its income and expenses. Once reasonable projections are made for every important product line or department, the owner-manager has set targets for employees to meet for sales and expenses. You must plan to ensure a profit. And you must prepare a budget to plan.

Part XV: Material to Ask For

- Sales brochures
- Price lists
- Public relations materials
- Product description and photographs
- Special forms
- Annual report
- Financial statements
- Sample advertisements and promotional materials
- Information given out at recent trade shows
- Organizational charts

Appendix D

An Extensive Consulting Proposal

**A Proposal for a Project Planning and Control System
Procedure Development Program**

Submitted to:

[*company name and address*]

Attention: [*name*]

Submitted by:

Decision Planning Corporation
3184-A Airway Avenue
Costa Mesa, California 92626

All pages of this document contain information proprietary to Decision Planning Corporation. All data furnished in connection with this proposal shall not be duplicated, transmitted, used, or otherwise disclosed to anyone other than _____ , and then only for the purpose of evaluating the quotation. This restriction is applicable to all sheets of this proposal.

[*date*]

Table of Contents

Description

Section

1.0   Executive Summary
      1.1   Program Background
      1.2   Proposed Services
      1.3   Decision Planning Corporation Qualifications

2.0   Technical Proposal
      2.1   WBS Element 1.0—Project Planning and Control (PP&C) System Review
      2.2   WBS Element 2.0—Project Planning and Control System Specification
      2.3   WBS Element 3.0—PP&C System Procedures
      2.4   WBS Element 4.0—Overall Program Management

3.0   Cost Proposal
      3.1   Estimate of Cost Elements
      3.2   Cost Estimate Rationale
      3.3   Cost Summary
      3.4   Invoice and Payment

4.0   Management Proposal
      4.1   Program Organization and Staffing
      4.2   Staffing Restrictions
      4.3   Program Schedule

1.0 Executive Summary

Decision Planning Corporation (DPC) submits this proposal to _____
_____ to develop project planning and control system procedures. The proposal contains a description of proposed services, associated
schedule and costs, and DPC qualifications to assist _____
_____ in this program.

In order to facilitate evaluation of the subject matter, DPC has subdivided
the proposal into four sections and two appendixes. Following is a brief
description of each part.

EXECUTIVE SUMMARY	The Executive Summary section provides an overview of the proposed program and the proposed approach to accomplishing contract work. The section concludes with a description of DPC qualifications to perform the proposed tasks.
TECHNICAL PROPOSAL	The Technical Proposal section begins with a detailed description of work to be accomplished and products/services to be delivered to _____. In addition to defining program scope, Section 2.0 identifies responsibilities of _____ _____ and DPC for development, review, and approval of individual products and services.
COST PROPOSAL	The Cost Proposal section contains a detailed estimate of labor hours and other elements of cost necessary to accomplish the proposed scope. This section also presents assumptions upon which the proposal is based, labor rates, terms and conditions, and other information necessary to fully understand the Cost Proposal.
MANAGEMENT PROPOSAL	The Management Proposal section begins with a discussion of the approach and methodology that will be used in accomplishing the statement of work. A summary schedule of events is also shown. The section closes with a detailed examination of DPC's project organization, in terms of both personnel to

be assigned and the organization of personnel into the Project Team.

APPENDIXES

DPC concludes the proposal by providing two appendixes containing data that describe DPC's overall qualifications and performance record. These appendixes are presented outside the body of the proposal in order to maintain proposal continuity and thus facilitate its review. The subject appendixes are described below:

Appendix A—DPC believes that its experience and knowledge in providing services offered in this proposal are the foremost in the industry. Appendix A, Relevant DPC Experience, provides a synopsis of representative DPC accomplishments.

Appendix B—DPC is convinced that the qualifications and experience of the staff proposed for this program cannot be excelled by any of its competitors. Appendix B, DPC Staff Résumés, depicts career accomplishments and the academic record of the DPC Program Team.

[*Appendix A and Appendix B have been intentionally deleted.*]

1.1 Program Background

_____ has initiated a corporatewide effort to upgrade existing management information system hardware and software systems. In parallel with this effort, the engineering department has initiated an effort to upgrade its project planning and control system by revising existing procedures and/or developing new procedures that describe how _____ organizes, plans, monitors, and controls project work on its engineering and construction projects.

Decision Planning Corporation recognizes the desire of _____ _____ to have these procedures defined, written, and implemented as soon as possible. The development of these types of procedures is normally accomplished in three distinct steps. The first step involves defining the project planning and control system requirements. The second step takes these general requirements and restructures them in the form of a detailed system specification. The final step is the development of each procedure from the specification. Each procedure contains a logic diagram, narrative text, and instruction related to the fulfillment of the procedure requirements.

DPC is currently engaged with _____ to develop a customized training program on project planning and control concepts. This program is based on DPC's public seminar, which is currently being presented nationwide. DPC has, however, made substantial changes in the presentation material to be _____-specific. This training program provides a perfect base for developing system procedures. Having DPC execute the proposed procedures development program will assure_____ of maximizing its investment in the training program and make procedure implementation much easier.

1.2 Proposed Services

Decision Planning Corporation offers to accomplish the scope of work outlined below and defined in the Technical Proposal. To assure a clear and complete understanding of the work scope between _____ _____ and DPC, the proposed program has been subdivided into its component parts by means of a Program Work Breakdown Structure (PWBS) shown in [*Figure D-1*]. Following is a brief description of the elements of this scope at the second level of the DPC PWBS.

WBS ELEMENT	*Project Planning and Control System Review:* WBS Element No. 1 includes: a review of the existing _____ Project Planning and Control (PP&C) System documentation to gain an understanding of the current _____ project planning and control techniques; a survey of sample _____ projects to assure a clear understanding of planning and control needs of projects by size and type; and interviews with _____ _____ management personnel to understand unwritten practices, procedures, working relationships, and attitudes.

Figure D-1. Program Work Breakdown Structure.

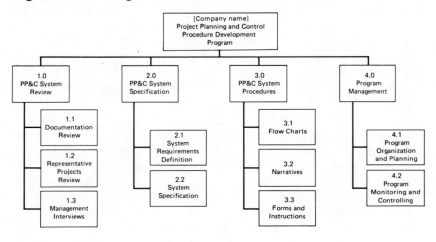

WBS ELEMENT 2	*Project Planning and Control System Specification:* This WBS element includes activities related to defining requirements for organizing, planning, authorizing, monitoring, and controlling project work and resources, and preparation of a specification that will be the basis for preparing each procedure.
WBS ELEMENT 3	*Project Planning and Control System Procedures:* This WBS contains development of system procedures, including system flow diagrams, procedure narratives, and forms design and completion instructions.
WBS ELEMENT 4	*DPC Program Management:* This WBS element includes the organizing, planning, monitoring, and controlling of the work and resources necessary to assure the successful and timely completion of this engagement.

A detailed description of each WBS element is provided in Section 2.0, Technical Proposal. An overview of the approach DPC proposes for accomplishing the program work is shown in [*Figure D-2*]. DPC's work methodology is described in the form of a logic diagram depicting the

Figure D-2. DPC approach for accomplishing program work.

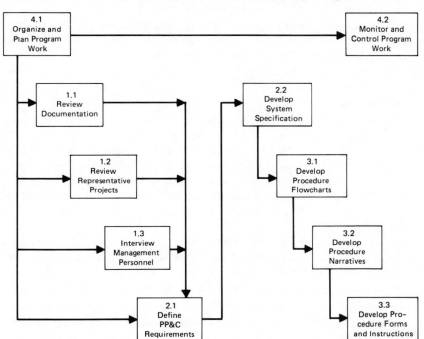

relationship of WBS subelements. In Section 4.0, this logic diagram was used as a basis for development of a realistic program schedule.

1.3 Decision Planning Corporation Qualifications

Decision Planning Corporation has an outstanding record in the field of project management. Formed in 1972, Decision Planning Corporation has built a nationwide consulting practice and provided services to over one hundred organizations from a variety of industries and several branches of the federal government. Among DPC's clients are electric utilities, construction companies, architectural/engineering firms, reactor manufacturers, aerospace/defense contractors, the U.S. Departments of Energy and Defense, the Canadian federal government, and many other organizations. These organizations received assistance from Decision Planning Corporation in virtually every aspect of project management.

Appendix A indicates the extent of DPC experience in the areas of project management relevant to this proposal. Of special interest to _____ _____ is the assistance provided to the Bonneville Power Administration, the Northwest Energy Corporation, the General Public Utilities Services Company, the Gas-Cooled Reactor Associates, and Southern Company Services. These engagements were performed in essentially the same environment and included the same scope of work as described in this proposal.

DPC personnel possess diverse experience in all aspects of project management, ranging from participation in the development of original concepts of Integrated Project Management to achieving remarkable results in the management of projects utilizing these concepts. For this proposed work, Decision Planning Corporation has selected a team of experienced project management professionals. Each has extensive experience in project management control system design, documentation, training, implementation, and operation.

Their experience will assure that the _____ Project Planning and Control System Procedures will reflect the needs of the company and will be the correct combination of proper structure and practical knowledge of the needs of the project manager/engineer.

Decision Planning Corporation is uniquely qualified to assist _____ _____ on this program. Following is a summary of the benefits that will accrue to _____ by selecting Decision Planning Corporation for this assignment.

- DPC is intimately familiar with the _____ project management environment. By selecting Decision Planning Corporation for this assignment, _____ will gain the benefit of DPC's extensive experience in the design, documentation, implementation, and operation of project management systems, thereby assuring that the PP&C procedures effort will be accomplished expeditiously.

- DPC is an expert in project planning and control techniques of the electric utility industry. DPC offers, as perhaps the only one of its kind in the United States, a public seminar entitled, "Project Planning and Control Within the Electric Utility Industry." _____ will gain the benefit of this know-how and experience in this engagement.

- Decision Planning Corporation personnel contemplated for this assignment possess a balance of business and engineering backgrounds, thereby providing the disciplines necessary to conceptualize the system, utilizing a project manager's awareness of what is practical and what is not.

- Decision Planning Corporation experience with project management assignments in the project planning and control environment has extreme depth and breadth. Over the past five years, Decision Planning Corporation has assisted twenty major organizations involved in engineering/construction activities in the development, implementation, and operation of project management.
- Decision Planning Corporation's entire corporate mission is dedicated to the business of assisting clients in the design, implementation, and operation of project management systems. Therefore, this effort is not secondary to other Decision Planning Corporation services. It is the central focus of its corporate experience and expertise.

In order to support the statements made and confirm the capabilities and performance records of Decision Planning Corporation, the following is a list of references provided to_____ for review.

[List of references intentionally deleted.]

2.0 Technical Proposal

Decision Planning Corporation proposes to provide the necessary services and related support to _____ in the conduct of a management system procedure development program outlined below. The program scope is presented in a modular fashion to enable_____ _____ to identify how those services are best suited to its present management needs.

SCOPE   The proposed scope of work involves the performance of ten (10) specific tasks. The individual tasks are structured as elements of a Work Breakdown Structure as shown in [*Figure D-1*]. The purpose of the Work Breakdown Structure is to define the deliverable products and services necessary to complete the program scope and to assure that the management of the engagement WBS is coded by a unique identification number. This number is used to identify the WBS element on all cost and schedule documents contained in this proposal. By using the WBS identification number, _____ _____ may correlate all proposed cost and schedule information to the work scope defined for that element.

RESPONSIBILITIES

Since the WBS describes the products and services associated with management system procedure development, and not the responsibility for preparing the product or performing the service, an identification of the responsibilities for various tasks regarding each individual WBS element product/service is set

Figure D-3.   Responsibility matrix.

Responsibility Matrix		Responsible Organization							
		DPC				[Company name]			
Work Breakdown Structure Element		Execute	Review	Consult		Execute*	Review	Approve	
Number	Description								
1.0	PP&C System Review								
1.1	Documentation Review	x							
1.2	Representative Project Review	x				x			
1.3	Management Interviews	x				x			
2.0	PP&C System Specification								
2.1	System Requirements Definition	x		x		x		x	
2.2	System Specification	x				x		x	
3.0	PP&C System Procedures								
3.1	Flowcharts	x	x			x	x	x	
3.2	Narrative	x	x			x	x	x	
3.3	Forms and Instructions	x	x			x	x	x	
4.0	Program Management								
4.1	Program Organization & Planning	x						x	
4.2	Program Monitoring and Control	x						x	

*XXXX effort is expected to take one equivalent person.

forth in [*Figure D-3*]. The matrix contains the following information.

- The vertical axis provides a listing of all WBS elements, products, and services.
- The horizontal axis contains a listing of activities associated with product/service development.
- Where axes intersect, a symbol is used to indicate responsibility for performance of the activity under consideration.

Activities associated with accomplishment of the proposed scope of work are identified as *execution, review, consulting,* and *approval.* Statements shown below describe program activities in terms of the content of work and deliverable products, where applicable.

EXECUTION
System review and analysis, flow chart preparation, development of procedures, and their presentation to the _____ personnel. All executed activities have clearly defined end products and/or services.

REVIEW
Analysis of results of execution activities for completeness and adequacy. Results of all reviews will be documented on the marked-up copies of program documentation, through memoranda, or by means acceptable to _____ and DPC.

CONSULTING
Activities related to advisory program administration, management, and other "level of effort" work that does not result in a tangible end product.

APPROVAL
Work associated with formal acceptance of various products and services by _____ _____ .

Decision Planning Corporation believes that material contained in this proposal presents a precise definition of the scope of work and responsibilities for its execution. It should be noted that the proposal quantifies the program scope to the maximum practical extent and avoids level of effort activities wherever possible. This provides a sound basis for management of the DPC work scope and assures adequate visibility into the progress of each product.

2.1 WBS Element 1.0—Project Planning and Control (PP&C) System Review

Decision Planning Corporation will review _____'s PP&C System documentation, survey its project plans and reports, and conduct interviews with _____ management personnel, as needed. This effort will involve a three-step process. Each step is described below.

WBS ELEMENT 1.1

PP&C Documentation Review: DPC will review existing PP&C documentation and "take inventory" of current _____ _____ practices associated with organizing, planning, authorizing, monitoring, and controlling labor, materials, and associated resources. This "inventory" will consist of the following:

a. Review of organization charts and position descriptions to develop an understanding of rules and responsibilities of people and organizations, and to identify the key interfaces of various project participants.

b. Review of other management policies, procedures, manuals, and related documentation to gain familiarity with current PP&C methods and practices.

c. Review of existing accounting and information systems to develop an understanding of: (1) labor distribution; (2) procurement/material commitments and distribution; (3) other direct costs distribution; and (4) other pertinent project and accounting information resources.

WBS ELEMENT 1.2

Project Review: DPC will review the character of the current engineering, construction, and maintenance projects. The review will consider a sample drawn from each of the major project groups—fossil plants, hydro plants, and transmission lines. The sample will be used to profile the project management requirements of _____ pro-

jects of each type and size. The review will
address, as a minimum, the following:
a. Work Breakdown Structure and other
    project definition documents as presently
    exist.
b. Schedules throughout all levels.
c. Budget and/or expenditure forecasting
    documents.
d. Work authorization documents, includ-
    ing contracts and purchase orders.
e. Work progress/accomplishment and
    problem analysis documents/reports.

WBS ELEMENT 1.3   *Management Interviews:* Decision Planning
                   Corporation will hold interviews with man-
                   agers and other key personnel in engineering,
                   project services, and other appropriate func-
                   tional management areas to gain understand-
                   ing of unwritten practices and procedures,
                   working relationships, and relevant attitudes.

2.2 WBS Element 2.0—Project Planning and Control System Specification

Decision Planning Corporation will develop a specification for the en-
hancement of the_____ Project Planning and Control
System. This specification will define criteria for organizing, planning,
monitoring, and controlling project work and resources, and analyze
_____ practices against these criteria.

WBS ELEMENT 2.1   *PP&C System Requirements Definition:* DPC
                   (with the assistance of _____
                   _____) will analyze project management
                   practices identified in WBS Element 1.0 in
                   light of existing project management require-
                   ments, and identify any additional require-
                   ments, as well as those which require further
                   development. This approach will assure that
                   the PP&C System reflects the state of the art
                   in project management thought, as well as
                   management style, values, and philosophy of
                   _____.

WBS ELEMENT 2.2   *System Specification:* The results of the system
                   requirements analysis will be documented in

a System Specification. The specification will contain project management requirements and identity of the priorities that should govern the PP&C System procedure development. The report will also document the satisfactory features of the existing management systems so that eventual system modification effort can be undertaken with minimum change to existing practices.

2.3   WBS Element 3.0—PP&C System Procedures

Following the documentation of _____ system requirements, DPC, with _____'s assistance, will prepare the system procedures that meet those requirements.

WBS Element 3.1   *Flow Charts:* DPC and _____ _____ will prepare graphic flow charts of the existing management practices. These flow charts will be compared to the requirements in the System Specification. Any shortcomings will be resolved jointly between DPC and_____. The outcome will be a flow chart of each intended procedure in the PP&C System. These flow charts will identify existing practices, modified practices, and any new practices and forms required to implement the practice. Upon completion of the flow charts, narrative explanations (text) of each step will be prepared. The flow charts and narratives will allow each reviewer to understand the flow and interaction of each step by viewing the graphical flow chart and understanding the contents of each step through review of the adjacent narrative. The ultimate goal is to assure that each intended procedure has consisted and clarified all necessary steps and interfaces.

A preliminary list of minimal system documentation follows:

- PP&C System Overview
- Work Definition and Responsibility Assignment Matrix
- Project Budgeting
- Project Scheduling Procedure
- Control Point Plan Development Procedure
- Authorizing Procedure
- Performance Measurement Procedure
- Baseline Measurement Procedure
- Analysis and Forecasting Procedure
- Change Control/Revision Procedure
- Control Point Manager's Guide

The complete/final list of procedural documentation will be identified prior to any procedure development work. Each procedure will contain a flow diagram, flow diagram narrative, existing forms and/or new forms, narrative describing the purpose and scope of the procedure, definition of unique or new terms, and procedure requirements.

WBS ELEMENT 3.2 *Procedure Narratives:* Utilizing the flow chart narratives, DPC, with _____ _____'s assistance, will prepare the series of procedures which will totally define the PP&C system.

WBS ELEMENT 3.3 *Forms and Instructions:* DPC will, if necessary, develop/revise PP&C forms and form instructions to be compliant with system procedure requirements. This task includes developing preliminary drafts, coordinating and reviewing preliminary drafts, and developing final drafts of both forms and form instructions.

2.4   WBS Element 4.0—Overall Program Management

In order to assure successful and timely completion of the proposed effort, this program must be organized, planned, monitored, and controlled effectively. The scope of work described below is designed to accomplish the above goals.

WBS Element 4.1   *Program Organization and Planning:* Near the outset of the program, DPC will finalize the following documents and submit them to _____ for review:

- Work Breakdown Structure   [*Figure D-3*]
- Organization Structure   [*Figure D-1*]
- Detailed Program Execution Network   [*Figure D-2*]
- Program Schedule   [*Figure D-6*]

      These documents will be designed to assure that all project activities have been thoroughly defined, assigned, and planned, and that adequate manpower is available for their accomplishment.

WBS Element 4.2   *Program Monitoring and Control:* DPC will continuously monitor the cost and progress of the program work and performance of DPC personnel. DPC recognizes that, during the execution of this program, a need may develop to alter the program scope, schedule, and/or budget. DPC will monitor the need for such changes, present them formally to _____'s management, and mutually agree upon the course of corrective action.

3.0 Cost Proposal

3.1 Estimate of Cost Elements

As described in Section 2.0, DPC has subdivided the _____ _____ PP&C Procedure Development Program through three (3) levels of the WBS. The activities necessary to accomplish the statements of work were scheduled in a manner that considers the relationships and interdependencies of the various work elements.

DPC's cost estimate to perform the work described in Section 2.0 is shown in [*Figures D-4 and D-5*]. The figures show the labor and other resources necessary to accomplish each element of the DPC WBS. The labor categories depicted are: director of projects, senior consultant, and consultant. Estimates are shown in man-hours by labor category.

Figure D-4.   Cost estimates by cost elements.

Estimate by Cost Elements	Labor*			Other				
	Director of Projects	Senior Consultants	Consultants	Airfare	Hotel/ Per Diem	Car Rental (Days)	Parking (Days)	Misc.
1.1 Documentation Review	8	8	10					
1.2 Representative Project Review	8	8	10					
1.3 Management Interview	8	8	12					
1.0 Total Review	24	24	32	3	13	5	13	3
2.1 System Requirement Definition	12	40	8					
2.2 System Specification	12	16	8					
2.0 Total System Specification	24	56	16	2	10	5	10	2
3.1 Procedure Flowcharts	4	80	120					
3.2 Procedure Narratives	3	120	160					
3.3 Procedure Forms and Instructions	3	40	56					
3.0 Total Procedures	10	240	336	9	43	24	43	9
4.1 Program Organization & Planning	16	24	12					
4.2 Program Monitoring & Controlling	16	24	12					
4.0 Total Program Management	32	48	24	2	10	5	10	2
Total Program	90	368	408	16	76	39	76	16

*Labor estimate is in man-hours.
Note: Use or disclosure of the data set forth hereon is subject to the restriction on the cover page of this proposal.

Decision Planning Corporation developed its cost estimate based on the labor rates shown below. [*Note that the rates have been intentionally deleted.*] These rates are based upon uniform market prices for services provided in substantial quantity to the general public. DPC labor rates are:

Director of projects	$____/day
Senior consultant	$____/day
Consultant	$____/day

Figure D-5. Cost estimates for proposed services.

Estimated Cost for Proposed Services	Quantity/Cost	Labor				Other Cost Elements						Total Price
Unit Price (Hr) / Quantity Cost / WBS Element	Q / $	Director of Projects	Senior Consultants	Consultants	Staff Consultants	Airfare	Hotel/ Per Diem	Car Rental (Days)	Parking (Days)	Mileage (100 mi.)	Visual Aids	
1.0 PP&C System Review	Q	24	24	32		3	13	5	13	3		
	$											
2.0 PP&C System Specification	Q	24	56	16		2	10	5	10	2		
	$											
3.0 PP&C System Procedures	Q	10	240	336		9	43	24	43	9		
	$											
4.0 Program Management	Q	32	48	24		2	10	5	10	2		
	$											
Total Program												

[Rates and costs intentionally deleted.]

The above rates are valid only for the resources shown and for a period of five months. If, during the course of this engagement, DPC is requested to provide services requiring special expertise in areas other than project planning and control, billing rates for such services will be negotiated with _____ at that time.

Other cost elements shown are estimated in units appropriate to the cost element. The cost elements and the units estimated are as follows:

Cost Elements	Unit of Estimation
Airfares	Round-trips from Costa Mesa to _____ _____
Hotel/per diem	Days × number of on-site consultants
Car rental	Days × number of cars rented
Parking	Days × number of cars parked
Miscellaneous	Dollars per trip

At present, DPC anticipates that the only materials that may be required are the general office supplies, light graphics, and reproduction.

3.2   Cost Estimate Rationale

The cost estimate for the proposed services is based upon the following assumptions:

- Timely completion and total cost of this program are dependent on the strict adherence of all participants to the project schedule.
- _____ will provide office space and all necessary facilities for the DPC personnel while engaged in on-site services. On-site activities include approximately 60 percent of the total effort.
- The term *site* refers to the _____ offices located at _____ . Travel to locations other than the "site" shall be regarded as out-of-scope activity and shall be negotiated/billed separately.
- Total project duration is assumed to be ten to twelve weeks.
- DPC currently reimburses its personnel for lodging at cost and provides a food and incidentals allowance rate of $_____ per day. For the _____ area, DPC estimates $_____ per night, which represents the middle range of a single hotel room. The total of $_____ per day has been multiplied against the estimated number of per diem days. [*Rates and costs have been intentionally deleted.*]
- Substantial cost savings can be realized by taking advantage of airline discounts and/or price reductions. However, to take advantage of these reductions, a firm schedule must be established. As soon as a firm

schedule is established, DPC will attempt to take advantage of all possible cost savings related to travel, reducing the overall travel-related expenses.

3.3   Cost Summary

The cost estimate for the proposed statement of work associated with procedure development has been summarized in [*Figure D-5*]. The total cost estimate is for all services/products described in Section 2.0. [*Cost has been intentionally deleted.*]

3.4   Invoice and Payment

DPC will invoice _____ each month for the costs incurred at the billing rates and actual expense costs incurred to date. Refer to [*Figure D-6*]. DPC anticipates payment will be received from _____ within thirty days of submission of the invoice.

All payments should be made to:

> Decision Planning Corporation
> 3184-A Airway Avenue
> Costa Mesa, California 92626

4.0   Management Proposal

This section describes the organizational approach that DPC uses on its consulting assignments, the specific team proposal for this program, and the schedule for accomplishing the statement of work.

4.1   Program Organization and Staffing

Decision Planning Corporation controls all of its assignments with a matrix organization as shown in [*Figure D-7*]. The left side of this chart depicts DPC officers, and the right side shows the organization of the Program Team.

DPC will appoint Mr. Richard Brodkorb as director of this program to provide for adequate interfacing with _____ management and to assure complete control of project resources. Mr. Brodkorb will be supported by a team that possesses a unique blend of technical and business management backgrounds chosen specifically for this assignment. All team members will not be utilized at the same rate; three team

Figure D-6. Program schedule.

PROPOSED SCHEDULING FOR PROJECT PLANNING & CONTROL PROCEDURE DEVELOPMENT

No.	Activity Description	\multicolumn{12}{c}{Weeks from Start}
		1	2	3	4	5	6	7	8	9	10	11	12
1.1	Documentation Review	▮											
1.2	Representation Project Review	▮											
1.3	Management Interview	▮											
2.1	System Requirement Definition		▮										
2.2	System Specification			▮									
3.1	Flowcharts			▮	▮	▮	▮	▮					
3.2	Narratives				▮	▮	▮	▮	▮				
3.3	Forms and Instruction				▮	▮	▮	▮	▮	▮			
4.1	Program Organization & Planning										▮		
4.2	Program Monitoring and Controlling										▮		

Figure D-7.   DPC matrix organization.

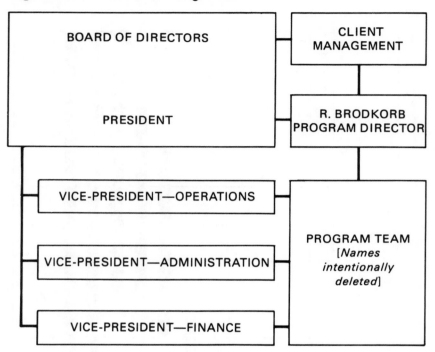

members are proposed in order to assure that qualified individuals are available to support peak periods. A synopsis of the proposed team members and their experience related to this assignment is presented below. A more detailed résumé on each member is included in Appendix B.

[Synopses intentionally deleted.]

4.2   Staffing Restrictions

The proposed staff is available to support _____ within three weeks of the date of this proposal. However, should authorization to proceed be delayed beyond _____, 19___, DPC may be required to assign a portion of the proposed personnel to other engagements. If this occurs, DPC will replace the reassigned personnel with staff members of equal qualifications. Replacements will be made with the approval of _____.

4.3 Program Schedule

The proposed schedule for accomplishment of the _____ _____ Project Planning and Control Procedure Development Program is shown in [*Figure D-6*]. The schedule was developed in the framework of the Work Breakdown Structure [*Figure D-1*], and it depicts time phasing and duration of all activities identified in the Execution Logic Diagram [*Figure D-2*].

Rather than being oriented toward specific calendar dates, the schedule is constructed based upon working days and weeks after commencement of the engagement. A minimum of two weeks' advance notice should be given in order for DPC to support desired dates.

Appendix E

Associations of Consultants

American Association of Healthcare Consultants—11208 Waples Mill Road, Fairfax, Va. 22202 (703/691-2242)

American Association of Medico-Legal Consultants—2200 Benjamin Franklin Parkway, Philadelphia, Pa. 19130 (215/563-5343)

American Association of Political Consultants—1211 Connecticut Avenue, NW, Washington, D.C. 20036 (202/546-1564)

American Association of Professional Consultants—9140 Ward Parkway, Kansas City, Mo. 64114 (816/444-3500)

American Consulting Engineers Council—1015 15th Street, NW, Washington, D.C. 20005 (202/347-7474)

Amercan Society of Consulting Pharmacists—2300 9th Street, Arlington, Va. 22201 (703/920-8492)

Association of Consulting Management Engineers—230 Park Avenue, New York, N.Y. 10017 (212/697-9693)

Association of Executive Search Consultants—151 Railroad Avenue, Greenwich, Conn. 06830 (203/661-6606)

Association of Fashion and Image Consultants—1133 15th Street, NW, Suite 620, Washington, D.C. 20005 (202/293-5913)

Association of Management Consultants—500 North Michigan Avenue, Suite 1400, Chicago, Ill. 60611 (312/266-1261)

Independent Computer Consultants Association—Box 27412, St. Louis, Mo. 63141 (314/997-4633)

Institute of Certified Financial Planners—3443 South Galena, Suite 190, Denver, Colo. 80231 (303/751-7600)

Institute of Management Consultants—19 West 44th Street, New York, N.Y. 10036 (212/921-2885)

Professional and Technical Consultants Association—1330 South
    Barcom Avenue, Suite D, San Joses, Calif. 95128
Professional Image Consultants Association International—4 For-
    est Laneway, Suite 509, Willowdale, Toronto, Ont., Can. M2N
    5X8 (416/229-4077)
Society of Professional Business Consultants—221 North LaSalle
    Street, Chicago, Il. 60601 (312/922-6222)
Society of Professional Management Consultants—16 West 56th
    Street, New York, N.Y. 10019 (212/586-2041)

INDEX

[Italics *(ii)* refer to illustrations.]

ability, individual, *ii*

absences, sole proprietorship and, 183

accounting firms, with consulting divisions, 5

accounts receivable ledger, 215, 217

acid-test ratio, 276

activity, in PERT chart, 113

advertising
  direct response space, 35–36
  in Yellow Pages, 37

advertising copy, for direct mail letters, 21

advice, giving in initial interview, 70–71

age discrimination, 9

agent, 194–195

AIDA formula, 36

Allis-Chalmers, 159–160

annuity contracts, 207

answering machine, 209

answering service, 209–210

Apple Macintosh computers, 233–234

articles, writing, 50, 54

assignment, objectives of, 68

associations, 49, 307–308

assumptions, in proposal, 79

attorney
  contract review by, 97, 107
  for incorporation, 186
  for partnership formation, 184

audience, 180

audit, of company, 75, 253–282

authority, of corporate personnel, 69

automobile insurance, 200–201

average collection period, 276

backup contact person, 69

Bain, William, on billing, 16

bedside manner, in client relations, 12–13

benefits, including in direct mail letter, 24–25

Bermont, Hurbert, 17

billing, 16
  daily, 91
  disclosure of fee structure, 95
  ethics in, 164
  fixed-price, 93–95
  methods of, 91–95
  performance, 93

blackboards, 176–177

Blitstein, Dr. Allen, on corporate attitudes toward recent graduates, 13–14

Bluestein, Ilene Gordon, 18

board of directors, 187

bodily injury, 199

body language, 71–72

book writing, 54–55

Booz, Allen, and Hamilton, 113
brain, right and left halves of, 147
Brandt, William, 11
brochures, 28–33
  basic contents of, 29–30
  sample of, 45–48, 243–252
Brock, Dr. Luther, 23
Brodkorb, Dick, on skills of consultants, 14–15
Building a Mail Order Business (Cohen), promotion of, 50
burglary insurance, 203
business, consulting for, 3–5
business cards, 39, 193–194
business interruption insurance, 202–203
business license, 190
business operations, 181–224
  anticipating expenses in, 210–211
  legal structure of, 181–190
  minimizing overhead in, 207–211
  record keeping in, 211–215
business phone, 209–210
business tax kit, IRS 454, 223
Byrne, John H., on executive searches, 7–8

calendar week, in PERT chart, 114
call to action, in direct mail letter, 27
capital
  for corporation, 187
  need for, 9
  partnership and, 185, 186
  sole proprietorship and, 183
cartels, 159
central problem, defining, 133–134, 142–143

Chan, Dr. Pedro, and building a consulting practice, 38–39
clients, 20–65
  analysis of consultants by, 12
  quoting from, in direct mail, 26
  request by, to delete report information, 161
  standard contract from, 97
  varying price for different, 90–91
  see also interviews, with clients; negotiations, with clients
codes, product/service, 58
Cohen's Maxims, *ii*, 39
coinsurance clause, 198–199
cold calls, 33–35
Commerce Business Daily (CBD), 59
communication skills, 13
company audit, 75, 253–282
company politics, 8–9
compensation, *ii*, 15–16
  in proposal, 77
competition price strategy, 89
competitive proposals, 74
competitive research, 153
comprehensive insurance coverage, 196
computers, 225–235
  Apple Macintosh, 233–234
  managing finances on, 228
  reports on, 226–227
  requirements for, 232
  selecting, 233–234
conclusions, in problem solving, 136, 146–147
construction, insurance for, 199
consultant(s)
  beginning as, 16–19
  need for, 6–7, 11–12

consulting
  defining, 2–3
  eleven areas of, 3
  firms, types of, 5–6
  industry, size of, 3
  types of expertise offered by,
    4
consumer acceptance theory,
    60–61
consumer credit protection, 9
contact person, 69
contract(s), 96–107
  converting proposal into, 81
  developing, 97
  elements of, 106
  formal, 98
  necessity of, 96–97
  negotiating, 64–65
  proposal as basis of, 77
  sample, 106–107
  sample of, *99–101*
  types of, 102–106
  ways of creating, 97–102
copywriters, for direct mail
    letters, 21
corporations, 186–189
  income taxes and, 218
cost contracts, 103–104
costs, in proposal, 81
county licenses, 190
court costs, liability for, 200
creative visualization, 178–179
credibility, 25–27
  of corporation, 187
  credit cards and, 193
credit cards, client use of, 193
crime insurance, 203–204
current ratio, 275
customer preference, 61

Dartnell's Cambridge Associ-
    ates, 40, *41–44*

data flow charts, 80
debt to net worth ratio, 276
defensiveness, in negotiations,
    127
demonstrations, in presenta-
    tions, 173
desktop publishing, 227
Diebold, John, on becoming a
    consultant, 18–19
direct mail marketing, 21–28
  cold calling with, 34–35
  writing your own copy for,
    23–28
direct marketing
  computers for, 228–229
  magazines, 23
  methods for, 20–38
directories, listings in, 36–37
direct response space advertis-
    ing, 35–36
direct writer of insurance, 194
disability insurance, 206
disk drives, 232
Disk Operating System (DOS),
    232–233
distractions, in decision mak-
    ing, 148
dot matrix printers, 234
dress, 66–67
Drucker, Peter F., 8, 15, 158
duty, *ii*

earliest expected date (TE), in
    PERT chart, 114–115
efficiency, 9–10
emotions, identifying from
    facial expressions, 73–74,
    73, 75
employee compensation record,
    211, 215, 216
Employee Retirement Income
    Security Act of 1974 (ER-
    ISA), 207

employees
  evaluating potential of with computer, 230
  insurance for, 205–207
  withholding income taxes of, 219
employer identification number, 223
employers, consulting for former, 37–38
employment agencies, pricing by, 90
endorsements, 26
enthusiasm, in presentations, 167–168
equal employment opportunity, 9
Espinosa, Luis, 18
Estimated Tax for Individuals Form 1040-ES, 218
ethics, 151–164
  and advertising, 35
  in billing, 164
  in Japan, 158–159
  of marketing research, 152–154
events, in PERT chart, 113
excise taxes, federal, 222
executive searches, 7–8, 157–158
  consultants for, 35
  pricing for, 90
expected lapse time, in PERT chart, 114
expense journal, 211, 213
expense ledger summary, 211, 214
expenses, anticipating, 210–211

facial expressions, identifying emotions from, 73–74, 73, 75

false information, in decision making, 148
fax machines, 210
federal crime insurance plan, 204
federal government
  buying process in, 60
  consulting for, 58–59
  contract negotiation with, 120
  regulations, 9, 187
federal tax deposit coupon, 218
federal taxes
  excise, 222
  income, 218–219
  remitting, 221
fees, average, 15
feedback, 173
fictitious name registration, 191–193
finances, managing on computer, 228
financial ratios, 275–277
fire insurance, 196–199
fire legal liability insurance, 200
first impressions, 66
fixed expenses, insurance for, 202
fixed fee, and cost-plus contract, 103
fixed-price billing, 93–95
fixed-price contracts, 102–103
fleet insurance policy, 200
flip charts, 175
forecasts, with computer, 229–230
Form 508, Federal Unemployment Tax Deposit, 222
Form 940, Employer's Annual Federal Unemployment Tax Return, 222
Form 941, 221
Form 1040, Schedule C (Profit or Loss . . .), 218

Form 1040-ES, 218
Form 1065, 218
Form 8109, Federal Tax Deposit Coupon Book, 221
Form SS-4, 223
Form W-2, Wage and Tax Statement, 219
Form W-4, Employee's Withholding Allowance Certificate, 219
formal contracts, 98
Fuchs, Jerome, on the eleven areas of consulting, 3

gamesmanship, 126–130
Garfield, Charles, on superior performance in presentations, 178
Garvin, Charles, on communication skills, 13
General Electric, 159–160
glass insurance, 204
goals, in negotiations, 120–124
good-guy–bad-guy technique, in negotiations, 128
government, *see* federal government
grammar, computer correction of, 229
Greene, Mark R., insurance checklist of, 195
group health insurance, 206
group life insurance, 205

handouts
    for presentations, 175–176
    and speaking before groups, 39
handwriting analysis, 230
Harvard Case Study Method of Problem Solving, 132–137
headhunters, ethics of, 163

headlines, 23–24
health insurance, group, 206
Hewlett-Packard Deskjet printer, 235
high-price strategy, 87
home office, 208
hourly billing, 91
Howe, Elias, and problem solving, 149

IBM computers, 233–234
ideas, from consultants, 8
incentive contracts, 105–106
incentives, costs plus, 103
income, retirement, 206–207
income received, daily summary of, 211, 212
income taxes
    for corporations, 188
    federal, 218–219
    reporting, 221
    for S corporations, 189
    withholding, 219
independent consulting, 1
independent insurance agents, 195
indirect marketing methods, 38–57
industrial spying, 161
industry
    consulting firms specializing by, 5
    and pricing, 89–90
information
    electronic access to, 231
    omitting from report, 161
information exchange, with noncompeting consultants, 57
information gathering, ethics in, 154
initial presentation, 63

insistence, by customer, 61
insurance, 194–207
  automobile, 200–201
  business interruption, 202–203
  cancellation of, 198
  checklist, 195
  comprehensive, 196
  crime, 203–204
  disability, 206
  as employee benefit, 205–207
  fire, 196–199
  glass, 204
  group health, 206
  group life, 205
  key-man, 207
  liability, 199–200
  rent, 204–205
  workers compensation, 201–202
intelligence gathering, 63
interviews, with clients, 66–75
  company audit in, 75
  giving advice in initial, 70–71
  note taking in, 69–70
  obtaining, 27
  questions for, 66–69
inventory purchase journal, 211, 215
Invitation for Bid (IFB), 60

Japan, ethics in, 158–159
job orders, 157

keyboard, 232
key-man insurance, 207

laser printers, 234–235
latest allowable date (TL), in PERT chart, 115–117
layout, for brochure, 30
leadership, *ii*

lead time, for visual aids, 177
legal structure, of consulting firm, 181–190
letter contracts, 98
letter proposals, 78–81
  sample of, 82–84
letter-quality printers, 234
letters, *see* copywriters; direct mail marketing
letters to the editor, 55
liability, 194–207
  with corporation, 186–187
  in partnership, 185–186
  in sole proprietorship, 182–183
liability insurance, 199–200
licenses, municipal, 190
licensing, 182, 190
Liddy, G. Gordon, as example of consultant, 13
life insurance, group, 205
listening techniques, 72–73
lists, mailing, sources for, 32–33
"Letter Doctor, The," *see* Brock, Dr. Luther
local taxes, 223–224
Lockheed payoff scandal, 151–152
lying, 162–163
  during negotiations, 126

magazines
  on direct marketing, 23
  writing articles for, 50, 54
mailing list, for direct mail, 31–33
mail order, computers through, 234
management consultant, 3
management skills, of consultant, 14

marketing
    ability, 14
    indirect methods for, 38–57
    preproposal, 60–62
    relationship, as aids in, 49
marketing, direct
    magazines, 23
    methods for, 20–38
marketing consulting services
    to government, 63–64
    time requirements for, 16
marketing research
    computers for, 230
    ethics of, 152–154
MasterCard, client use of, 193
Masters of Business Adminis-
    tration, 3, 10
medical payments insurance,
    201
memorization, of report for
    presentation, 169
merchandising theory, 61
modems, 231
mouse, 234
MTA Group Management and
    Technology Advisors, Inc.,
    and direct mail, 32

naming products, computer
    program for, 229
national general management
    firms, 5
National Speakers Association,
    39
near-letter-quality printers, 234
negligence, insurance coverage
    and, 199
negotiations, with clients, 64–
    65, 119–131
    gamesmanship in, 126–130
    goals and objectives in, 120–
    124

hints for, 130–131
    planning for, 125–126
    preparation for, 124
    by telephone, 124–125
new ideas, and proposal writ-
    ing, 78
newsletters, 40–49
    sample of, 41–44
newspapers
    advertising in, 36
    and fictitious name registra-
    tion, 192
note taking, in client interview,
    69–70
not-to-exceed clause, 103

objectives
    of assignment, 68
    in negotiations, 120–124
    in proposal, 79
office, 208
office politics, and assignment
    completion, 68–69
order agreements, 98
organization, of presentations,
    168–169
organizations, social, 49
overhead costs, 92, 95
    minimizing, 207–211
overhead transparencies, 175
    on computers, 227
ownership of proprietary infor-
    mation, 162

paperwork, 187
    minimizing tax, 224
partnership, 183–186
    federal taxes for, 218
Patton, General George S., and
    enthusiasm, 167–168
payment information, in pro-
    posal, 81

penetration pricing, 85
performance
  billing, 93
  contracts, 104–105
  superior, in presentations,
    178
personal injuries, 199
personal liability, 194–207
personnel, and consultants, 7
PERT (Program Evaluation and
    Review Technique) chart,
    80, 113–118
  samples of, *114–117*
Phyllis Hillings & Co., 40, *45–48*
planning, *ii*, 108–118
  with computer, 229–230
point of contact, 69
potential problems, listing in
    proposal, 80
practice, for presentations, 169–
    174
preferences, of customer, 61
preparation, for negotiations,
    124
prepared handouts, 39
preproposal marketing, 60–62
presentations, 165–180
  controlling time during, 170–
    172
  demonstrations in, 173
  enthusiasm in, 167–168
  initial, 63
  objectives of, 165–166
  organization of, 168–169
  practice for, 169–174
  professionalism in, 166–167
  questions during, 179–180
  stage fright and, 177–179
  visual aids for, 175–177
pressure, in decision making,
    148
pricing, 85–95
  checklist for, 262–267

high-price strategy for, 87
industry and, 89–90
meet-the-competition strat-
    egy for, 89
and quality, 86
strategies for, 85–89
varying for different clients,
    90–91
printers, selecting, 234–235
problems
  diagnosis of, 13
  listing potential, 80
problem solving, 8, 10, 132–150
  alternatives in, 135–136,
    144–146
  case study on, 137–147
  conclusions in, 136, 146–147
  defining central problem in,
    133–134, 142–143
  Harvard Case Study Method
    of, 132–137
  psychological techniques for,
    147–150
  questioning client about, 67
  recommendations in, 136–
    137, 147
  relevant factors in, 133–134,
    143–144
product description, in pro-
    posal, 80–81
productivity, computers and,
    227
Professional Analyst (software),
    230
professional associations, 49
professionalism in presenta-
    tions, 166–167
profits, 278–279
  and performance contract,
    104
  sole proprietorship and, 182
project development schedule,
    108–113

proposals
  computers for, 227–228
  converting into contract, 81
  form for, 74
  preparing, 64
  sample of, 283–305
proposal writing, 76–84
  letter form for, 78–81
  necessity of, 76–77
  process for, 77–78
proprietary information, 161–162
publicity releases, 56
public sector
  firms, 5
  marketing consulting services in, 58–65
public speaking, 38–39
public utility company, business interruption due to, 203
purchase orders, 102

quality, pricing and, 86
questions, during presentations, 179–180
quick ratio, 276

RAM (random access memory), 233
reading, of report for presentation, 169
recess, in negotiations, 129
recommendations, in problem solving, 136–137, 147
record keeping, 211–215, 279–282
referrals, from other consultants, 57
registration, of fictitious name, 191–193
rejections, from cold calls, 33
relationship marketing, 49

rent insurance, 204–205
Request for Proposal (RFP), 60
resale permit, 190
responsibility, ii
retainer, 92–93
retirement income, 206–207
Riggio, Ronald E., and identification of emotions, 73
right half of brain, 147
right of subrogation, 199
Ringer, Robert, Winning Through Intimidation, on negotiating, 119
risk, ii, 64, 194
robbery insurance, 203
Ross, Phil, as example of a consultant, 17–18

safety standards, 9
sales improvement, 9
sales tax, 190–191
scheduling, 108–118
S Corporation, 189
screening, 63
search consulting, 17–18
secretaries, cold calling and, 34
security deposit, for resale permit, 191
self-confidence, ii
self-employment tax, 221
selling ability, 14
seminars, 40, 55–56
shareholders, for S corporation, 189
Shenson, Howard L., 16, 17
sickness
  partnership and, 185
  sole proprietorship and, 183
slack, 117–118
slide presentations, 175
Small Business Administration, xii, 60

Small Business Institute, xii–xiii
social organizations, 49
Social Security taxes, 219, 221
  reporting, 221
software, 232
sole practitioners, 6
sole proprietorship, 182–183
  federal taxes for, 218
  vs. partnership, 184–185
solutions, predetermined,
  studies with, 160–161
speaking before groups, 38–39
spelling, computer correction
  of, 229
split-focus technique, 179
spreadsheets, 229
spying, 164
Staff Study Method, 132–137
stage fright, 177–179
state taxes, 223–224
  sales, 190–191
stationery, 193–194
straw issues, in negotiations,
  128–129
study methods, in proposal, 79–
  80
subconscious mind, decision
  making by use of, 148–150
subrogation, right of, 199
success, ii
Svatko, James E., on need for
  consultant, 11
symptoms, vs. problems, 133

target market, 29
tasks
  length, 110
  time, 110
tax deductions, losses as, 188
taxes, 215, 218–224
  federal excise, 222
  federal income, 218–219

sales, 190–191
  Social Security, 219–221
  state and local, 223–224
  unemployment, 222–223
tax preparation, on computer,
  228
teaching, 55
technical expertise, 13
telephone, 209–210
  negotiations over, 124–125
thesaurus, 229
think tanks, 5–6
third party, placing blame on,
  127
time
  as basis for billing, 16, 91
  controlling in presentation,
    170–172
time constraints, in decision
  making, 148
time frame, 77
time squeeze, in negotiations,
  129–130
training
  for consulting, 2–3
  of employees, 10
transparencies, overhead, 175
  on computers, 227
turnaround specialists, 10–11

unconscious mind, 147
unemployment taxes, 222–223
Ungar, Bernard, and product/
  service codes, 58
uninsured motorist protection,
  201
U.S. Department of Commerce,
  190
U.S. government, see federal
  government
U.S. Navy Special Project
  Office, 113

vacant buildings, insurance on, 197
vacations
    partnership and, 185
    sole proprietorship and, 183
verbal contracts, 102
veterans' rights, 9
Visa credit card, client use of, 193
visual aids, for presentations, 175–177
vocational counseling, 230

walkouts, in negotiations, 129
Washington Researchers, 153–154

Survey of Company Information Techniques, 154–156
Westinghouse Co., 159–160
white lies, 162
win-win outcome, 121
withholding
    income taxes, 219
    Social Security taxes, 219, 221
word processing, 226–227, 232
workers compensation insurance, 201–202, 206
working hours, 1

Yellow Pages, listing in, 37, 210